Growing Up Wise

Growing Up Wise

a memoir

Susan Wise O'Hearn

LUMINARE PRESS
WWW.LUMINAREPRESS.COM

Growing Up Wise: A Memoir
Copyright © 2021 by Susan Wise O'Hearn

All rights reserved. This book or any portion thereof may not be reproduced or used in any manner whatsoever without the express written permission of the publisher, except for the use of brief quotations in a book review.

Printed in the United States of America

Luminare Press
442 Charnelton St.
Eugene, OR 97401
www.luminarepress.com

LCCN: 2021910402
ISBN: 978-1-64388-657-2

*For my children and grandchildren
and their children*

Table of Contents

Acknowledgment ix
Preface xi

Chapter 1
  The Beginning 1

Chapter 2
  The Wise Family 12

Chapter 3
  Dad 27

Chapter 4
  Mom, Marriage, and Me 42

Chapter 5
  Laguna Beach 70

Chapter 6
  Harper Avenue and Holt Avenue 77

Chapter 7
  Bedford Drive 92

Chapter 8
  La Grange Avenue 111

Chapter 9
   Stanton Avenue 194

Chapter 10
   Bellaire Avenue 274

Chapter 11
   San Francisco 304

Chapter 12
   Magnolia Boulevard 333

Chapter 13
   Rhodes Avenue 344

Chapter 14
   Last Chapter of Our Family 369

Afterword 376
Filmography 379

ACKNOWLEDGMENT

My sister, Sally, is my forever friend on this journey of life that we started together. She has been my sounding board and first-look story editor. Her suggestions and encouragement have kept me going. Viewing our shared childhood from an adult perspective has given us new insights. Reliving the good times brought us pleasure and laughter. Remembering the bad times brought us closure. I am so fortunate and grateful to have Sally as my sister.

PREFACE

My father was a motion picture writer and a wonderful storyteller, and Mom was the keeper of our family history, passing down the stories of her life and what she knew of my Dad's life. Now that they are gone, preserving the past is my job.

I was left with a wealth of stories to tell, but first I had to find the answers to some burning questions. Where did my mother's and father's families come from in Germany? How did my father's grandfather make his fortune? Where did my father live in Germany for a year as a boy? Who did he stay with in Germany? What movies did my father write while working at Metro-Goldwyn-Mayer Studios?

My journey to find answers started before we had the internet. I began with the research of my father's side of the family because some of his relatives were prominent figures in Manhattan, New York, and it was easier. I spent countless hours at local libraries and the Los Angeles Family History Library.

I found a video store in North Hollywood specializing in classic films. The owner had a large book on the counter that held a list of my father's movie credits from his days at the studio. I wrote them down in my notebook, but I knew there were other movie credits to uncover.

In Bennett Cerf's book, *At Random*, I found a kernel of information about Nathan Wise, his grandfather, and my great-grandfather. I learned more when Bennett's oral history was available on the internet.

As the internet grew, I subscribed to Ancestry.com, and my research world opened up. From the comfort of my home, I could look at census records and ships' records. Everything changed the day I found the ship's record of my great-grandfather. He had listed his exact town of origin in Germany: Lengsfeld (changed to Stadtlengsfeld in 1896).

Letting my fingers do the traveling, I looked at pictures of Stadtlengsfeld. The town was part of East Germany following World War II. I hired genealogist Esther Bauer to do research for me. She was originally from Germany and able to read the Old German writing. She pored through the records of my father's family in Lengsfeld, borrowed from the Family History Library in Salt Lake City, and sent me her findings.

Researching my mother's side of the family from Baltimore, Maryland, was more difficult. Baltimore had a devastating fire in 1904 that destroyed many records. My mother's family was of modest means, and newspaper articles about them were limited. I found a family tree on Ancestry.com and learned about my maternal great-great grandfather from a distant cousin in Indiana. I visited my mother's sister and her daughter who had moved from Los Angeles to Tucson, Arizona. Happily, I came away with new stories that added to my understanding of my mother's early life.

During a vacation and research trip to Manhattan, my granddaughter and I combed through microfilms and record books in the New York Public Library, noting information about my father's family. We drove by the addresses where the family had lived. We visited the Castle Clinton National Monument where my paternal great-grandfather entered the United States through the Castle Garden immigration center.

Wanting to know more about Stadtlengsfeld, I searched the internet for someone who lived there and spoke English. I discovered the website of a genealogist from Tiefenort who worked in Stadtlengsfeld, Astrid Adler, and thus began a fortuitous and heartwarming friendship that brought answers to many of my questions.

Astrid Adler's newly published book, *Vergessene Menschen*, documented emigration in the nineteenth century from her village of Tiefenort and the Grand Duchy Saxe-Weimar-Eisenach region in Thuringia, including Stadtlengsfeld. She spoke of Mr. Rolf Leimbach, who was a retired teacher in Stadtlengsfeld and the town's historian. Astrid said he didn't speak English, but she would translate for me and wondered if I had thought about visiting Germany.

A few months later, my granddaughter and I made the trip to Germany and enjoyed spending time with Astrid and her husband. We met with Mr. Leimbach, and he took us on a walking tour of Stadtlengsfeld. We took pictures and thought about my father's people who had lived there for decades before World War II. Mr. Leimbach unlocked the iron gates of the Jewish cemetery where we wandered among the headstones of our ancestors and saw the gravesite of my father's grandmother, Fanny.

Astrid and her husband subsequently came to the United States, and we became better acquainted. She wanted to divide the content of her German-language book into two English-language books, and she asked for my help with editing. We worked together by email for more than a year on the project. I returned to Germany for a two-week stay at her home in Tiefenort where we did some final editing, visited Stadtlengsfeld again for more pictures, and had dinner with Mr. Leimbach.

Since then, Astrid has visited the United States numerous times, sometimes staying at my home. What a delight it was to help her with speaking engagements and promotional tours for her books: *Goodbye Forever, Life Beyond Germany* and *Our Ancestors Were German*.

It came time for me to write my own book. In so doing, I have placed a strong emphasis on the houses I lived in. For me, home represents security and comfort in a special way. My life unfolded and evolved in those homes where the rooms absorbed the sounds of my laughter, tears, and prayers. Growing up in the 1940s and 1950s was a unique time in history. I could not have imagined then that the memories created—some good and some not so good—and my fascination with family history and the Golden Age of Hollywood would come together in this memoir.

Susan Wise O'Hearn

CHAPTER 1

The Beginning

———⚬⚬⚬———

Autumn arrives late in Los Angeles. A subtle cooling trend doesn't end the dog days of summer until about mid-October. November is a transitional month, bringing some overcast days and a rainstorm or two but also plenty of sunshine. The big Pacific storms that deliver much-needed water to thirsty landscapes usually hold off until December or January. As the evenings progressively turn chilly, living room fireplaces flicker to life, sending skyward the smoky aroma of logs burning. Just when everyone thinks that winter has finally arrived—shorts and bathing suits have been stashed away—along come the devilish Santa Ana winds off the Mojave Desert, fanning another heat wave. Darn if it's not like summer all over again.

The day I was born, November 21, 1936, Los Angeles was having one of those late-season hot spells. The thermometer hit the mid-eighty mark. My mother spent the day at the Good Samaritan Hospital near downtown—a short labor, she said—giving birth to me just after sunset.

Fall colors are plentiful in late November thanks to deciduous trees such as the Modesto ash, sweet gum, birch, poplar, and sycamore. It's the same every year. Twisting leaves turning vibrant shades of mustard, amber, and rust-red stand out against an otherwise green landscape. While this is usually not Mother Nature's prolific fall celebration as Easterners know it, I think it's a beautiful time of year in Southern California. The scenery does change if you care to notice, and I look forward to the season and the upcoming Thanksgiving and Christmas holidays, and, of course, there's my birthday.

My parents, Walter and Ethel Wise, were delighted with the birth of their first child: me, a daughter. Mom sheepishly admitted when I was older that she had hoped for a boy. Dad celebrated my arrival at a restaurant close to the hospital where he ordered a New York steak dinner, his favorite meal, and proudly handed out cigars to everyone.

Financially, these were easy times for my parents. While many American families were struggling from the effects of the Great Depression, my father was earning a good living working as a screenwriter at Metro-Goldwyn-Mayer Studios (MGM) in Culver City. Before her pregnancy, my mother also worked at MGM. She started out in the stenographers pool and later earned a coveted promotion to a secretarial position in the publicity department headed by Howard Strickling.

Our home was a rented two-bedroom, English Tudor-style bungalow in West Los Angeles on Wetherly Drive near Pico Boulevard. The location was desirable, considering its proximity to the MGM studios. My parents had many friends from the studio who shared the belief that this was a fortuitous time to work in the film industry. It was later recognized as the Golden Age of motion pictures. Stories about the studio, the film stars under contract, and my parents' industry friends were often topics for tantalizing conversations at the adult dinner table at our house while I eavesdropped.

I didn't happen to come from a particularly large family, and what relatives we did have were scattered on opposite coasts. The Wises lived in Manhattan, where my father was born and raised. He grew up in a fashionable apartment with servants. He was one of three surviving siblings and the middle child between his older sister, Delphine, and younger brother, Fred. Stanley, the firstborn, died when he was just five. Had I been a boy, my name would be Stanley.

My father's parents, George and Hulda Wise, were German and Jewish. George was a native of Manhattan, whereas Hulda arrived in her late teens at the end of the nineteenth century when she emigrated from Germany. George and Hulda were first cousins, which was not terribly uncommon in European Jewish culture during that era but a fact that probably affected the health of some of their offspring. Each was related to the New York Wises on one side and the Weiss family of Germany on the other. To further complicate their union, Hulda was not George's first wife. George was married to Hulda's older sister, Bertha, before her death. The children had different mothers: Stanley, Delphine, and Walter were Bertha's children, and Fred belonged to Hulda. Hulda was my great-aunt rather than my grandmother, but she was closer biologically than a step-grandmother. She was the mother who raised my father from the age of five, and I knew her by the nickname everyone fondly called her, Grandma Lovey.

Growing up, I was always intrigued by my father's account of the family money. His grandfather, Nathan Wise, accumulated a sizable fortune as a tobacco distributor in New York and a partner in the Metropolitan Tobacco

Company. When Nathan died, my grandfather inherited a share of his father's money as did his five siblings, including Frederika Wise Cerf, the mother of Bennett Cerf, cofounder of Random House, Inc., New York. Bennett was a day from turning sixteen when his mother died and the inheritance unexpectedly passed to him. A few years later, Bennett used that money to start his publishing company. Bennett was also a well-known celebrity face during the 1950s as the charming panelist on the immensely popular weekly television show, *What's My Line,* now available on the internet for all to enjoy.

Before the 1929 stock market crash, my grandfather was a wealthy man. The family enjoyed an affluent lifestyle. He lost the bulk of his inheritance after the crash, and his stock portfolio was practically worthless.

"That's because he was a stubborn fool and refused to diversify," Dad told me. "He wouldn't listen to anyone, not to me or his brother Herbert."

Uncle Herbert, the youngest of my grandfather's siblings, was remembered as being brilliant and talented with an outgoing charm. Herbert, a writer and aficionado of the arts, lived in a snazzy Park Avenue penthouse. My father said he had a permanent seat on the New York Stock Exchange where he watched his inheritance grow in value. Intuitively, he knew that diversifying his investments was a smart thing. After the stock market crash, Bennett Cerf wrote in his book *At Random* that "with luck and skill Herbert quickly rebuilt his fortune." After Herbert's death, the greater part of his wealth went to his live-in male companion of many years.

My grandfather was obviously not as intuitive or as fortunate as Herbert. His stubborn nature and shortsightedness cost him dearly. In the end, he joined ranks with the legends of other sorry investors who, like him, were wiped out after the stock market crash. It must have been awful. I heard at one point he even contemplated suicide. Finding the courage to go on and save face must have been incredibly difficult. My grandfather continued working, moved to a less expensive apartment, and no longer employed servants. Later on, he and my grandmother moved in with their daughter, Delphine, son-in-law, and Susan, the granddaughter they adored. Not a bad arrangement since my uncle had a silk-stocking factory in Havana, Cuba, and the family lived in Havana for a time. After Grandma Lovey died, my grandfather rented a room in Manhattan that his sister helped to finance, according to my father.

Dad always scoffed when, as a child, I pressed him for more details about the family money. "Tell me how we were almost rich and how you lost your inheritance," I begged him, wanting to hear the story again.

I imagined how my life might be different if I were a rich girl: I'd have my own room, a new bicycle, a closet full of pretty clothes, lots of toys, a huge playhouse, trips to wonderful places, and, of course, a maid, cook, and butler. I fantasized that maybe there was still some family money out there belonging to my dad. Amused, he'd insist, "I promise you there's no money, Susan."

When my father's Uncle Herbert passed away, my father and Fred inherited about thirty-five thousand dollars each. That was a good chunk of change at the time. With his inheritance money, my father established a small independent film production company and bought a bigger house. My fairytale wishes were not too far-fetched. Nevertheless, the inheritance was used up quickly, and I never saw any of the money.

My father's sister, Delphine, started off on better financial footing than her siblings. As the oldest, she reached the age required to cash out her share of a modest trust fund that had been established for all three of the Wise children. Lucky for her, because on Black Friday, what remained in the trust disappeared like a house sheared off its foundation and scattered to the winds in an Oklahoma tornado. As far as their inheritance was concerned, my father and Fred were out of luck. That's why a year later in 1930, my father had no qualms about moving to Los Angeles, bringing with him a thin wallet and high hopes for a better future on the West Coast.

My mother's parents, William Clayton Houck and Elizabeth (Debrick) Houck, were of the Christian faith with appreciably more modest means than the Wises. However, their heritage was also German. The Houcks hailed from Hagerstown, a working-class neighborhood outside of Baltimore, Maryland, where they married and had two daughters: my mother, Ethel Eleanor, and my aunt, Beulah Ovilla, who later changed her name to June.

My mother thought that some members of the Houck family came from Pennsylvania. She said they were Pennsylvania Dutch settlers, and I've often wondered if any of them might have been Amish or Mennonite, but realistically, they were probably Lutheran. My grandmother and aunt had a religious belief system that reflected a curious mixture of theologies, neither wholly Protestant nor Catholic. My aunt gave me a handwritten prayer and told me that she wore one just like it pinned to her underwear when she started elementary school. The prayer was supposed to keep her safe from harm. Since my grandmother's mother was German, it's likely the prayer was German in origin with an English translation.

The Houcks moved to California in 1910 when my mother was three and her baby sister was ready to celebrate her first birthday. They initially lived in Emeryville near Oakland with my grandmother's older sister, Anna, who had relocated from Maryland beforehand.

Aunt Anna was a strong-willed woman. She was married several times and for some years raised her children as a single mother. Rail thin with piercing blue eyes and a sharp nose, she was not very attractive and had a reputation for being strict and a no-nonsense kind of person. I kept a safe distance whenever she was around. However, she and my grandmother were close, and I sensed there was more fun underneath Aunt Anna's hard exterior than I could see.

Needing to find immediate employment, William Houck took a job as an engraver, etching intricate designs on plain glassware and mirrors to enhance their beauty and salability. It was a marketable profession that enabled him to find work quickly. He was artistic, but later, his youngest daughter, June, was recognized as the consummate artist in the family.

The Houck family didn't stay in Northern California long before deciding to head south for a better-paying job and a warmer climate. They arrived in Los Angeles filled with positive expectations for the future at a time when the city's population was mushrooming and economic opportunity seemed plentiful. Aunt Anna and her children moved to Los Angeles as well, which enabled the families to maintain their close bond. My mother and her sister developed a lifelong friendship with their cousin De Setta.

"Your mother is like a sister to me," De Setta often told me.

The Houck's relocation to Los Angeles was the right move. My grandfather found a job as a sign painter and later worked as a motion picture projectionist in a downtown theater. This was the time when Los Angeles vaudeville houses were shifting from live productions to the newest innovation in entertainment: silent movies. People couldn't get enough of this new art form, and they flocked to the theaters in droves. New silent films were being churned out every week like a cookie factory, and most of them took only a day or two to shoot. The motion picture business was booming, and this greatly influenced my mother. Growing up, she had dreams of being in show business. My grandfather's dreams, however, took him in another direction. At midlife, he enrolled in college and became a chiropractor, although his life was cut short, and he didn't work for long in his new profession.

In 1936, when I was born, my father and mother were happy and doing well on Wetherly Drive. Franklin Delano Roosevelt was president of the United States. The Yankees beat out the Giants in the World Series with help from baseball greats Lou Gehrig and Joe DiMaggio. I came into the world as Susan Delphine, befitting a new descendent of the Wise family.

A Rose by Any Other Name

Growing up, I disliked my middle name, Delphine. Dad naturally favored it because it was his sister's name. Later in life, I was surprised to learn that Delphine was also the name of my father's grandmother. It was a popular French name.

My friends always burst out laughing when I told them my middle name. It was unfamiliar and sounded peculiar to them. I wanted something simpler like Ann, Marie, or Diane. I began using my initial as Susan D. Wise.

For a while, I didn't even like the name Susan. That probably started after a playground incident when I was in the sixth grade. A bully from my class started calling me "Thuthee." What I did to deserve his lunchtime taunting is uncertain. When the other kids snickered, it got him going. "Thuthee, Thuthee, Thuthee," he chanted one day while my face flushed red. I should have kicked him in the shins.

When I was thirteen years old, I fell hard for a boy named Bob. We were an item at summer church camp that year in the San Bernardino Mountains. I went with the Lake Street Baptist Church when we were living in Glendale, and he was there with another Baptist church. As soon as I came home from camp, I decided to change my name. I asked Bob and everyone else to call me Jeannette, which I thought was a more sophisticated-sounding name. Since Bob lived a distance away in Bellflower, we wrote letters back and forth. Although the envelopes were addressed to Susan Wise, inside he obligingly started off "Dear Jeannette." Our pen pal relationship lasted only a short time. I had hopes of seeing him again at church camp the next year, but he didn't go. Happily, there were plenty of other boys.

Dad sometimes called me Sukie, but that nickname never caught on. Looking back, I guess my friends thought I was silly in insisting on being called Jeannette. No one else took on a different name except my friend Betty. In the sixth grade, she changed her last name when her mother remarried.

When I entered North Hollywood High School, after moving from Glendale, I finally made a name change. On the first day of school, I was waiting in the auditorium for my classroom assignments along with the other new students. I sat with the tenth graders who, like me, had just graduated from a junior high school outside of the area.

It was an exciting day, although at eight o'clock in the morning, the large auditorium was already stifling hot. The school didn't have air conditioning, nor did any of the schools. If I had known it was supposed to be over one hundred degrees, I would never have worn my new woolen skirt with the hipline pleats. I sat sweating in my seat, and the wool itched terribly. Fortunately, I had on a sleeveless blouse, although the white cotton piqué fabric didn't look right with the beige tweed skirt, and the metal circular buttons on the blouse kept popping open. Looking around and noticing some classier girls, I knew I was going to need some help in the dressing-for-popularity department.

A friendly girl sat down next to me. She asked my name, and I nonchalantly answered, "Sue." That was the nickname my cousin Susan in New York used, and I thought it sounded more grown-up. It was a spur-of-the-moment decision.

"Hi, Sue. I'm Marcia."

It was as easy as that. I went from Susan to Sue in one short conversation and met my first friend, Marcia, in high school. Since then, my name of choice has been Sue. Of course, Susan is required on legal documents, and there are some close friends and family members who affectionately call me Suzy. You could say I ended up with three names: Susan, Sue, and Suzy. Take your pick, but please don't call me Thuthee if you want to keep on living.

My mother, Ethel, and her sister, Beulah Ovilla, were obviously not bestowed with beautiful-sounding names. Mom never had a nickname except for a few years when she worked as a chorus line dancer at the Orpheum Theater in Los Angeles. Everyone in the theater company called her Babe Williams.

She never minded the name Ethel, but I knew for sure that she liked her middle name. "My name is Ethel Eleanor," she often told people, linking the names together proudly.

Just before her sixty-fifth birthday, Mom sent for her official birth certificate from Baltimore so she could apply for Social Security benefits. What she discovered was a shock. Eleanor was not her middle name. The birth certificate read Ethel Renetta Houck. She telephoned me in disbelief. "Who the heck is Renetta?" she asked.

The next person she called was her mother. My grandmother was also surprised. "I'm sorry," she said. "The midwife must have recorded that name."

Mom was upset and felt like she'd been robbed. "I want Eleanor back." She whined but never followed up to find out how that could be legally done.

Beulah did change her name. She explained, "I always hated the name Beulah. When a boy straight off the farm embarrassed me in front of the neighborhood kids saying, 'Our cow's name was Beulah, and she had big, brown eyes just like yours,' that was the last straw. Since I was born in the month of June, I decided it was a good name."

Beulah became June in her late teens, and the name stuck for the rest of her life.

CHAPTER 2

The Wise Family

Walter Wise, my father, was born and raised in Manhattan, the same as his father, George Wise. How my father's family came to have money speaks to the American dream coming true for my father's immigrant grandfather, Nathan Wise, who made his fortune in the tobacco industry.

My grandfather George, grew up as one of six children, all born in Manhattan and of German heritage: Minnie, Emma, George, Frederika (Freda), Arthur, and Herbert. A seventh child, Blanche, died in infancy. The children's mother, my great-grandmother Delphine, tragically passed away in 1893 at the young age of forty-four, one month after Herbert was born. Grandfather George was twenty-two years old and still living at home. His early life is hidden in the archives of history, but there's a hint that he might have attended college.

Early on, George worked as a bookkeeper, sold real estate, and for a time had a business venture with his younger brother, Arthur. The Wise & Jacobs Company sold hosiery, underwear, and gloves.

In an oral history taken by Columbia University, Bennett Cerf said about his uncles, "They had a hosiery business, which was quite successful, and they loved being recognized by officials. They used to give free socks to the entire police department of New York, so that when they'd ride in their car down Fifth Avenue, they'd be recognized. My uncles agreed that it cost them a fortune, but they were hailed by the police!"

The bulk of George's money came from an inheritance after his father passed away. My great-grandfather, Nathan Wise, was an astute businessman who amassed a great deal of money in the tobacco distributing business. While enjoying a pleasure trip abroad with his second wife, Bettie, and son, Herbert, in the summer of 1908, Nathan died unexpectedly of unknown causes in the spa town of Marienbad, Germany, two months short of his sixty-sixth birthday. Half of Nathan's fortune went to Bettie, and the rest was divided among his six children, including my grandfather.

Nathan Wise

My great-grandfather's life is a fascinating story. Regrettably, my father never knew his grandfather, because Nathan died one year after my father was born. Nathan's rise to prominence and prosperity in the tobacco distributing business points to his intelligence and business savvy considering he spoke only German when he came to this country. Though my father was a sensitive boy and found his career in writing and the creative arts, he would have admired his tough-thinking grandfather and his hard-fought accomplishments.

Nathan cannot compare to the richest tycoons of the era such as Cornelius Vanderbilt, John D. Rockefeller, or Andrew Carnegie, but he does share some things in common with them. Creating a business from the ground up like those men, Nathan and his partners, the Bendheim brothers (Wise, Bendheim & Company), built their tobacco distributing company into the largest jobbing house in Manhattan. They went on to dominate the New York tobacco distributing business, and in 1909, they went through a reorganization and founded the Metropolitan Tobacco Company. One of the partners throughout the years was Nathan's brother-in-law, Julius G. Miller, the younger brother of my great-grandmother Delphine.

Nathan and Delphine's firstborn child, Minnie, married a cigar salesman, and they moved to Portland, Oregon, in the early 1900s for business opportunities there. Since selling tobacco products appeared to be a family career path, it is surprising that neither my grandfather nor his brothers followed in their father's footsteps. Then again, in those unregulated times, it was a tough business to be in. There was intimidation from competitors, price gouging, undercutting, and lawsuits to fight. The federal government was breathing down their necks. Buyouts and mergers were negotiated as "Big Tobacco" worked to gain a monopoly. George Wise and Arthur Wise chose to work in a variety of sales jobs that were probably much less stressful, while Herbert Wise became a financial investor in the stock market as well as a writer associated with Manhattan's artistic and literary community.

Some of the most successful entrepreneurs of the nineteenth century ran their businesses during this time when monopolies went unchecked. Teddy Roosevelt became president after the assassination of William McKinley, and his relentless drive to break up monopolies led to the federal government initiating lawsuits under the Sherman

Antitrust Act of 1890. The lawsuits eventually broke up the monopolies and changed the way business in America is conducted.

The American Tobacco Company and the Metropolitan Tobacco Company, as its sole distributor in New York, were deemed monopolies in the federal lawsuit brought against them and ordered to disband. The Metropolitan Tobacco Company closed down in 1911, and Nathan retired. This is the short version of what happened, as there were earlier lawsuits against my great-grandfather's company. In New York, "tobacco jobbing" had a complicated history.

Interestingly, Nathan could have joined James Buchanan Duke in the founding of the American Tobacco Company in 1890. In his oral history, Bennett Cerf explained why Nathan turned down the opportunity. "At one time a young man came to him and suggested a partnership that my conservative grandfather didn't think was very good. The man's name was Duke, and he became the great tobacco magnate. My grandfather thought he was a wild young fellow, which indeed he was."

What Nathan lacked in common with America's notable tycoons was the willingness to take unimaginable risks or the ruthless ambition to win at all costs, which describes men like Vanderbilt, Rockefeller, and Carnegie. Nathan was a devoted family man, widowed in 1893 when his last child, Herbert, was a newborn. He married his second wife Bettie in 1897 when Herbert was about four years old. Bettie was thirty-three, much younger than Nathan, and had no children. Nathan's daughter, Emma, who never married, might have raised Herbert with the help of servants until Nathan remarried. Bettie then took over raising Herbert and was the only mother he knew.

Lengsfeld, Germany

Nathan arrived in Manhattan in the fall of 1863 at the age of twenty-one. His surname was Weiss, but in a few years, he changed it to Wise. He came from Lengsfeld in Thuringia, which after 1896 was known as Stadtlengsfeld, meaning "city of Lengsfeld." The town had a large Jewish population with a synagogue, mikveh, kosher meat market, and cemetery that has remained intact to this day, though it has deteriorated appreciably. My father's people are buried in the cemetery including his maternal grandmother, Fanny (Ullmann) Weiss, and generations of ancestors that can be traced back to at least the mid-1700s. Since my father's parents were first cousins, both sides of his family originated in Lengsfeld. I discovered there were other intermarriages going back in time.

Stadtlengsfeld circa 1900

Nathan Weiss was the youngest son of the trader Salomon Weiss II and Mindel (Ullmann) Weiss. Nathan's older brother, Salomon (Salomon III), was a merchant. During his first marriage, Nathan's brother resided in Tiefenort with his wife, Regina, and their two young daughters, although he was born and raised in Lengsfeld.

Tiefenort is about fifteen minutes by automobile from Stadtlengsfeld and is the village where my friend Astrid Adler lives. Astrid wrote three books about nineteenth-century emigration from this Thuringian region of Germany. In one of them, she includes a newspaper announcement from 1863 that shows that Salomon Weiss III gave a financial guarantee to Catharine Elizabethe (Ziller) Isleib and her three minor children who intended to immigrate to America at the same time as his brother, Nathan. The person giving a guarantee agrees to assume all debts that might be owed by the person who is leaving the country. Because of the financial implications, guarantees were normally issued only for family members or a very close personal friend. The ability to give a guarantee shows that Salomon Weiss III was financially secure and a man of good character in the community.

Ziller happens to be Astrid Adler's maiden name. Astrid and I were amazed that our ancestors had a close connection in 1863, more than a century and a half before we met by chance (or divine intervention) on the internet. Our mutual interest in family history and genealogy led to us becoming good friends.

In 1870, two years after his first wife, Regina, died, Salomon Weiss III married Fanny Ullmann, my future great-grandmother, and they resided in Lengsfeld. Salomon and Fanny had a son named Siegmund, who died at the age of five. They also had four daughters: Bertha, Golda, Hulda, and Esther. Assumedly, Salomon's daughters from his first marriage, Gella and Minna, stayed with him and were raised by his second wife, Fanny. Bertha and Hulda eventually moved to New York and became the wife (at separate times, of course) of my grandfather, George Wise.

To explain why Nathan Wise left Germany in 1863, it helps to know some history of Germany and Lengsfeld at the time. Germany was not unified as a country until 1871. Until then, it was a collection of kingdoms, duchies, and principalities run by kings, princes, and dukes. The House of Boyneburg owned the land on which the town of Lengsfeld was situated as well as the surrounding countryside and forest. Life was difficult for the town's inhabitants whether Jewish, Catholic, or Protestant. Many families earned a small income working in a weaving mill. However, weaving at home was considered the most important occupation. The townspeople were not allowed to collect wood or other natural resources in the forest. A citizen was not even allowed to keep sheep in his own yard for wool and meat, because only the lords had the privilege of sheep farming. Agricultural farms were few, since farmers were unable to secure financing to pay taxes and duties.

Jewish men in Germany were not allowed to have certain kinds of jobs. Hence, they traditionally worked as cattlemen, traders, traveling merchants, and shopkeepers. Young men of all religions sought to escape inscription into the military to fight in the numerous wars. No wonder that between 1843 and 1869, many Germans immigrated to countries throughout the world, including my great-grandfather who left Lengsfeld for a better life in America.

When I visited Stadtlengsfeld with Astrid and my granddaughter, I was surprised that the town looked much the same as it did in photos from the late 1800s. The streets were laid out the same, the houses were the same, the small Felda River ran on the edge of town, and the trees lining the main street were the same kind and even the same size. Fortunately, Stadtlengsfeld was not bombed during World War II.

My great-grandmother, Fanny Weiss, had a brother named Nathan Ullmann, who had a mercantile store on the main street with living quarters above. The building still exists, is in good repair, and is painted white. Of course, now cars are parked along the street instead of horses, carts, and buggies. While residents refer to Stadtlengsfeld as a town or sometimes even a city, by American standards it is small—a village, in my opinion.

Three story Ullmann house (2014)

A fire in 1878 set by a disgruntled employee destroyed a third of Lengsfeld including seventy houses, twenty that were owned by Jews. Dankmar Adler (no relation to Astrid Adler) was born in Lengsfeld. He moved to Chicago and became one of America's best-known architects and the father of the modern skyscraper. Dankmar Adler spearheaded a large event in Manhattan to raise money to rebuild Lengsfeld. I imagine Nathan Wise attended the event or at least contributed money.

In 1878, a railroad line came to Lengsfeld. This was welcome good news for the residents who now had a much easier time traveling, especially to connections that led to the northern seaport.

Coming to America

My great-grandfather's arrival in the United States marks the beginning of the Wise family in this country. He paid for his cabin passage aboard the steamship *America* and set sail from the German port city of Bremerhaven near Bremen. In those days, it took about three weeks to cross the Atlantic Ocean.

Nathan, using his original surname Weiss, arrived in New York City on November 8, 1863, and was processed through the Castle Garden immigration center. There is no evidence of a brother coming to the United States before him, though Nathan's father noted in one record that he had two sons living in America. The mystery is yet to be solved.

On the ship's manifest, Nathan Weiss listed his occupation as "merchant," the same as his father in Lengsfeld. Selling cigarettes and cigars was an easy way to get started making a living in America, and that's what he did. In 1863, Abraham Lincoln was the president of the United

States, and the country was embroiled in a civil war. My great-grandfather avoided the fighting and remained in Manhattan where business ventures were available if you were a smart man like him.

Census records taken seven years after he arrived in the United States show that Nathan Weiss (age 28) was married to Delphine (age 21), and they had three children: Minnie (age 3), Emma (age 2), and George (age 1), my future grandfather. They were living in an apartment on Attorney Street in an area in Lower Manhattan known as Kleindeutschland (Little Germany). One servant lived with them. Nathan listed his occupation as tobacconist. Clearly, my great-grandfather was doing well after being in the country for only a short time.

Delphine's parents, Abraham and Caroline Miller, were my great-great grandparents. They also lived in Kleindeutschland with two of their children, Arthur and Louise. Another son, Julius G. Miller, was grown and lived elsewhere. The Millers emigrated from Luxembourg when my great grandmother Delphine was two and her brother, Julius, was eight months old. They made the trip across the Atlantic Ocean on a sailing vessel, a journey notoriously fraught with danger and life-threatening illnesses. It was a difficult crossing with small children. They left Hamburg on May 1, 1850, and it took six weeks or more, depending on the winds and weather, to reach New York Harbor. They endured the hardships of such travel for a better life in America, which they found. In Luxembourg, my great-great grandparents' surname could have been different than Miller (maybe Mueller or Muller).

Young Nathan Weiss and Delphine Miller probably met through friends or as neighbors in Kleindeutschland, where the German culture and language thrived. Encompassing an area between Fourteenth and Division Streets, the East River, and the Bowery, Kleindeutschland was the first large, urban-language settlement in an American city. Between 1855 and 1880, it was the third-largest German-speaking community in the world, outranked only by Berlin and Vienna.

By 1880, Nathan was going by the surname of Wise. He was the head of a large extended family living together at 667 Madison Avenue, including his wife, Delphine, five children, parents-in-law Abraham and Caroline Miller and their young adult children, Arthur and Louise, and two servants. Four years later, the large family was living in a multilevel, single-family home at 14 E. Seventy-Sixth Street, a block from Central Park.

My father enjoyed explaining how our last name changed from Weiss to Wise. The story goes that his grandfather needed a truck to transport his tobacco goods. He bought one with the name WISE already lettered on the side. Why not Americanize his surname and avoid having to repaint the name on the truck? Nathan was an opportunist and a frugal man. By the time the 1880 census was taken, the family name had officially changed to Wise. When Nathan became a naturalized American citizen on March 27, 1884, it was under the surname Wise, and his children carried the surname forward.

In Lengsfeld, Nathan's brother, Salomon Weiss, and his wife, Fanny, were active in the synagogue. Salomon was a board member of the Jewish community for many years. Fanny was active in the Jewish Women's Association, which saw to the needs of the ill and indigent.

In this country, Nathan Wise and his family were not

religious, nor was my father's immediate family. However, their friends and business associates were predominantly Jewish. Over the years, Nathan invested in real estate, buying and selling open land in locations including the Bronx and what is now Harlem. He made donations to the Hebrew Sheltering Guardian Society of New York, an orphanage for Jewish children. Given his wealth, he might have given money to his relatives in Lengsfeld, where life was difficult.

Life presumably grew harder for my great-grandmother, Fanny Weiss, after her husband died in 1891 at the age of sixty-one. She was twenty-four years younger than him and had children at home to raise, one as young as two years old. There is no proof, but Nathan probably sent his sister-in-law money, or perhaps she received help from other relatives living in Lengsfeld or from the Jewish Women's Association. In a tight-knit community like theirs, people helped one another as best they could.

This also explains why Fanny's daughters Bertha and Hulda went to America in their late teens and married (at different times) their cousin George Wise. He had the means to give them a better life.

Travels to Germany

Nathan Wise retained close ties to relatives in his hometown of Lengsfeld. According to Astrid Adler, many emigrants left Germany never to return, relying on letters to stay in contact with loved ones. Some who left were never heard from again, hence the title of her first book on emigration, *Vergessene Menschen*, which translates "Forgotten People."

In 1891, Nathan took his family on a trip to Germany and arrived back in New York aboard the steamship SS

Kaiser Wilhelm II on October 5. His wife, Delphine, and their five children (before their son Herbert was born) were aboard as well as Delphine's brother, Julius G. Miller, his wife, Virginia, and their two children.

In those days, New York did not retain records of ships leaving port, only those returning. Given the two weeks or so it took to cross the ocean by steamship, and from the itinerary on their passport application, it is clear they were gone for the whole summer. Nathan's brother, Salomon Weiss, died in April 1891, so perhaps the main purpose of the trip was to attend a memorial service for him in Lengsfeld. My grandfather, George Wise, was twenty-one years old, and it appears to be his first trip to Lengsfeld. If so, then this is when he met his cousin Bertha Weiss, whom he married on April 24, 1900.

The record shows that in the summer of 1905, Mrs. George Wise (Bertha) returned to Stadtlengsfeld for a visit with her son, Stanley (age 4), and daughter, Delphine (age 2). Bertha's sister, Hulda Weiss (age 17), returned to New York with them.

Nathan Wise made another voyage to Germany fourteen years later. On this trip, he was with his second wife, Bettie, son Herbert, and daughter, Emma. They arrived home on August 23, 1905, aboard the SS *Kaiser Wilhem Der Gross* after enjoying an extended vacation.

As mentioned, my father never knew his grandfather. His cousin Bennett Cerf, however, was nine years older than his cousin Walter and remembered him well. In his book, *At Random*, Bennett said the Cerf family was loaded with charm but little money, while the Wise family had little charm but a lot of money.

Everybody kowtowed to my Grandfather Wise, a rather stern man with a beard—he looked like one of the Smith Brothers then pictured on cough-drop boxes. I saw him mainly on Sundays, the day reserved for having dinner with him and the rest of the family. My mother was one of six children, three boys and three girls, Grandfather had a private house and lived in some elegance, and he had the first automobile I ever saw. He also had a great backhand. At the dinner table he'd reach across and wallop you so fast, you couldn't see it coming. So, the object was to sit as far as possible from Grandpa at Sunday dinners. In the afternoon when he would take a nap, the house had to be silent as a church. I never was quiet in my life, and I was usually the one who woke him up and got the back of his hand.

My father and mother met each other in a rather curious way. Not too many girls went to college then, not in the circle my family moved in, anyway. But when my parents were young, it was considered quite the thing for respectable young ladies to take elocution lessons and recite things like "The Boy Stood on the Burning Deck." So, a teacher was hired for my mother, Frederika Wise, and the gentleman who gave her those lessons was my father. The teacher and pupil fell madly in love, and eloped—to the outrage of my grandfather, who looked upon my father as a charming fly-by-night. And those two people were gloriously in love for their entire lives together. So, I was born into a happy family. (Bennett Cerf, At Random [New York: Random House, 1977], Pages 3-4).

Sadly, Frederika (Wise) Cerf passed away in 1914 after a later-in-life pregnancy the day before Bennett's sixteenth birthday. The inheritance from her father, Nathan Wise, passed to Bennett, purportedly in the amount of $125,000. (In 2021 dollars, that equates to $3,256,000.) Shortly after the death of Bennett's mother, her brother, Herbert, moved into the Cerf household. He was just five years older than Bennett, and Bennett said his uncle became a strong literary and social influence on him. In 1925, Bennett and his friend Donald Klopfer formed a partnership to purchase rights to the Modern Library and began a publishing business that became Random House, Inc., New York.

CHAPTER 3

Dad

Walter Julius Wise was born on April 23, 1907, in Manhattan. His sister, Delphine, was four years older, and his brother, Fred, was eight years younger. They grew up in an upscale apartment in Manhattan.

Dad was super smart and good looking. He was six feet tall with a slim build and broad shoulders. When walking down the street, he took long, purposeful strides with an air of confidence, and it was hard for me to keep up with him as a little girl. He had blue eyes and dark-brown hair before it turned silver gray. His naturally curly hair was kept short, creating ripples on the crown of his head that reminded me of corrugated cardboard. At times, he came across as arrogant with a superior attitude, but he knew how to make a good impression when it counted and made lasting friends and loyal business associates over the years. In my youth, I thought of him as impatient and sometimes aloof, which bothered me. He was reserved, yet in a group of people, he could entertain with charm, sharing stories and anecdotes that often made him the center of the conversation. He was definitely opinionated. He had an innate ability to accurately judge a person's character, something

I wanted to learn from him. While not demonstratively affectionate with me or my sister, a reflection of his German upbringing, he was a man of his word. He always told me, "I'll never make a promise I can't keep."

Dad went to a public school in Manhattan, except for one year, at age six, when he attended school in Germany. In Manhattan, he played stickball in the street. I thought kids living in the big city didn't have the freedom to play outside like I did in Los Angeles. Dad said, "When I was young, the streets weren't as crowded, but we still had to watch out for vehicles."

Dad said it was an advantage to grow up in the city. He bragged about New York's excellent schools. The city offered an abundance of activities, places to go, and things to see. He enjoyed going to museums and cultural centers with friends. He was an avid reader, learned to play bridge, and studied violin for twelve years. He also loved the theater and was naturally drawn to the words, music, and stories of writers who captured his imagination and acclaim. His parents took him to the opera. For those occasions, they dressed in their finest attire and wore velvet capes instead of coats.

Walter in New York.

What he didn't like about New York was the humidity in the summer and the bitter cold and snow in winter, especially when the streets became slushy and dirty. One winter in his boyhood, he underwent a double mastoidectomy, the result of continuous ear infections that threatened his hearing and even his life. He recovered but bore the surgical scars behind each ear.

Dad didn't talk about the early days of his youth, presumably because they were marked by a terrible tragedy. He did tell me about his mother's suicide, but there was more to the story than he revealed. My father was born eleven months after his older brother, Stanley, died of spinal meningitis and pneumonia. Five years later when my father was five, his mother, Bertha, was being cared for in the home by a nurse. What happened next was detailed in *The New York Times*. The article described how on the morning of October 10, 1912, Bertha had enjoyed breakfast with the family. After her husband left for work, Bertha sent her son and daughter with the maid to see the ships in the harbor. Escaping the watchful eye of her nurse, she jumped from the roof of their building. Neighbors found her body. She was only thirty-nine years old.

What a disturbing and painful memory for the family to endure, especially for her young children. My father and his sister, Delphine, must have asked themselves a thousand times, "Why?" We know that in those days, there were no miracle drugs for depression. There was little hope for relief or recovery. Bertha must have suffered greatly.

What I'm about to say may have nothing to do with Bertha's depression or suicide, but there are some coincidences. Bertha was her mother's firstborn child, although there were two half-sisters living in their Lengsfeld home. There were no more children until Bertha reached the age of seven, and then her brother, Siegmund, was born. Bertha was twelve when Siegmund died at the age of five. It leaves me wondering if Bertha was haunted by not only her son's death but also that of a beloved brother, as both died at age five. She took her own life when my father was five. Sadly, we will never know why.

The months following Bertha's death must have been terribly difficult for the family. A year later in 1913, when my father was six years old, he traveled to Stadtlengsfeld with his father. He remained there for a year while his father returned home. He presumably lived with his grandmother, Fanny Weiss, and perhaps his maiden aunt, Golda. He went to the schoolhouse on the hill above town, which still stands there today. Since German was spoken at home, my father had no trouble speaking or understanding the language.

The following summer, George Wise, his new wife, Hulda, and daughter, Delphine, returned to Stadtlengsfeld to bring young Walter home. They arrived back in New York on October 25, 1914, aboard the SS *Rotterdam* and were lucky their steamship reservations were honored. World War I had just started, and American citizens were clamoring to leave Germany. Passenger ships were full and shortly thereafter stopped service altogether.

Though my father said nothing of his time in Stadtlengsfeld, he did say how much he enjoyed watching the cargo transfers while traveling onboard the ship. The SS *Rotterdam* carried passengers as well as some cargo. (Dad also raved about the bread in Germany, saying it was the best bread he had ever tasted.)

By the way, this was not my father's first trip to Stadtlengsfeld. In the summer of 1910, when he was three years old, he traveled there with his father, mother (Bertha), and sister (Delphine).

My grandfather, George, married Bertha's younger sister, Hulda, seventeen months after Bertha's death. In May 1915, Hulda gave birth to Fred. In Jewish culture, it was not uncommon for a widower to marry his wife's sister in the belief that a close family member could better help raise the children. Hulda was already living in the home and knew the children well. She spent considerable time with the family in New York since traveling there from Germany in her late teens. Perhaps she came to help her sister with the children or care for Bertha when she was ill, or maybe she just came for the advantages of being in America.

For Delphine and Walter, there was undoubtedly more stability with a mentally sound mother now caring for them. There were also two servants living in the home to help with the household chores. By everyone's description, Hulda was a kind and loving woman—hence her nickname, Lovey—and Fred was welcomed into the household as the new baby brother.

Walter, Fred, George, Hulda

The Wises had a large extended family and many friends. They had an active social life and enjoyed get-togethers with relatives. Unfortunately, there were times when those get-togethers meant gathering for a funeral. My father said he was once at a funeral with his parents. It was the fourth death of a relative in a short time. At the end of the funeral, trying to get a laugh, he announced loudly, "Now they have a fourth for bridge." He said no one laughed.

My father must have inherited the love of jokes from his father, who also told jokes. Dad became an excellent joke teller and had a large repertoire for just about every occasion. Sometimes he told off-color ones, which made me feel uncomfortable. Mostly he specialized in good ethnic jokes that he could tell with the appropriate accent. One of my Dad's favorites was this one.

An old Irishman, Paddy, was about to go to his eternal reward. He looked at his grieving friend, Mike, and said, "I have one last request, Mike."

"Anything, Paddy," Mike said. "What is it?"

"In me kitchen pantry, you'll find a one-hundred-year-old bottle of whiskey. When they put me in the ground, will you pour it over me grave?"

"I will, Paddy," Mike said, "but would you mind if I passed it through me kidneys first?"

In a conversation with my mother, Grandma Lovey told her, "Walter was a difficult child." She said he had an awful temper. Dad himself told the story of the time he was twelve and quarreled with his sister. He became furious with Delphine and impulsively threw her new watch out of the high apartment window. "I felt terrible afterward," Dad said. "I usually just teased her about her boyfriends."

Temper or not, Dad was a sensitive child. My cousin Susan said that his father referred to him as "the proverbial waterworks."

Dad had his bar mitzvah at age thirteen. "We weren't religious," he said. "I just wanted a party and presents like the rest of my friends."

Given the death of his mother and a father who by all accounts was emotionally unsupportive and critical, Dad's boyhood was no doubt unhappy, yet he was remarkably uncritical when talking about his upbringing. He did call his father stupid for losing his inheritance money in the stock market crash and said he resented his father for never attending any of his basketball games at school. Underneath it all, my father probably felt aggrieved that none of his grandfather's fortune passed down to the children of George Wise.

One of my Dad's sayings was this: "Money doesn't make you happy, but if you have to be unhappy, it's better with money than without."

In 1921, my father's family spent another summer vacation in Germany, leaving New York in June and arriving home on September 9, 1921, aboard the steamship SS *Nieuw Amsterdam*. George and Hulda Wise, Delphine Wise (age 18), Walter Wise (age 14), Fred Wise (age 6), aunt Emma Wise, and niece Renny Huhn were on this voyage. Although my father was older, true to form he said nothing about his time in Germany or the relatives he visited in Stadtlengsfeld.

In his mid-teens, Dad lived away from home at boarding school at the Worcester Academy Prep School in Massachusetts. He was on the basketball team and cross-country team, and he belonged to the history club. Coming to Worcester Academy with fifteen college credits, he had a jump on college.

A good story comes from Dad's school days at Worcester Academy. It was the first day of a new class. His professor, a lorgnette over one eye, was taking roll. Failing to call out Dad's name, the professor turned to my dad, saying, "What is your name?"

My father politely answered, "Wise, sir."

The professor looked puzzled and repeated the question. Same response. Irritated, the professor told him to stop asking *why*. The class started laughing, and the professor, losing all professionalism, shouted, "Tell me your name."

"Wise, sir" came the predictable response.

The headmaster walked by the class at that moment and opened the door to see what the commotion was about. The professor said, "I keep asking this insolent young man his name, and all he says is 'wise sir.'"

The headmaster smiled and said, "For goodness sake, my good man, that is his name."

Dad entered Yale University at the age of seventeen to study banking. He was on the Yale basketball team and joined Pi Lambda Phi, the Jewish fraternity his cousin Bennett Cerf belonged to when he attended Columbia University.

Another story is about my father's allowance when he was attending college at Yale, money that he habitually used up before the month ended. Dad sent a letter to his father, asking for additional funds. Fed up with his son's mismanagement of money, Dad's father sent back a postcard reading "Enclosed please find check."

Sometimes I tell people that my father graduated from Yale, but that's not true. He finished most of his studies but quit before graduating. After college, he worked at a bank in Manhattan for a short time before deciding to drastically change careers.

My father's parents made one more trip to Germany with Uncle Herbert during the summer of 1929, arriving home on October 1, days before the stock market crashed on October 29. This would be their last trip to Europe.

Relatives Escape Germany

My grandfather may have had some unlikable traits, especially from his son Fred's point of view, but to their credit, he and Hulda graciously welcomed numerous relatives into their home for extended stays. George's sister, Emma, lived with them for a few years and traveled with them. George's brother, Herbert, also lived with them for a while.

Other family members came from Stadtlengsfeld and Tiefenort to live with my grandparents. The Wise home became a port in the storm for Jewish relatives leaving Germany. The first to come at the age of twenty in 1914 (as World War I started) was Renny Huhn. When I saw her listed as a niece on the census, I wondered, *Who the heck is Renny Huhn?* My father never mentioned her name—not once—yet she lived with the family for about six years, beginning when my father was seven.

It turns out that Renny was his mother's half-sister's daughter, a niece as indicated, and she was also his father's uncle Salomon's granddaughter. Oh, how confusing it is to figure out our convoluted family tree!

Renny Huhn worked as a seamstress. She became a US citizen in 1920 and eventually moved to a rooming house.

As the Nazi regime threatened the lives of Jews, my grandparents opened their home and assisted other members of the family leaving Stadtlengsfeld before escape from Germany became impossible. My grandmother's sister, Esther Norring (known as Else), came in 1937 with her daughter, Inga. Else's sons, Alex and Fred, arrived in New York the year before.

Thankfully, Renny was able to bring the rest of her family to America. Her sister, Eva Huhn, arrived in 1936. In

January 1937, her sister, Helene Blau, brother-in-law, Herbert Blau, and father, Jacob Huhn, all came from Tiefenort. Jacob Huhn was a merchant in Tiefenort and a widower since 1924 when his wife, Minna, died. The surname Blau became Blair in America.

By 1940, Renny and her sisters, brother-in-law, and father were all sharing an apartment in Manhattan. Renny enjoyed several trips abroad during her lifetime, and she passed away in 1985 at the age of ninety-one.

Kristallnacht (night of broken glass) in 1938 was the turning point for the forty-eight Jews remaining in Stadtlengsfeld. On November 9–10, the Nazi SA paramilitary forces and civilians carried out a pogrom against the Jews as German authorities looked on without intervening. Windows of Jewish-owned stores, buildings, and synagogues were smashed, and Jewish homes, hospitals, and schools were ransacked. Rioters destroyed 267 synagogues throughout Germany, Austria, and the Sudetenland. Thirty thousand Jewish men were arrested and incarcerated in prison camps.

The Jews in Stadtlengsfeld on November 9, 1938, were witness that night to the burning and destruction of their synagogue. They were doomed—rounded up, sent to the nearest city of Eisenach, loaded into boxcars, and sent to concentration camps. Golda Weiss, my great-aunt, unfortunately and for some unknown reason, never joined her sisters in New York. She died in Auschwitz in 1942 at the age of sixty. Thank goodness her mother, Fanny Weiss, passed away in 1930 before any of that happened.

After World War II ended in 1945, Stadtlengsfeld and Tiefenort became part of East Germany, trapped behind the Iron Curtain under Communist rule. Freedom for the people living in the state of Thuringia was not realized until Germany's reunification in 1990.

Felda River (2014)

Today, Stadtlengsfeld is a picturesque, peaceful town nestled in the rolling hills of the Rhön Mountains. As it travels from Tiefenort, the road goes over the small Felda River Bridge before reaching the main part of town. When my granddaughter and I were there in the month of June, we stood on the bridge and watched as the shallow, meandering river gurgled below us on its way toward the Werra River, which eventually joins the larger Fulda River. We could see children playing on the walking path next to the river. Trees alongside the path shaded a few fishermen who were trying their luck. A family of ducks waddled by, and we thought about what life was like for our ancestors who lived in this idyllic setting before they were forced to leave.

Stadtlengsfeld (2014)

Fanny Weiss's side of the family escaped to New York and Palestine (later settling in Israel). One descendant living in New York is my distant cousin, Jonathon Ullmann, whose grandfather was Fanny's brother. Astrid Adler put us in touch. Jon and his family visited Stadtlengsfeld shortly after my granddaughter and I were there. They planted an almond tree in the Jewish graveyard next to the gravesite of Isaac and Sara (Weiss) Ullmann, his great-grandparents and my great-great grandparents. Jon and I had a nice telephone conversation filled with additional family information, and we have since kept in contact.

It's curious that my father never talked about any of his relatives living in Stadtlengsfeld, not even his grandmother,

Fanny. I can hear him saying from heaven, "Well, Susan, I left all of that good family history for you to discover one day when you're writing a book."

Hollywood or Bust

In 1930, movies with audible dialogue had only recently replaced silent films, and the demand for "talkies" was insatiable. Producer Irving Thalberg and studio president Louis B. Mayer of MGM Studios responded to the public demand by cranking out new feature films by the dozens, sometimes completing a movie in a month or two. Scriptwriters were recruited and hired from across the nation.

My father left New York at the age of twenty-two in 1930 and moved to Los Angeles on the heels of his close friend, Felix E. Feist, to work in the film industry. This was a year after the stock market crash, and with the loss of the trust fund money he was due to inherit, Dad was on his own. Young Felix was the son of Felix F. Feist, vice president of sales for the New York division of MGM, and the nephew of Leo Feist, head of the Feist Sheet Music Publishing Company in New York. Clearly, the Feist connection had everything to do with my father getting a job at MGM.

When Dad arrived in Los Angeles, he took an interim job as a bank clerk and rented a room near Sixth and Vermont. Soon he was hired at MGM. While Felix started out as an assistant director in charge of screen tests, Dad was hired as a staff writer in the writing department under story editor Samuel Marx.

Screenwriting was quite a departure from the banking industry. Rather than developing into a clever businessman, which would have pleased his father, Dad gravitated toward the language arts. Words were his game. He was an excellent storyteller and a talented writer, and the career change from banking to motion picture writer suited him perfectly. He loved Los Angeles—the laidback lifestyle and ideal weather—and made it his forever home. As luck would have it, he met my mother at MGM.

CHAPTER 4

Mom, Marriage, and Me

My mother, Ethel Eleanor Houck, was born on September 23, 1907. She was three years old in 1910 when her family moved from Baltimore, Maryland, and settled near downtown Los Angeles where she grew up with her sister, Beulah (June). Ethel was outgoing and popular. She was student body president at Budlong Elementary School and a graduate of Manuel Arts High School.

Beulah and Ethel

Ethel

Ethel's mother, Elizabeth Houck, was a housewife, as were most married women in those days. She went by "Lizzie" as a child and "Elizabeth" as an adult, and her grandchildren called her "Nanny."

My mother's father, William Clayton Houck, worked as a glass engraver, sign painter, and movie house projectionist before going to college in his forties and becoming a chiropractor. My mother told the story of how as a little boy, her father traveled by horse-drawn, covered wagon with his family. He sat on a small, wooden footstool in the wagon. My mother kept the stool for many years as a treasured memory of her father.

My grandmother's parents were John and Ann Debrick, and they had six children, my grandmother being the youngest.

Ann Debrick

John Debrick emigrated from Saxony, Germany, and settled in Baltimore, where he worked in a factory as an iron molder and later as a store porter.

John Debrick

According to my aunt, he was known to waste money from his paycheck at the neighborhood saloon. Aunt June said, "One time, I heard he got so drunk that the saloon keeper had to sling his half-conscious body across his horse and send the horse homeward with no one holding the reins."

My grandmother was five years old when her mother passed away. Nanny said, "My mother died from the change of life, and I went to live with my older sister, Bertha."

Bertha was about twenty-two years older than my grandmother and was married for two years to Leon Weitsaw at the time of her mother's death. Leon emigrated from Saxony, Germany. Interestingly, before his marriage, he joined the US Army in 1879 as a cavalry soldier and was assigned to Fort Niobrara in Nebraska. The fort mission was to contain the Lakota Indians on their reservation after the Great Sioux War of 1876 and to provide protection for the settlers in the region. Leon was discharged in 1884, and he married Bertha that same year. Two years later, my grandmother, age five, came to live with them. Leon was then working as a laborer on the railroad. He and Bertha never had children of their own.

Elizabeth, Bertha, Ethel, Beulah

My grandmother mentioned nothing about her upbringing in her sister Bertha's home except to say she only went to the sixth grade in school. I was surprised to discover that at age eighteen, she had a job working as a gum wrapper in a chewing gum factory in Philadelphia. She lived with a girlfriend named Lettie Houck and her married sister and husband, all originally from Baltimore. In 1906, my grandmother and William Houck were married in Baltimore. She was twenty-five, and he was twenty-two. How they met is unknown, but clearly my grandmother had friends in the Houck family prior to her marriage.

About my grandmother's brother, Charley, Aunt June had this story: "Uncle Charlie owned the first circus in Baltimore. It was a covered wagon on wheels with four horses. He tied himself up with ropes and knots and showed people how it took him three minutes to get out. To fund the circus, he illegally sold horse medicine to cure aches and pains for one dollar a bottle. It was called Charlie's Liniment, but it was just wine and water. He was run out of town."

Nanny's father, John Debrick, who was a widower, prepared a will. In a simple and touching document, he named his two sons and two of his daughters, who were not yet married, as the recipients of his meager belongings. It reads in part:

> *First, I give and bequeath to my son Charley fifty dollars to be given him at the age twenty-one with what interest may accrue.*
>
> *Secondly, I give unto my youngest daughter Lizzie two-thirds and unto my daughter Sadie one-third of what money is over after all funeral expenses and tombstone have been paid at the age of 18 years or in times as the Executor may deem best.*
>
> *Unto my son George the framed photograph of myself and the wife.*

I give unto my daughter Sadie the washstand and chamber pot.

I give unto my daughter Lizzie my Bedstead and all bedding. The balance of my furniture what is not mentioned to be divided among my children the Executor of my will may deem best.

All my clothing to be given to my son Charley.

I give and bequeath unto C. H. Lighthiser whom I appoint as my sole Executor of this my Last Will and Testament my four books of Moses.

C.H. Lighthiser was the son of John Nickolas Lighthiser, who was Nanny's grandfather and my great-great grandfather. John came to America from Sonneberg, Germany, about 1837 with his wife, Anna Barbara, and daughter, Ann Debrick. Whether Anna Barbara is actually the mother of Ann Debrick or John Lighthiser's second wife is a mystery. Coincidently, Sonneberg is in Thuringia, an hour and forty-five minutes by car from Stadtlengsfeld where my father's ancestors once lived. John Lighthiser was a shoemaker and had a cobbler shop in Baltimore on Welcome Alley. He and Anna Barbara had four children in America including the aforementioned executor of John Debrick's will.

Happy being a married homemaker, my grandmother was the kind of person who never needed riches or worldly trappings, only people to love. Quoting Will Rogers, Nanny used to say that she never met a man she didn't like. "That goes for women too," she'd add with a chuckle. If a man had an obnoxious trait, she excused the behavior with a shrug and a kind thought. "You know the good Lord loves him," she'd say.

My mother never said she had aspirations to attend college, but she often told me how proud she was that her father went to college and became a chiropractor. There was never a doubt that Mom wanted me to go to college. "You can be whatever you want to be, Susan," she told me.

The Houck family prospered in Los Angeles and eventually moved into a Craftsman-style bungalow on West Fifty-Fourth Street. Mom always bragged, "My father built the house for us." Presumably, he had plans drawn up and hired a contractor, or perhaps he bought the home from a speculation builder after it was already built. Mom told me many times, "I loved that house on West Fifty-Fourth Street."

House on West Fifty-fourth Street

My mother idolized her father and was the apple of his eye. She talked about the good memories they shared: the times he took her shopping downtown on the red streetcar, going to the big department stores together, or shopping at the corner market where she bought a pickle out of a barrel for five cents. They were confidants and spent time sitting on the covered front porch of their home, talking about life and things.

William Houck

One thing they didn't talk about was my grandfather's family. There are no stories, but an obituary in a newspaper, *The Democratic Advocate* of Westminster, Maryland, confirmed the names of my grandfather's parents as Henry H. Houck and his wife, Sarah Ehrhart Houck. They were born in Maryland and had four children. The prior generations of Houck ancestors were Pennsylvania Dutch, a German cultural group, and they lived in York, Pennsylvania.

William Houck had many talents. He was an artist and a good writer who enjoyed writing short stories and poetry. My father said he had a big ego and a chip on his shoulder, a Napoleon complex of sorts. Perhaps it was compensation for having a short stature and a disability—a lame leg that caused him to limp. When he was a baby, his sister accidently pushed him too hard in his cradle, and it overturned, injuring his hip. Mom recalled how, as a child, she sometimes walked beside him and limped on the same leg, hoping it seemed normal so no one would notice that her father was limping.

Houck Family

One thing was for sure. My grandfather didn't like noise in the house once he came home from work. He worked hard, often at two jobs, and lived by a fairly strict schedule, according to my mother's sister. Aunt June said, "He'd go straight to the bedroom after work to be alone. He liked to relax with a glass of beer or wine."

On the other hand, my grandmother enjoyed having a lot of people around. My aunt said there was always someone staying for dinner or sleeping overnight. "Daddy didn't particularly like the social activity and had no qualms about telling people to leave. Sometimes the fun could end quite abruptly," Aunt June said.

My grandmother's days were spent keeping house, an all-consuming job. Unworldly, yes, but she was kind and wise about things having to do with home and family. A strong Christian faith and the uncanny ability to love everyone unconditionally were at the core of her goodness.

My grandmother told me, "One time Grandpa Billy gave me the money from his weekly paycheck. I hid it behind the gas heater in the bathroom until I could go to the bank. He came home from work, turned on the heater for his nightly bath, and burned up the money. He sure was mad at me."

The differences in lifestyle preference may be one reason my grandfather had an affair with Percy (Priscilla), a younger woman of Mexican decent. He supposedly met her while working at the motion picture theater where he was a projectionist. Percy was a clever woman. She worked for many years, starting out with nothing and ending up owning several houses on the same block in East Los Angeles. My grandmother was very sweet and loving but never someone described as clever.

After my grandparents divorced, my grandfather married Percy, and they had a happy union until his death in 1942. My mother liked Percy and joined her father and Percy on occasional vacations. One was a camping trip to Idlewild in the mountains near Palm Springs. In the early years of their marriage, my grandfather and Percy adopted a young boy from a Mexican family who had more children than they could afford to raise. His name was Delbert (Bobby) Houck.

Percy visited my mother throughout the years until I finished high school, and then they lost contact. By then, Percy had remarried. She stunned the medical community by giving birth to a daughter in her early sixties. When Percy visited our home, I enjoyed seeing her. She was nice and taught me words in Spanish. My grandmother, God love her, never said an unkind word about Percy or her former husband.

As a teenager, my mother often accompanied her father to his work at the movie theater on a Saturday afternoon. It was a short ride by streetcar. She spent hours in the projection booth with him, watching the images on the screen and dreaming of becoming an actress or a dancer. Unable to afford dance lessons, she earnestly studied the steps and choreography of film and stage performers and practiced at home.

Armed with a little bit of talent, no experience, and a lot of grit, she landed a job as a dancer in a live production theater. Only seventeen and petite at five feet one, Ethel had to lie about her age to win a spot in the coveted chorus line on the Orpheum Circuit. Her friends, all eighteen or older as required, nicknamed her Babe. Her stage name was Babe Williams. She moved into an apartment with a few of her chorus line girlfriends. She admitted it was a rowdy bunch but also said, "I had the time of my life."

In the apartment, they had an upright, black telephone. If they placed a penny on the receiver, the jiggle of an incoming call knocked the coin to the floor, letting the girls know they'd missed a call. "I called my mother right away to see if it was her," Mom said. "She called practically every day, which was annoying. We wanted it to be a fellow, asking for a date. Mama liked to keep tabs on how I was feeling. 'Are you eating all right?' she'd want to know. 'How are your bowels, dear?' Having good bowel elimination for some reason was important to Mama. I told her not to call so much, but she always did."

The house on West Fifty-Fourth Street was sold after the divorce, and my grandmother used her share of the funds to buy a smaller home. Just fourteen years old, June was thrilled when she was asked to help decorate the rooms. Nanny took in male boarders who needed a place to sleep and a home-cooked meal. In the end, she couldn't afford to keep the house and went on public assistance for a while.

Elizabeth and sister Anna.

Nanny rented a house on Baltimore Street in Highland Park. She lived there with June and a lodger named Ole Tvedt from Norway, who was a chauffeur for the Goodwill Company. June was nineteen by this time and worked as a telephone operator. Soon she would marry her first husband, Albert Van Nattan, and have a daughter, Beverly Jean. Nanny and Ole moved in with them.

My mother was spunky, street smart, and willing to go after whatever she wanted. What she wanted was to marry well and have children. When her parents divorced, my mother was deeply saddened. She adored her father, and when he left home for another woman, it was upsetting. In some way, she blamed her mother for his leaving, because there were incidences over the years when she exhibited a mean-spirited attitude toward my grandmother.

On September 10, 1927, at the age of twenty, Ethel married Albert Scholes after he professed his love for her. Albert was ten years older, a widower, and a family friend who worked as an auto mechanic and lived with his mother. Mom was looking for love and stability, but the marriage was a mistake. She said, "I knew Al's first wife and liked her very much, but he was still caught up in her memory. He kept a picture of her on our bedroom dresser."

That and the fact that he couldn't have children were the reasons Mom cited for leaving Albert after two years of marriage. "It broke his heart," Mom said, "but I couldn't stay."

Metro-Goldwyn-Mayer Studios

The desire for a good-paying job, and perhaps an acting career, led Ethel to MGM in Culver City. Armed with the ability to type and take Gregg shorthand, worthwhile skills she had acquired at Sawyer Business School, my mother talked her way into the stenographers pool. By her account, she aced out quite a few young women who were also competing for a coveted entry-level steno job at the studio. Some, like herself, had dreams of being discovered as actresses.

Once on the MGM lot, Ethel made a point to volunteer for assignments with the toughest producers and directors. She said, "None of the other girls in the steno pool wanted to work for some of those brash, hard-driving executives."

It was well known that their story conferences could go on into the night. Besides the grueling work hours, they also had a reputation for having foul mouths and smoking smelly cigars. "Fuck that idea. What the hell are we talking about here? Goddamn those sons of bitches—we'll do the story our way."

"That's the way they talked," Mom said.

Some of the profanity bothered her, but she kept a professional demeanor while her fingers captured their words in shorthand—squiggly little lines and curves that no one else could read—as they dictated story ideas and changes to their scripts. The next day, she typed up her notes.

She talked about one balding director who vigorously snapped his fingers behind her back so she'd get the words down faster. His cigar smoke curled under her nose as she fought the urge to gag. Putting up with things like that was worth it, she said, because she wanted to meet and impress the most influential studio bosses. It was a plan she hoped would get her promoted out of the stenographers pool and into a more prestigious assignment.

The job at MGM was exciting and paid well. Mom bought herself a black Ford convertible with a rumble seat and became immersed in life at the studio. She was proud of her accomplishments, especially the Ford that she drove right off the showroom floor.

Mom made good friends at the studio. One was named Tootsie. However, Rose De Luca was her closest friend. "A barrel of fun," is how Mom described Rose, who was a petite, feisty redhead. When I was almost three, my mother and I visited Rose at her home in Encino in the San Fernando Valley. Mom and Rose sat in the kitchen, drinking black coffee and smoking cigarettes. They talked nonstop and laughed about all sorts of things that I couldn't understand.

Mom told a great story about Rose. She worked as the switchboard operator at MGM, handling incoming and outgoing calls except those for the studio head, Louis B. Mayer. Mayer had a private line, and his calls didn't go through the main switchboard. In those days, switchboards were large, wooden behemoths. The operator sat at a stool in front of the switchboard and fielded calls. The switchboard had numerous paired cords with metal tips on the ends that fit into small, round holes called lines that had lights above them. When someone on the lot lifted the receiver to make a call or a call came in from the outside, a line lit up, and a buzz alerted the operator. The operator hand-connected the calls. Paired cords were connected from extension to extension: from an incoming call to an extension or from an extension to an outside line.

One morning, Rose responded to an inside call. "May I help you?" she politely asked.

"This is L. B." a gruff voice announced. He asked her to dial a number for him.

"My ass," she said, disconnecting the line immediately. Rose was wise to the antics of those brazen young guys on the lot who were always fooling around and making crank calls.

In a few minutes, Louis B. Mayer showed up at her switchboard, and Rose almost fell off her stool. Something was wrong with his private phone. He couldn't make an outside call and needed to reach someone right away. Naturally, she apologized all over the place.

"I hope this doesn't get me fired," she told Mom as they ate lunch in the commissary.

Mayer apparently took it in stride and even seemed amused. The story spread rapidly throughout the studio lot and brought plenty of laughs from the commissary lunch crowd.

Ethel Meets Walter

The ability to handle the tough story conferences eventually earned my mother a promotion to a coveted secretarial position. She was assigned to the publicity department headed by Howard Strickling, where she joined forces with the other secretaries working in his office. It was there, seated at her desk, that she met Walter Wise. He sauntered up to her desk with the bold confidence of an up-and-coming motion picture writer, introduced himself, and unabashedly asked for a date.

"No thanks," she said. "I'm not interested."

"Your father was too pushy." That's what she said when I first heard the story, although she admitted that she thought he was good looking.

Undaunted, Walter repeatedly came into the publicity department, hoping to score a date with her, and she continued to turn him down. Not someone who easily took no for an answer, he gave my mother flowers. She learned he drove a snazzy Packard convertible and paid for his dinner dates with a hundred-dollar bill. Much later, she was amused to discover there was only one such bill in his possession at any given time.

"He'd have to save like crazy until he had enough money for another one, and then I guess he could ask someone out again." Mom laughed, rolling her eyes, when she told me the story.

It was obvious that my father enjoyed acting like a millionaire, and my mother never denied that she wanted to marry one. One night, after his cocky request to "give me a call when you're ready to go out with me," my mother was lonely and dateless and reluctantly made the call. The fellow she really wanted to see, Logan, had moved on after several dates with her. He was a handsome, happy-go-lucky young man who had taken her to Lake Arrowhead one weekend for a group outing in the snow.

My dad was different—more intense and sometimes intimidating—but he was handsome and could be charming. His persistence and charm obviously won Mom over, because she continued dating him, and they became a regular couple.

While my folks came from very different backgrounds, they connected in their interests in movie making and story development. Dad read his scripts out loud to Mom so she could make suggestions. Each had an excellent eye for visual composition, which my father expressed through his work as a motion picture writer and Mom enjoyed through her hobby of taking photographs with an Argus camera.

In the years before I was born, my parents went out dancing. Mom was a good dancer, and Dad made a wonderful partner with his slim build, broad shoulders, and excellent posture. He had a carriage about him that oozed confidence and a bit of mystery. He could have easily played an on-screen leading man. With his good looks and natural wavy hair, some of my friends thought he looked like Victor Mature, who was a handsome leading man of the day.

They won first place in a Charleston contest, and when I was a little girl, they showed me how they beat out the others with their fancy steps. They moved their arms quickly back and forth in unison, rolling their legs in and out as they grabbed their knees. Mom smiled while Dad turned up the side of his mouth in a silly grin. It always made me laugh to see them do this, and I applauded loudly. "Dance with me," I'd beg. Dad let me stand on his shoes, and we'd cut a rug.

Before they were married, my parents frequented Hollywood nightspots and parties given by their studio friends. However, they preferred more intimate settings and informal dinners. Barney's Beanery in West Hollywood was known for its good steaks and chops, and they went there frequently.

In 1932, Ethel and Walter moved in together. They rented a home at the top of Laurel Canyon in the picturesque Santa Monica Mountains that divide Hollywood from the San Fernando Valley. Laurel Canyon seemed a million miles away from the city but was only minutes from Hollywood. Local artists and movie people favored the funky canyon residences for the country atmosphere and seclusion.

My dad loved dogs, and at the time, he and my mother had Doberman Pinschers named Gretel and Satan. Mom was driving with Satan one time and described how he saved her from getting a speeding ticket on Laurel Canyon Boulevard. As the policeman approached the car, Satan growled menacingly from his perch on the rear shelf of the Plymouth coupe. Afraid, the officer cautiously backed away. "Never mind, lady," he muttered. "Consider this a warning."

My parents lived together for a while before they married. Although Dad was persistent about his intentions, Mom resisted a rush to the altar. She had some real concerns. His quick temper and possessiveness worried her, but Dad had a few tricks up his sleeve. On what was probably her twenty-sixth birthday, Mom arrived home from work to find a piano sitting in the corner of their living room. A bright-red ribbon with a huge bow on top was tied around it. She said, "It was quite a shock but a wonderful surprise. I'd always wanted to learn how to play the piano."

Mr. and Mrs. Walter Wise

My parents finally agreed to tie the knot and decided on June 30, 1934 for the wedding. Instead of a traditional church ceremony, they opted for an informal exchange of vows. My father found the perfect setting in an orange grove out in the country and made arrangements for their wedding to take place underneath the orange trees. A romantic setting indeed!

The wedding party traveled to their destination on a two-lane highway going south from downtown Los Angeles. The scenery unfolding along the way was lovely and worth the long trip. Beyond the city limits, orange and lemon groves were visible as far as the eye could see. Rows of stately eucalyptus trees stood like sentries between the squared-off plots of land, protecting the citrus crops against winter frosts and fierce Santa Ana winds. Along the way, clapboard produce stands welcomed travelers to stop and purchase fresh fruit, packaged nuts, and vegetables in season.

Today those beautiful orchards are gone. What you see instead are walled-in housing developments, office buildings, industrial complexes, and shopping malls. Freeways have replaced the scenic highways. This is Orange County, home of Disneyland, where millions of people live and work.

The small group of wedding guests included friends Felix and Dorothy Feist, Sam and Marie Marx, Arthur Hyman and his wife, and a few others from the studio. My grandmother was there, but no other family members attended. What had been planned as a joyous occasion started off on a sour note. Angered by the minister showing up late and inebriated, Dad flew off the handle and royally told him off. No doubt my father had every right to be upset and angry, but his outburst in front of the wedding guests caused his bride-to-be considerable embarrassment.

"I had serious misgivings at that moment," Mom told me. "However, he settled down, and we went ahead with our marriage vows."

They had selected fashionable outfits. Mom wore a brown tweed two-piece suit accessorized with a small felt hat that held a feather and a short veil. Dad wore a nice suit.

Ethel and Walter on their Wedding Day

Soon after their marriage, Mom was thrilled to learn that she was pregnant. Sadly, after carrying the baby for five months, she miscarried, delivering the premature infant at home. The frightening circumstances and loss were devastating. She blamed herself. "The day before, I lifted a large throw rug over the clothesline and beat the dust out with a broom," she told me.

Mom was soon pregnant again, this time with me. Fearing another miscarriage, Mom found a leading obstetrician and followed his orders to the letter, which was to stay off her feet and in bed for almost the entire nine months.

Susan

My parents had moved out of Laurel Canyon and were renting a house on Wetherly Drive near Hollywood. During her pregnancy, Mom worked from home, writing synopses of movie scripts for Columbia Studios. This kept her busy and brought in extra money. A friend built her a sturdy work table painted white that spread across the entire bed—floor to floor—and had recessed circular holes on top to anchor the legs of her upright Underwood typewriter. She didn't resume any real physical activity until the beginning of her ninth month.

At dinnertime on that warm, summer-like evening in November, my mother had an easy delivery at Good Samaritan Hospital. My parents said hello to their daughter, Susan, and Felix Feist took some fine photos of me in the nursery.

My first year on Wetherly Drive was carefully documented in a baby album Mom put together with plenty of photographs and descriptions of the cute things I said and did. Mom was pleased that I had inherited my father's natural curly hair, since hers was straight. Everyone thought I was smart and adorable. Dad continued working at MGM, and the year was financially good. Mom stayed at home and enjoyed being a full-time mother.

Mom and Me

Needing help with the baby and the household chores, Mom came up with a clever idea to hire a live-in mother's helper without having to pay anything. Several young girls lived in our home and worked in exchange for typing and shorthand lessons my mother gave. The arrangement worked well with one exception. Mom said, "I caught one girl slapping you across the face with a wet washcloth during your evening bath. I was furious and fired her on the spot."

Since writing assignments and film shoots kept my father busy, Mom was left at home to play with me and encourage happy smiles. Gretel and Satan had a litter of twelve puppies, and Aunt June adopted one of them and named her Greta. Greta had the most incredible dog smile. When we visited my aunt's home, Greta displayed her teeth and joyfully wagged her stubby rear end.

Family life meant visits from friends and other children, but Gretel and Satan were too big and potentially untrustworthy around little children. The dogs were given to my parents' friends, the Retzlaffs. They lived in a country home with acreage on Ventura Boulevard in Sherman Oaks, which was then a two-lane road. Chain link fencing surrounded the property, and a large circular driveway led to the front porch.

Ernst Retzlaff had a dog training school and raised Great Danes. Dad learned a lot about dog obedience from him. Sometimes they spoke to each other in German. One day when I was very small, we stopped at their home for a visit. Two giant beasts the size of ponies came bounding off the front porch onto the driveway, barking loudly to greet us. Terrified, I ran in the opposite direction, screaming as the dogs chased after me. Ernst called off his dogs, giving the command in German. The dogs stopped abruptly, thank goodness, and Dad scooped me up in his arms to safety.

Dad worked at MGM in the 1930s during what was considered the golden years. A collaborative team of writers churned out dozens of scripts, one after the other. One writer, someone Dad considered a friend, stole his idea for a script and sold it. Dad filed a lawsuit and discussed the subject on occasion, making a point about the importance of honesty and integrity. During his years at MGM, his biggest movie was *The Runaround* starring Rod Cameron and Ella Raines.

In those days, movie stars belonged to the studio under contract. The studio owned them and orchestrated their careers. Unflattering or sordid details of their personal lives were tightly guarded secrets the publicity department protected to ensure that their public image was a positive one.

Because of their jobs at the studio, my parents were privy to the truth. Table talk in our house included titillating stories about the lives of stars who were under contract at MGM. I remember overhearing dinner discussions about such things as how Clark Gable had his huge ears surgically pinned back. How Jean Harlow's husband had killed himself because of sexual impotence (later revised to indicate he was killed by his first wife). How Joan Crawford was a bitch to work with. What actor was sleeping with what actress. Looking back, I can't imagine allowing children to hear this kind of stuff, but in our home, it was commonplace.

My father played in golf tournaments with Louis B. Mayer and other studio executives. Several trophies and group photos adorned our bookshelves, memories of the good times spent working at the studio. Although Dad didn't socialize with actors or actresses, he did have some well-known and influential writer, producer, and director friends within the film industry.

Felix Feist played a prominent role in my father's life for a long time. One funny incident happened when we visited Felix at his home in Laurel Canyon. I was maybe three years old. I had to go to the bathroom, and Uncle Felix said, "It's right there," pointing to a door in the entry hall.

The adults stopped talking and watched as I opened the door and went in. The sight before me was extraordinary. The toilet sat three ceramic-tiled steps above the floor in a room with a ceiling high enough to accommodate this unusual expression of art. It took some doing to maneuver the steep stairs in order to assume my position on Uncle Felix's throne.

"Are you okay?" Mom called out.

"Yes," I said tentatively, hearing everyone laugh.

Early in my parents' marriage, Felix evidently showed my mother too much attention, and that made my father jealous. The story goes that Felix came to the house one afternoon, supposedly to return a book, which led to an extended visit over coffee. Dad showed up unexpectedly, although Mom claimed, "Your father was suspicious and purposely came home early."

When he heard the car door slam, Felix sought refuge in my parents' bedroom, only to be discovered hiding under the bed by my outraged father. "Get out!" Dad said, and Felix ran out of the house, laughing his head off.

One of my father's favorite stories was about Dorothy Feist. The story goes that Dorothy never ate rabbit, repulsed at the thought of devouring "cute little bunnies," as she referred to them. My parents were at a dinner party one evening with Dorothy, Felix, and several other guests. Rabbit was served. "This is the best chicken I've ever eaten," Dorothy remarked in her New York accent that sounded like the radio comedienne, Gracie Allen.

"Thank you," the hostess said. Everyone smiled knowingly, not letting on.

"How come the chicken has so many legs?" Dorothy asked, looking up quizzically from her plate.

My father spoke. "Well, Dorothy, there's just a lot of chickens."

"Oh…" Her voice trailed off as she continued eating. No one ever told her the truth.

Felix's outgoing charm and sense of humor won over many friends, although he did have a thing for the ladies and especially Hollywood starlets. This ultimately led to a divorce from his wife, Dorothy. My parents liked Dorothy very much, and the divorce was unpleasant. Dorothy and daughters Margorie and Jacqueline ended up in a rented apartment while Felix remarried and went on to establish a notable film directing career, including producing the original television series, *Peyton Place*.

Dorothy went to work as an elementary school teacher after once enjoying an affluent lifestyle. Dad was critical of Felix for leaving his family, which probably accounted for the end of their relationship. Mom continued to visit Dorothy and the girls for a while, taking Sally and me with her. After we moved from West Los Angeles, however, they didn't keep in touch.

"Felix is a scoundrel," I remember Dad saying. Sometimes he called him a slob, not meaning he was messy. Dad called many people a slob when they didn't live up to his ideals. Others he called a pinhead, screwball, or son of a bitch.

My dad was doing well at MGM, and my parents rented a larger home in Westwood. We lived there for a year.

Germany invaded Poland, and the war in Europe had significant ramifications here in the United States.

CHAPTER 5

Laguna Beach

In 1939, hard times hit. The economy was terrible, resulting in layoffs throughout the film industry, and Dad lost his job at MGM along with many other writers. After being out of work for a few months, my father decided to try his hand at writing an independent screenplay or maybe a novel. It was his idea to move our family to Laguna Beach, a sleepy artists' colony between Los Angeles and San Diego, idealized for its solitude and magnificent sea cliffs. Dad hoped the peaceful setting would inspire his creativity. Mom reacted to the idea with skepticism consistent with her practical nature. However, in the end, she agreed to go.

My parents rented a small hillside cottage near Laguna's main village. It was a cute but quirky house and not suited for a young child. Because of the downward slope of the property, the main floor was raised from street level to capture the view. A half dozen entry steps led to the front door. The house had a living room, one bedroom, a bathroom, and an alcove for dining next to the kitchen. A large bay window in the living room gave a view of the ocean and the sunset so long as there was no fog. A small bonus room was tucked underneath the house, and French doors opening to the front walkway were the only means of access. This was my bedroom. To get into the main part of the house, I had to come and go by way of the front door. It was an awkward arrangement, especially for a three-year-old child.

A brown wicker chair that had been inherited from the previous renters sat on a thin patch of grass in front of the house. It was a welcoming presence that encouraged a passerby to sit in the sun for a spell and enjoy the scenery. Geraniums in jewel colors blossomed everywhere, flourishing in the mild coastal climate. Bougainvillea vines cascaded down the hillsides like crimson-colored waterfalls. When all was still, we could hear the waves crashing against the sea cliffs in the distance. What a picturesque site!

The move to Laguna Beach from our rental home in Westwood was supposed to be easy, but that didn't happen. Short on funds, my parents chose the cheapest moving company. Right from the start, there were problems. On moving day, the movers showed up late with a truck that was smaller than ordered and had seen better days. The loading was painfully slow and finished much later in the day than planned.

Finally, the dilapidated, grimy, white moving van lumbered away from the curb, belching thick, black smoke, giving my parents more cause for concern. The truck was stuffed to the brim with our belongings including lovely wedding gifts from my parents' studio friends and prized pieces of furniture they had collected at local auctions before I was born. Dad led the way, sitting behind the wheel of our green 1934 Plymouth coupe. I sat between my parents and later shifted to Mom's lap so I could see out of the window better. The shelf behind the front seat was filled with last-minute items.

It was a tiring, hot drive on two-lane roads. By the time we reached Laguna Beach, the sun was drooping low on the western horizon. We were minutes from our destination as Dad turned left off the Coast Highway (now Pacific Coast Highway). The moving van was right behind us as we started up the steep hill leading to our new beach home, but halfway up the hill, the truck stopped dead in its tracks and hung there motionless for a second. The driver and his helper threw open the doors and jumped out.

"Oh my God," Mom gasped as she turned to watch in disbelief.

The driverless truck rolled backward down the hill and intersected with the highway where it twisted and toppled over on its side like a stricken elephant. Apparently, the brakes had failed. It was a devastating sight.

Most of our things were ruined. Boxes packed with kitchen items had broken open, mixing dishes, pots, pans, glassware, catsup, laundry soap, olive oil, vinegar, sugar, and other food items with clothes, bedding, and upholstered furniture. The inside of the truck looked like a giant antipasto salad. Glassware and many wedding gifts were broken. The furniture was soiled or gashed. Some of our belongings were snatched right off the highway by looters who got out of their cars when they were forced to stop and wait for clearance around the wreckage. Adding insult to injury, the moving company skipped town. My parents received no financial reimbursement for their loss.

Hearing the commotion, our new neighbors rushed to help us like Good Samaritans. Even with their assistance, the task of carrying everything up the hill by hand took many hours. We ended up sleeping on the living room floor with our mattresses and bedding spread out like an emergency Red Cross center. I went to sleep long before my parents were able to call it a day.

Early the next morning, as the sun peeked through the bay window—no curtains, shades or screens to cover it—I woke up with the enthusiasm of any curious three-year-old. As my parents slept, I crawled off the mattress, ready to investigate my new surroundings. After using a wooden chair to climb up on the kitchen counter, I got naked, lowered myself into the rust-stained sink, put a rubber cap over the drain, and filled the basin with cold tap water. I added to the water what was left in a bottle of Mrs. Stewart's Bluing, a product used to whiten laundry that the previous occupants had left on the windowsill. A rusty can half-filled with powdered ant poison was also abandoned on the sill. I generously sprinkled the contents over my shoulders and chest, thinking it was baby powder.

The next thing I heard was my mother's panicky voice. "Susan, where are you?" She rushed to the bay window, fearing the worst.

"Here I am," I called out from the kitchen. "I'm taking my bath."

Mom was shaken but relieved that I was safe and in the house. I might have been a mess, but she had to laugh at the sight of me.

For the brief time we lived in Laguna Beach, my constant companion was a boy my age named Sonny who lived next door. We took turns giving each other rides in my red wagon. We also played with Hash and Widget, the small, mixed-breed, curly haired mutts that we adopted shortly after the move.

Sonny, Susan, Hash

One morning, Sonny wasn't around, and I had nothing to do. I spotted my father in a neighbor's garage and rode my red tricycle over there to say hello. Dad wasn't particularly happy to see me. He and the man were looking at girly magazines, something I didn't learn until I was much older. "Go home, Susan," my father said, and I turned around and headed back.

The road we lived on ran perpendicular to that steep hill that our moving truck had failed to negotiate. As I pedaled toward home, I lost control of the tricycle and found myself heading down the hill toward busy Coast Highway. The momentum caused my feet to fly off the pedals. Holding tightly to the handlebars, legs outstretched, I was moving fast when I heard my father holler, "Turn the steering wheel."

I turned the wheel, and the tricycle rammed into the hillside, spilling me onto the asphalt. Dad rushed down the hill, scooped me up, and carried me home. It was a pretty terrifying experience.

Felix visited us several times in Laguna Beach. One afternoon, he came while I was napping. He set up his camera tripod in the living room and waited for me to wake up. When I opened the front door, my rag doll in one hand and flowers I'd picked as a surprise for Mom in the other, a blinding flash greeted me. Afraid, my arm flew across my mouth, partially covering my face.

"It's Uncle Felix," Mom told me. "He's here to take your picture."

The next flash caught my smile. Those two photos, mounted in a double maple frame, sat on my parents' bedroom dresser until I was grown.

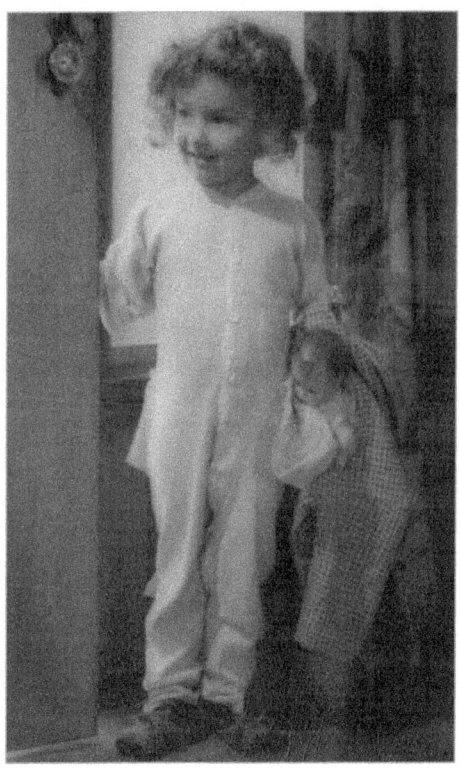

We didn't stay long in Laguna Beach—maybe six months. Dad never did get his screenplay or book written. Mom did get pregnant. She was thrilled, because she wanted another child. Before the baby was born, we left our seaside cottage, moved back to town, and settled into a small, one-story duplex on Harper Avenue in West Hollywood. Hash and Widget didn't come with us.

CHAPTER 6

Harper Avenue and Holt Avenue

Mom was in the early stage of her pregnancy and expecting in the month of June when we moved to Harper Avenue. Her sister, now married to Paul Clay, was pregnant with her son, Gary, and had a due date in February.

Before the babies were born, Mom and I took a short vacation with my aunt and cousin Beverly to a beach house in Santa Monica. The rental was one of many white clapboard cottages on one side of Ocean Avenue, facing bluffs that overlooked the ocean. A parklike strip of grass with a walking path and shady palm trees ran along the bluffs. Our cottage had a front patio enclosed by a wooden fence with clear glass inserts to protect against the wind and salt air. We had a nice view of the park and the ocean beyond.

Dressed in my bathing suit that first morning, I waited impatiently on the patio with my cousin. "Hurry up, Mama," I hollered, wanting to get down to the sand and stick my feet in the water. Before we could leave, however, my mother and aunt had to finish their morning coffee.

Cottages like the one we rented were plentiful when I was a child. Over time, the properties became increasingly valuable. Long ago, the white cottages along the Santa Monica bluffs were torn down and replaced by high-rise apartments, expensive condos, and hotels. With that came more tourists, traffic, and then the homeless. It's not a sleepy seaside retreat anymore. Nothing is the same except the cliffs and the beautiful Pacific Ocean.

Another time, my mother took me with a friend of hers and her friend's daughter to the mountains for a short get-away. We stayed in a log cabin in a grouping of small cabins fronted by a main lodge. The weather was chilly, and I had to wear a warm coat. I remember hearing and feeling the wind as it whistled through the pine trees. We were going to take a ride in a rowboat, but the lake had receded, leaving the docks and rowboats mired in mud. After some pushing and pulling, we gave up trying to get the rowboat into the water.

A bunch of scraggly gray cats showed up at our front door. Mom's friend gave them a bowl of milk. "The cats are wild, so you can't pet them," Mom said.

That was the weekend I fell in love with the mountains. Where was this place? Years later, I discovered it was Ducey's Lodge at Bass Lake near Yosemite.

My sister Sally arrived on June 12, 1940. Her birth was destined to change my world in profound ways, all of them wonderful, I eventually discovered. Dad wanted to name the baby Penelope, but Mom wasn't about to let that happen. Can you imagine being called "penny wise and pound foolish"? That was a popular English saying. They named her Sally and used Penelope in the middle: Sally Penelope Wise.

Sally's birth initially wasn't all that positive from my

point of view. She was too little to play with yet big enough to steal my parents' affection and attention. The problem began the day they brought her home from the Queen of the Angels Hospital. As Mom crawled into bed, I gleefully pounced on her stomach in my excitement to have her home again. Angry, Dad snatched me up by one arm. "You're hurting her," he said, swatting my rear end. This was the only time my father ever spanked me. Miserable and hiding my tears, I sulked off to my bedroom.

A three-year-old has a way of getting even. It happened one morning while Sally was taking a nap in her carriage on our covered front porch. This is where I kept my playthings, a chair, and a yellow toy box that a family friend had built. When the baby let out a high-pitched cry, Mom rushed out. "What's wrong? Why is Sally crying?" Mom looked me square in the eyes.

"I don't know," I said, shrugging like kids do when they don't want to tell the truth. "I pinched her," I then said, feeling no shame. A scolding followed. No matter. I had proven my dominance over this tiny intruder and decided that maybe it would be all right if Sally stayed in our family.

As the months passed, I began showing signs of independence and defiance. There was definitely sibling rivalry going on. While Mom was preoccupied with Sally on another morning, I used her inattention to my advantage. When crossing the street by myself, something that was forbidden, I stopped a little girl pushing her doll carriage down the sidewalk. I'd never seen her before. "Go home," I said, wanting to flaunt the fact that I owned the street. She seemed scared, and that made me feel powerful.

I was grabbed by one ear and nearly yanked off my feet. "Just what do you think you're doing, young lady?"

I'd been caught by the mother police. Given Mom's usual method of discipline, I surely spent some time sitting on a chair in the corner, my face to the wall, contemplating my actions.

On another day, feeling bored in the backyard and with no one to play with, I saw a stray cat amble out of the bushes. Instead of giving it a loving stroke, I picked it up by the tail, swung it around in a circle, and released it midair as it let out a frightened yowl. The cat landed feet first and a whisker from the prickly cactus that grew along the fence. I knew this was not a nice thing to do, but somehow it didn't matter. A three-year-old is not quite civilized, you know.

Dad started his new writing job at Tradefilms, Inc., working for Shirley Burden, who started his commercial motion picture company at a perfect time in history.

Dad with script.

The company soon played an important role in making training films during World War II that were in high demand by the US Navy, the US Office of Education, and Lockheed Aircraft Company. While other men were not as fortunate during the war years, Dad enjoyed steady employment that paid well.

In 1940, Lockheed in Burbank released the film *Look to Lockheed for Leadership*. My father wrote it, and Tradefilms produced it. Commercial aviation was in its infancy, and the film showcased Lockheed in the forefront of aviation history. The wife of Charles Lindbergh, the pioneer aviator who was first to fly across the Atlantic Ocean, took part in making it. According to reviews, the film contains interesting and rare factory footage including information about how test pilots tried out the newest inventions and set records for speed. There was also footage of the Wright Brothers, Charles Lindbergh, Amelia Earhart, and Howard Hughes. Dad was very proud of this film.

Birthday parties for close family friends and relatives were becoming something special in my life. A neighbor boy I barely knew surprised me with an invitation to his birthday party. He lived across the street and a few doors down, but I was shy and afraid to go by myself. Mom said, "You'll have fun. There'll be ice cream and cake." She knew I loved ice cream. That's what sold me on going.

After the party, Mom walked me home. I had a sour look on my face.

"What's wrong? Didn't you have a good time?"

"There wasn't any ice cream," I said, grumbling, "just cake and Jell-O."

"I'm sorry," she said. "Maybe they couldn't afford ice cream."

Hands on hips, I made my point. "Don't you know it's not a party without ice cream?"

The next birthday party was a snazzy affair for Richard Marx, the son of Samuel and Marie Marx. Sam was Dad's former boss at MGM. They lived in a beautiful estate home in Beverly Hills and had a tennis court. I wore my best dress, and we ate cake and ice cream wearing party hats, sitting at a long, decorated table in the large dining room. To my delight, there was plenty of ice cream. However, the pony that showed up to give us rides around the tennis court was something special.

My mother and I took a walk one day and met a little girl named Suzette and her mother, Amelia Winters. Suzette and I were both three years old, and she became my first girlfriend. While I was shy, Suzette had boundless energy with a bubbly, outgoing personality, all enviable qualities. Mrs. Winters, on the other hand, admired my quieter, more reserved nature. She told Mom, "Suzette's a pistol. She's hard to handle."

Susan and Suzette.

Amelia Winters was a registered nurse before Suzette was born, and her husband, Vernon, worked as a fireman. The family eventually moved to an attractive home in Culver City on Club Drive where they lived for many years. We continued to move often, but Suzette and I met up at the park, attended the same kindergarten class, and went to each other's birthday parties. After we moved from West Los Angeles, Suzette and I were more like distant cousins. The relationship was sustained by the lasting friendship between our mothers, who visited each other throughout the years. When it came time for college, Suzette and I chose rival universities: I went to the University of California, Los Angeles (UCLA), and Suzette went to the University of Southern California (USC).

While I was in high school, Suzette and her mother

came for a visit. Suzette and I sat in my bedroom chatting and comparing notes. We knew that our moms bragged about us and had a penchant for embellishing the facts. I thought Suzette was the most popular girl in school and that she made terrific grades. She laughed and said, "Hey, that's what I heard about you."

While we lived on Harper Avenue, Mom made another good friend named Mrs. Powers. She was Norwegian. Her daughter, Patty, babysat for us off and on. Patty graduated from UCLA and became a social worker. I initially chose sociology as a major at UCLA, hoping to follow in Patty's footsteps.

Mom could sew, but Mrs. Powers taught her some advanced dressmaking skills. With her help, Mom made a beautiful winter coat for me. Mom had an old-fashioned Singer treadle sewing machine. With her right foot moving the treadle up and down, she could drive the needle faster or slower as she deftly fed the material into place. Watching her do this was fascinating. I remember concentrating on her skillful hands and listening to the rhythmic sounds of the machine, thinking how difficult it must be to coordinate hands and feet. Years later, Mom had her treadle machine converted to run on electricity.

In addition to dressmaking, Mrs. Powers taught Mom how to make Norwegian pancakes. This recipe became a Sunday breakfast favorite in our house and has been handed down to family members. Somewhere along the way, we started calling them Swedish pancakes.

SWEDISH PANCAKES

Whisk together 12 eggs

Add sifted flour until the mixture is a medium-thick consistency

Thin the mixture down with milk to the consistency of a creamy soup

Add a pinch of salt

Add ½ to 1 tsp. of cinnamon (optional)

Melt butter in a frying pan (or two pans at a time)

Pour pancake mixture into the pan (and tilt pan to spread evenly)

Turn pancake when firm enough, and cook for another few seconds

Roll pancake, remove from pan, and place on a plate

Top with sifted powdered sugar, serve with maple syrup or jam

12 eggs serve about 6 people (two pancakes each)

My grandmother visiting us on Harper Avenue is my earliest memory of Nanny. Her permanent home was with Aunt June's family in Glendale and then Eagle Rock. She normally stayed at our house for at least one week out of the month. She was a big help to my mother, helping with the laundry, doing the ironing and, of course, giving Sally and me lots of loving attention.

Nanny.

Holt Avenue

From Harper Avenue, we moved to an apartment building on Holt Avenue in Los Angeles near Pico Boulevard. We were the first tenants in a new apartment. There were many new apartment buildings being built along the street, interspersed with duplexes. The street was uncongested at a time when Los Angeles was developing westward from downtown. Open lots were still plentiful. Families typically had one car, and very few cars were parked curbside along the street. Today, the area is congested with people and traffic. Finding a parking place is difficult.

Our apartment had two bedrooms. However, the master bedroom was another quirky setup, occupying an open loft area on the second floor that overlooked the living room. An iron railing for safety was not enough to quell Mom's fears, and she warned me repeatedly, "Stay away from the railing."

She had good reason to be afraid, because climbing was one of my newest skills. One day, a neighbor girl and I decided to investigate the apartment building under construction behind us. There was no fencing between our yard and the construction site, so we had easy access. The two-story building was in the framing stage, and the workmen never noticed two little girls climbing up to the first floor. My friend got scared and went home, but I continued to climb the crude stairway to the upper level. I was walking around on the second floor and heard my mother's voice. "Susan," she called out sweetly.

I could see her standing below with an ice cream bar in her hand. The Good Humor man had just come down our street, the music from his truck trailing off in the distance.

"Here I am," I hollered, getting close to the open edge so she could see me.

"Don't move," Mom said in a trembling voice.

Fortunately, one of the carpenters showed up and carried me down to safety. By then, the ice cream was melting down my mother's arm, but she was just relieved to have her daughter safely back on the ground.

I celebrated my fourth birthday on Holt Avenue. Aunt June made me a beautiful party dress the color of pale-orange sherbet with rows of ruffled netting.

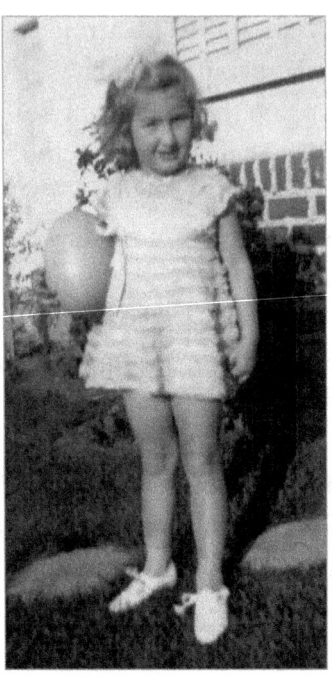

4th Birthday Party

Unfortunately, she had miscalculated the length, and it barely covered my underwear. The stiff netting felt prickly. During my birthday party, I started scratching my legs and arms to relieve the itching. Mom noticed that I wasn't my usual energetic self and discovered a rash all over my body. Unfortunately, the rash had nothing to do with my prickly party dress. I had the measles. Party guests Suzette Winters, my cousin Beverly, and my other friends were all exposed. I was sick for two weeks, and thankfully, no one caught the measles from me, not even Sally.

Cousins Beverly and Gary

On Holt Avenue, I demonstrated a monumental act of righteous rebellion. The reason was jealously and rejection or perhaps just the foibles of being four. A girl my age lived across the street. She was an only child and spoiled. I loved playing with dolls and envied her big collection. For no reason, she often turned down my invitations to play. On those few occasions when we did play together, she demanded her own way and didn't share her dolls. Thus, my plan for revenge was set in motion.

One afternoon, the girl's mother unexpectedly rang our doorbell. "Susan stole two of my daughter's dolls," she angrily told my mother. She wanted them back.

Mom was surprised, because I'd never stolen anything before. "I'll look into it," she said and went to find me in the backyard where I was playing alone. "Do you have your friend's dolls?"

I shrugged and ignored her question, but Mom had a way of getting at the truth. She asked again about the dolls.

"I didn't play with them," I said, an important point for sure. I pointed to a spot in the dirt. "They're under there. I buried them."

Sure enough, Mom found the dolls buried a few inches beneath the topsoil where no grass grew. She cleaned them up, gave me a lecture about stealing, and returned them.

The woman thanked her and said curtly, "I don't want Susan playing with my daughter again."

That was fine with me, and that was the first and last time that I ever stole anything.

Stella Orbach, Grandma Lovey's best friend in New York, came for lunch one day expressly to see Sally and me. She was in Los Angeles on business for Orbach's Department Store, the national chain that she and her husband owned. For this special occasion, Mom tidied the house, prepared a nice lunch, and dressed me in a cute outfit.

When Mrs. Orbach arrived, I showered her with hugs and kisses. During the visit, I sat on her lap and barely gave her a chance to hold Sally. Mrs. Orbach was flattered and returned the affection.

Mom was surprised. "Susan is usually shy around strangers," she said. "She's probably confused and thinks you're her Grandma Lovey."

That was exactly what I thought despite being told otherwise. Mrs. Orbach was kind and gracious, and when she left, she said, "Your Grandma Lovey says hello and loves you very much."

Shortly after Mrs. Orbach's visit, we went apartment hunting for a larger and safer place to live. Sally and I were in the narrow backseat of the car that was added to the Plymouth coupe in place of the back shelf. Dad was at the wheel, eyes scanning for rental signs as he drove slowly down the street in a dense apartment area. He didn't see the little dog that ran out between two parked cars. Suddenly, there were screams from people standing on the sidewalk and a dog's dying squeals. Dad stopped and jumped out of the car. Sadly, it was too late to help the dog. I saw the whole thing from the car window. It was an awful and traumatic end to an otherwise pleasant day.

My parents found a large apartment and started packing for the move. We also received happy news. I would soon meet the real Grandma Lovey when she and my grandfather traveled to Los Angeles by train for a long-waited visit.

CHAPTER 7

Bedford Drive

From Holt Avenue, we moved to Bedford Drive between Olympic and Pico Boulevards, close to Beverly Hills and just around the corner from Roxbury Park. The spacious apartment was on the ground floor of a Mediterranean-style duplex. There was a large, grassy backyard enclosed by a chain link fence that was perfect for small children. A quiet couple and their college-age daughter lived in the apartment upstairs.

Our apartment had hardwood floors, a large living room with a fireplace, a separate dining room, an eat-in area in the kitchen, two bedrooms, one bathroom, and an alcove in the hallway with a shelf that held our black candlestick telephone. French doors in the living room led to a covered side porch with iron railings and steps leading down to the backyard.

I started kindergarten with my friend from Harper Avenue, Suzette Winters. Her father drove us to the public school in his station wagon, an authentic Ford "Woodie." Suzette and I sat in the far back of the wagon and squealed with laughter every time the car went around a corner, causing us to slide from side to side on the polished wooden floor.

I loved going to school in the Woodie and looked forward to learning how to read. Before going to bed at night, I tried to read some of my Random House books that were gifts from Cousin Bennett Cerf, but try as I may, I couldn't make sense out of the jumble of letters. I thought if I concentrated hard enough, maybe somehow I'd be able to read the mysterious words. In the end, I had to make up my own stories and pretended to read while using the pictures as a guide.

Unfortunately, reading was not part of the kindergarten curriculum as I had hoped. Instead, I was introduced to watercolors. I enjoyed painting pictures of houses while standing at one of the child-sized easels. The day I brought home my favorite painting of a house, Mom made a huge fuss over it and had it framed. The picture hung in the bedroom I shared with Sally, next to my spoon collection of the Canadian Dion quintuplets, until I was too old for such things. The watercolor depicted a square house with a square door, two square windows, and a square chimney. Everything was square except for a few thick lines running horizontally across the painting.

"What are those?" Mom asked.

"Water pipes," I said proudly. "Don't touch them, or else you'll get hurt."

Later, I realized that I would never be an artist like Aunt June. Mom certainly knew that, but my interpretation of the water pipes grabbed her heart. Aunt June gave us one of her oil paintings of Humpty Dumpty, a character in a nursery rhyme. Sally and I had it our bedroom for many years, and it was saved for Sally's children.

War Starts

One Sunday morning, Mom was working in the kitchen while I sat at the breakfast table. The date was December 7, 1941. The music playing on the radio was interrupted by a man delivering a solemn message. Mom dropped what she was doing, went over to the radio, and stood there quietly listening.

I asked her, "What's the matter, Mommy?"

"Oh, Susan, we're at war," she said with tears in her eyes. I knew something bad had happened.

The early years of World War II were scary. We lived near the Pacific Ocean. After the bombing of Pearl Harbor, people living near beach communities were terrified that the Japanese might launch an air attack on the West Coast. Santa Monica was the home of Douglas Aircraft Company. For protection, camouflage netting, which looked like green fields from the air, hung over the Douglas facility, adjoining airfield, and other strategic sites nearby. From the ocean to several miles inland, silver metal canisters the size of fire hydrants sat curbside along the major streets. They were designed to emit thick, black smoke to obscure the ground in case of an enemy attack.

Air raid drills were frequent. When the ominous sirens went off, we were supposed to close the window coverings, turn off the lights, and seek cover. I remember one time my mother held Sally in her arms as the three of us huddled under the phone shelf in the alcove. I shook with fear. We never knew if the sirens meant it was a drill or the real thing. That was the most frightening thing.

The start of the war turned into a favorable opportunity for Tradefilms and my father. Already in the business of making training films, the company became successful in meeting the high demand for military training films. Dad was the writer, and Hal Walker, a former navy pilot, was the photographer. This was a job Dad loved, and it paid well. Writing technical films about airplanes and working with the pilots who flew them was challenging and exciting for him. He had a great deal of affection and respect for his boss, Shirley Burden, and Hal Walker. They became good friends as well as working partners.

That first Christmas on Bedford Drive was something special. Santa Claus brought me a large tricycle with a step platform on the rear. Sally found a musical rocking chair and a baby doll under the Christmas tree. My parents put up a folding screen around the tree, hoping to catch our excitement on film. Up early, I saw the screen and moved it aside, causing it to come crashing down. My parents woke up to the noise, knowing what had happened, and came rushing to the living room. I was scared and tearful, but they weren't mad. Seeing the tricycle, my tears turned to smiles, and I couldn't wait to go outside and go for a ride.

Sally spent the better part of the day sitting in her rocking chair, cradling her doll. "Bye, bye, baby," she sang over and over, trying to sing "rock-a-bye baby."

At two, Sally was talking pretty well. At dinner one evening, she tried to join the conversation. If I said something, she'd repeat it. Annoyed, I told her, "Stop being a copycat."

She thought that meant something good and ran around the table, singing, "I am a copycat." I had to admit she was cute.

Sally and Susan.

Mr. and Mrs. Poppins were good friends of my parents. They came for visits to have dinner and play bridge. Their daughter, Sandy, came with them, and she was my age. We liked playing together and going to sleep side by side in my bed. When the bridge game ended, her parents lifted her quietly from the bed without waking me.

One day, Mom sat me down for a serious discussion about someone dying. She said that Sandy's illness had come on suddenly, beginning with flu-like symptoms that worsened quickly. At that time, leukemia was untreatable. The doctors at Children's Hospital couldn't save her. It was my first encounter with death, and I took it hard.

Mrs. Poppins visited one more time after Sandy died. It was an awkward visit. My mother had two healthy little girls running around the house while Mrs. Poppins had just lost her precious Sandy. During lunch, without thinking, Mom apologized for the dirty fingerprints on the dining room wall.

Mrs. Poppins said, "I'd give anything to have fingerprints on my wall."

Mom was so embarrassed. This became one of my mother's important lessons in life. When Sally and I became mothers ourselves, she told us, "Treasure the fingerprints left by your children. It means they're alive and well."

Not long after Sandy passed away, I was admitted to the same Children's Hospital to have my tonsils and adenoids removed because of many sore throats and fevers. I was normally a good patient, but knowing that Sandy had recently died in the same hospital made me uneasy.

Mom explained that my situation was different. "Everything will be fine," she said. "Be brave, and after it's over, I'll buy you whatever you want."

Once back in my room after the surgery, I started vomiting from the ether and had to return to the operating room to repair broken stitches in my throat. Back in my room again and coming out of the sedation, I saw that my mother was there with me, and I remembered her promise. It hurt to speak, so I whispered, "I want a black Betsy Wetsy doll,"

Betsy Wetsy dolls with sweet, cream-colored faces were all the rage with girls my age. They were made of rubber and went potty like a real baby when fed water from a miniature bottle. Where I got the idea for a black doll is anyone's guess.

True to her promise, Mom said, "I'll do my best to find one for you, honey." Hours later, she showed up with a black Betsy Wetsy doll. She drove to South Los Angeles near where she used to live on West Fifty-Fourth Street, which was now an all-Black neighborhood. She found a toy store that carried the black dolls. I remember thinking my mother was ingenious and could do almost anything. I asked for more ice cream, because that's what kids were allowed to have after a tonsillectomy.

The next surgery was a simple dental procedure called a frenectomy to remove the thick, cord-like tissue from between my upper two front teeth. Mom had the same large space. She felt self-conscious about the gap in her front teeth and made sure mine was corrected. After the surgery, I wore a gold cap over the teeth for a short time, and they came together perfectly.

First Grade

At the suggestion of Dad's boss, Shirley Burden, I was enrolled in the first grade at Good Shepherd Catholic School (Beverly Hills Catholic School) on Linden Drive. The school had a fine reputation for scholastic excellence and was on a par with more expensive private schools. Uniforms were required, and Mom liked the idea. The girls wore sturdy cotton dresses in royal blue with white cuffs and collars and a matching blue belt at the waist. They needed to be ironed and looked best when starched. The boys wore corduroy pants and blue, short-sleeved shirts.

An orientation was held before the first day of school, and Mom took me to meet my new teacher, Sister Kathleen Mary. She was young and had a sweet, angelic face despite the old-fashioned wire-rimmed glasses she wore. Before the orientation, Mom did her best to prepare me for the meeting. I had never seen a nun or attended a church of any faith, and I knew nothing about the Catholic religion.

"Nuns dedicate their lives to God and Jesus," Mom told me. "Sister will be wearing a long, black robe, which is like a costume, only she wears it every day. If you have any questions, wait until we get home."

When I met Sister Kathleen Mary, no amount of preparation would have mattered. I was awestruck and couldn't take my eyes off her robe, headpiece, and the rosary beads that jangled from her waist as she moved gracefully about the room. Even her name sounded peculiar to me, being a sister and not a Mrs. somebody.

Sister seemed genuinely pleased to meet me. As we talked, I stared at her heavy, black robe. I was unable to hold back my thoughts, and they tumbled out. "It's hot today," I said shyly.

"It certainly is," Sister said.

"I bet you can't wait to go home and put on your sunsuit."

Sister laughed with twinkling eyes, and I knew I was going to like being in her class. She was a wonderful teacher, so kind and patient with her young students. Four years later, Sally started elementary school in Sister Kathleen Mary's first grade class.

Learning to read felt like my biggest accomplishment. Who in my generation doesn't remember reading their first *Dick and Jane* books? I started reading right away.

In addition to reading, I loved everything about school: learning how to print, how to add and subtract numbers, and especially making new friends. One of the Crosby boys was in my class. I thought he was the son of crooner Bing Crosby, who was probably the most popular singer and movie star of the day, but I later learned that his sons' ages didn't match mine. Perhaps it was the son of Bing Crosby's brother, though Bing did attend the Church of the Good

Shepherd in Beverly Hills. The Crosby boy wasn't in my class for long.

Judy lived up the street and was my age. We went to the same Catholic school and played together after school and on the weekends. One Saturday for lunch, Judy's mother served us a scrumptious potato soup. It was probably nothing more than leftover mashed potatoes and warmed milk, but I never forgot how good it tasted.

On school mornings, I walked by myself to Judy's house. Together, we walked the rest of the way to the corner and waited for the yellow school bus. I loved Mary Jane shoes, the dressy party shoes with the rounded toe and thin strap. The black patent leather ones were my favorite, but for some reason, in the first grade I had a pair of white Mary Janes. They were soon outgrown, and Mom put them aside for Sally when she got older. One morning, I took the shoes from the closet and walked out with them under my coat. On the way to Judy's house, I took off my sturdy brown oxfords, hid them under a bush, and put on the Mary Janes. When coming home, I reversed the process. Mom never knew. I wore the white Mary Janes to school every day, scrunching my toes until I could no longer walk in them. Finally, I put them back in the closet.

This secret obsession for Mary Janes led to my third surgery a few years later. The big toe on my left foot had become painful in my shoe. Mom took me to an orthopedic specialist, and an x-ray revealed a sizable nonmalignant growth that needed to be surgically removed. Puzzled, the doctor didn't understand how this happened. "We see these things when people wear shoes that are too small," he said.

"I always make sure that Susan's shoes fit properly," Mom said adamantly, knowing that it couldn't be the reason.

I confessed, and Mom was shocked as the doctor flashed me a half smile. Surgery followed under a local anesthetic. I was brave and watched the whole thing propped up on my elbows—a piece of cake until the anesthetic wore off and my toe throbbed like it was going to explode. I had to wear mukluk slippers to school for a while and endure painful changes of gauze. I was near the monkey bars one day when a boy flew off the bar and landed on my toe. I saw stars and limped away in tears. It was a painful lesson about the importance of properly fitting shoes.

Uncle Fred, my father's brother, visited us while we lived on Bedford Drive. He was a songwriter in Manhattan. It was the first time I met him, and I thought he was fun and had a great sense of humor.

Mom, Fred, Susan, Sally.

After dinner one evening, the family took a walk around the block. Pointing up, I said, "Look, Uncle Freddy, there's a bird."

"Bird?" he said, emphasizing the *err* sound. "It's a boyd."

I argued back, saying it was a *bird*, not a *boyd*. I didn't suspect that it was the perfect setup for him to deliver a line from a favorite family joke. "Well, it sure choips like a boyd." He laughed.

It wasn't that funny to a five-year-old, but I heard my father repeat that joke many times as I was growing up.

My grandparents from New York finally came for a visit. It was their second trip to California, the first time being before my parents were married. I was thrilled to meet them and noticed right away how different they seemed from my California relatives—more proper and perhaps sophisticated. They had a bit of an accent, a combination of East Coast and German, and dressed more formally, Grandpa in a suit and Grandma Lovey in a tailored dress.

Grandma Lovey and Grandpa George.

Grandpa George paid a lot of attention to me, and I enjoyed feeling special. One day, the two of us took the blue bus to the Santa Monica Pier, had lunch, and watched the sea lions swimming in the ocean. It was a one-on-one outing and a good memory.

Grandma Lovey was sweet. Every night, she read a story to me before bedtime. Of course, she made a big fuss over my little sister, too, but the most memorable event was going to the big toy store on Wilshire Boulevard in Beverly Hills. "You can pick out anything in the store you want," she told me.

"Anything?" It was like she offered me the world.

There were so many choices as I searched the aisles. Then I saw her: a hand-sewn, imported doll made from sturdy felt with thick, auburn hair that could be styled, washed, and curled because it was real human hair. The doll came with a pink trunk that held different outfits and a drawer for the brush and comb.

"I want that one," I told my grandmother, pointing to the top shelf where the doll and the trunk were displayed. The doll was one of my favorite playthings, and I kept her in good condition until I was too old to play with dolls.

Mom loved telling one particular story about my grandparents' visit. Prior to their arrival, I had been prepped about manners and behavior. Mom was a little uptight, knowing they were New Yorkers and well-traveled. She wanted to make a good impression on her in-laws. I was in the kitchen with Mom while she was preparing lunch. Grandma Lovey came in and asked what we were having, and Mom told her, "Tomato soup and grilled cheese sandwiches."

"We're not having that damn soup again?" I blurted.

Mom's eyes enlarged, and her face turned red. I had never talked like that before. What got into my head?

I probably picked up the bad language from the kids in the neighborhood. There were some boys living nearby, ages seven, eight, and nine. They frequented a makeshift clubhouse behind the home of one of the boys who lived across the street from us. You had to know the password to gain entry to the clubhouse, but they wouldn't tell me the password because I was a girl. I'd go over there anyway and stand around, hoping to ingratiate myself. Soon one of the boys noticed me and said, "What are you doing here? Go home."

Shortly before Christmas, one of the boys made a smart-aleck remark. "There's no Santa Claus, you know. Your parents put the presents under the tree."

I took the news stoically and went straight home to

confront my mother. "I know there's no Santa Claus." Putting two and two together, I added, "There's probably no Easter Bunny, either."

Mom talked to me about the true meaning of Christmas and made me promise not to tell Sally.

Those same older boys taught me how to ride a two-wheel bicycle. They often rode their bikes on the sidewalk in front of our house. One boy had a miniature, rickety, two-wheel bike that had been around since maybe the 1920s. "Want to try this one?" he said one day.

I tried and failed maybe a dozen times before getting the hang of it. Mom came outside as I was riding down the sidewalk. "Look at me," I yelled. She was surprised.

Some older teenage boys scared me to death one afternoon. I saw them as I walked to Judy's house. They were gathered around a sycamore tree in the park strip. A frightened boy, struggling and pleading for his freedom, was tied with a rope around the trunk of the tree. I saw the fire. Several matches were stuck under the toes of his shoes, and the boys were lighting them one by one. A surge of adrenalin went through my body, and I tingled with fright. Would the boys turn their attention on a helpless little girl? Mustering all my courage, I turned around and began walking back the way I had come. With each measured step, I was terrified that one of the boys would grab me from behind. A safe distance away, I took off running for home and burst into the house. "Mom," I shouted, out of breath. "They're trying to kill a boy."

Mom was alarmed, but I don't think she went to investigate. In the future, I was on the lookout for those boys whenever I went outside. I never saw them again.

Mom arranged for me to take swimming lessons. She found a woman who gave individual instruction at a fancy home in Beverly Hills. The beautiful backyard reminded me of a park. It had a huge lawn, shade trees, and a pool that was enclosed by manicured hedges. On my first day, the swim teacher taught me how to float in the shallow end, which I mastered quickly.

"Can I dive off the diving board?" I asked her, unafraid.

Maybe it was a little risky, but the instructor assured Mom it was okay. I walked to the end of the board and followed her instructions to the letter: hands together and pointed down, dive in, come up, take a breath, assume the stomach position, and float to the side of the pool while kicking my feet. I did it perfectly, and Mom was amazed. Soon I was swimming all over the pool. I loved the water.

Many evenings, I waited on the front lawn for Dad to come home from work, especially in the summer when it stayed light longer. I spent the time creating a one-dimensional house with rooms on the grass, using my parents' poker chips. One day, instead of doing that, I was eating an apple. When my father drove up, I hollered, "Hi, Daddy," and a piece of the apple went down my throat the wrong way. I choked and couldn't breathe. My father was quick to notice that my face was turning blue. He jumped out of the car, flipped me upside down, whacked me hard on the back, and the apple dislodged. He saved my life that day.

From then on, Mom was always reminding me about the importance of taking small bites, chewing well, and not talking with food in my mouth. It had significant meaning a few years later. Sally and I had a regular babysitter named Mrs. Frank. For about three years, she took care of us on Wednesday night while Mom and Dad enjoyed an evening out together.

Mr. and Mrs. Frank were enjoying a steak dinner at home one evening when a piece of meat lodged in Mr. Frank's throat, cutting off his air supply. While his wife frantically started the car to take him to the hospital, he stumbled in circles on the driveway and choked to death. That was a story guaranteed to get any child's attention. It drove home the point that immediate action like using the Heimlich maneuver was necessary and lifesaving.

Another time, I was in front of the house, waiting for my father to come home, when a car pulled up and parked. A middle-aged man got out of the car and asked if the apartment next door was still for rent. I told him it was. He said, "I'd like to see it. Can you show it to me?"

The next thing I knew, I was standing in the empty apartment with the man. He asked me to take off my clothes. Just then, I heard my mother calling me. "I have to go now," I said, rushing out the door. The man made no attempt to stop me.

Maybe six months later, I was taking a bath. Mom was washing me and looking at me with affection, the way a mom does when she thinks her child's body is the cutest thing in the world. Out of the blue, I said, "That's the way the man looked at me."

"What man?" Mom asked, alarm in her eyes.

I told her what had happened, and that was that. The next day, the older girl living upstairs took me to Roxbury Park. I thought it was odd, because I had never gone anywhere with her before. Mom was always the one who took me to the park. When I returned home, two police cars were parked in front of the house, and several police officers were inside, talking to my mother.

The female officer asked me questions about the man.

"What did he look like? What kind of car did he drive? What did he say to you? Have you ever seen him before? Have you seen him again?"

"The car was green," I said. That was all I could remember.

The man was never found. Mom had a long talk with me about strangers, and I wasn't allowed to play in the front yard alone anymore. Arrangements were made for the school bus to stop in front of the house. The encounter had no impact on my life, though when I got older, I realized how close I'd come to being molested that day.

What did have an effect on me was a brief confrontation with the school bus driver. One morning he asked, "Where is your friend?" He meant Judy.

"Don't ask me." I shrugged.

"I am asking you," he shot back in an angry tone. It caught me off guard. The kids on the bus noticed, and I was embarrassed. I disliked and distrusted the bus driver from then on and was also more careful with my words when speaking to adults.

Mom's seemingly dormant desire to become an actress resurfaced on Bedford Drive. She was given the role of Mrs. Maurant in a little theater production of *Street Scene*. I was excited when she took me with her to the dress rehearsal. Seated there in the front row of the theater by myself, I was enthralled with the whole production. Suddenly there were angry words and loud gunshots. Next thing, Mom was being carried out dead on a stretcher, and I jumped up, screaming, "Mommy, mommy."

Mom raised her head from the stretcher. "Look, Susan, I'm still alive. It's just pretend."

How should I have known? I was the child who cried uncontrollably after seeing Pinocchio swallowed by a whale, disturbing the audience and having to leave the movie theater. I was the child with a vivid imagination and a sensitive nature. Thankfully, Mom wasn't in any more plays.

Listening to the radio was a favorite pastime. As a small child, I liked *Let's Pretend* and *Uncle Whoa Bill* and later *The Shadow* and *The Lone Ranger*. Mom and Dad always turned on the nightly news to hear the war updates. Dad also tuned to the daily rerun of the horse races, which aired around dinnertime. I had to be quiet when his races were on.

I can remember seeing my mother's father only once on the afternoon he came for a visit on Bedford Drive. Grandpa Billy sat at the dining room table with my mother, and they chatted over a glass of wine. Mom adored her father, and my father disliked him intensely. Spending time together as a family was out of the question. There were many things my father had against his father-in-law, including the belief that he was egocentric and left my grandmother for another woman. At the top of his list, however, was blaming him for encouraging Mom's drinking. "He always brought you wine," I overheard my father once angrily say to my mother.

Not long after that visit, my grandfather died of a massive heart attack. He was only fifty-seven years old and supposedly in good health.

This was yet another tragedy in my mother's life, counting her parents' divorce and the death of Wanda. Wanda lived with the Houck family for a time and was the same age as my mother. Mom said, "She was my adopted sister and best friend."

Wanda was a petite girl who had some health problems. She married a man in her early twenties and, against the advice of her doctor, got pregnant right away. There were complications when she went into labor a month early. The doctors worked to save them, but Wanda and her infant son died on the delivery table. Mom was devastated and consumed with grief. She blamed Wanda's husband for getting her pregnant and causing her death.

When tragedy struck again with the death of her beloved father, this led to a critical turning point in my mother's life. Alcohol was becoming the friend she could count on and an easy way to escape her emotional pain, but when I was six and living on Bedford Drive, none of this was apparent to me. As far as I was concerned, my mother was strong, capable, and invincible. She was the center of my life, and I loved her unconditionally.

CHAPTER 8

La Grange Avenue

My father's job at Tradefilms was going well and bringing in a steady income. The year was 1943. My parents had about $500 in savings for a down payment on a home of their own. Finding that first home came with a great story.

After working with one real estate agent and touring open houses on the weekends, Mom and Dad hadn't found anything they liked in their price range. Frustrated, they decided to try a different real estate office to change their luck. Mom told me the story and said this is what happened.

They sat down with the new agent as she thumbed through the listings book of homes for sale. "Here's a new listing on La Grange Avenue in Westwood," the agent said.

Mom quickly caught the knowing twinkle in my father's eye.

"Hmmm," Dad said. "It looks pretty nice."

"It's perfect," Mom said, not needing a second thought.

My parents knew the description of the house met their needs: two large bedrooms, two full baths, nice-sized living room with a fireplace, cozy den with a second fireplace, bonus space described as a sewing alcove, roomy dining room, and kitchen with space for a small table. The asking price was affordable at $7,000.

"We'll take it," they said.

"But you haven't even seen the house," said the realtor, eyeing them suspiciously.

With conviction, my father told her, "That's okay. We like it. Go ahead and draw up the offer."

The poor woman undoubtedly thought she was dealing with a couple of kooks. Finally, Mom told her the truth. "We rented the house in 1938 and lived there for a year before we moved to Laguna Beach. We loved the house and wanted to buy it, but we didn't have the money, and anyway, it wasn't for sale."

Relief showed on the realtor's face. It was undoubtedly the easiest sale of her career.

Soon our family moved from the duplex on Bedford Drive to our very own home in Westwood. The house on La Grange Avenue was in a desirable area, two blocks south of Santa Monica Boulevard and a block west of Fox Hills Drive, a short distance from the town center of Beverly Hills. The land directly east of Fox Hills Drive wasn't trendy Century City as it appears today with its sleek glass and steel high-rise buildings filling the skyline. Then, it was the back lot of Twentieth-Century Fox Studios where enormous movie sets and giant painted backdrops languished among tumbleweeds in a graveyard of forgotten movie memories.

House on La Grange Avenue.

At that time, Westwood was the suburbs. This was before huge tracts of cookie-cutter homes were built after World War II, attracting families and especially veterans to affordable housing in outlying areas such as the San Fernando Valley. It was long before home prices went through the roof. No high-rise condos and office buildings lined Wilshire Boulevard. The major streets were congestion free in contrast to the maddening gridlock that now clogs them. Driving was a leisurely experience without freeways. Back then, it was okay to park on La Grange Avenue for as long as you wanted. Today, signs warn drivers "Parking by Permit Only," and violators receive stiff fines.

In the median strip on Santa Monica Boulevard, the lumbering red streetcars made regular runs from Hollywood to the ocean where the cliffs overlook the white sands of Santa Monica Beach. The click-clack of the steel wheels on the rails and the motorman's clanging bell are nostalgic sounds of my childhood. The railroad tracks are gone now, and the boulevard is widened to accommodate the bumper-to-bumper traffic. In my childhood, there was no such traffic, and that meant life was pleasantly slower and more relaxed in every way.

Mom always said, "My favorite house was the one on La Grange Avenue."

Mom loved the style and the proximity to Beverly Hills, Westwood Village, and the ocean. Attractive custom-built homes lined the streets that meandered up and down a mostly hilly terrain. I rode my bicycle all over the neighborhood, developing strong legs going up the hills and enjoying the wind in my hair as I sailed down them.

The first time I went trick-or-treating was on those streets. I loved Halloween—dressing up and free candy. My sister and I wore homemade costumes. One year, I was Little Red Riding Hood and looked authentic in my red wool cape. I carried a paper-mache lantern with a lit candle inside, a common but dangerous practice. Another year I dressed in my Women's Army Corps uniform with a skirt and jacket like the enlisted women wore in the war.

One Halloween, I was trick-or-treating with Mom and Sally on Fox Hills Drive, and some kids ran by and hollered, "They're giving out Double Bubble gum on Dunkirk Avenue." This was something special, because during the war, you couldn't get Double Bubble gum. Mom took my sister home while I went to Dunkirk Avenue by myself. By the long line of kids standing out front, I knew I had found the right house.

"Only one to a customer," the homeowner said as he placed the prized bubble gum in my outstretched hand.

Hoping to get another piece, I ran home and changed my costume. However, when I got back to the house, the porch light was off. One piece would have to do. I chewed my gum off and on for about three days, saving it in a glass of water.

Over the years, many of the homes in our neighborhood were upgraded and remodeled as real estate prices climbed. Remarkably, our house stayed the same except that one owner added a family room that ate up most of the backyard. When our family lived there, husbands and fathers worked mostly at professional careers while mothers stayed at home and raised their children. Sally played with David, who lived up the street on the corner of Fox Hills Drive. Mom and his mother, Lillian, were good friends, and David's father was a violinist with the Los Angeles Philharmonic Orchestra.

Mom was also friends with Jeannie, who lived next door to Lillian. She had two small boys. Once, Mom drove us all to the beach so we could have a picnic dinner on the sand at sunset. Jeannie surprised us by bringing a hand-crank ice cream maker and all the fixings. Right there on the sand, we churned the most delectable chocolate ice cream infused with coconut flakes.

Our neighbors with young children were friendly; others, not so much. I felt a sense of formality in this part of town, or perhaps it was just the way it was in the 1940s. Children respected authority and their elders. Manners were taught at home and reinforced at school. In my home, with a father who was German, the adage that "children should be seen and not heard" was a given. Grown-ups were always addressed by their last name.

One thing for sure was I always felt safe playing in the neighborhood. During the summer months, Sally and I looked forward to playing outside until it got dark. Mom's rule was "Come in when the street lights go on."

The streetlights on La Grange were notably vintage and handsome. They remain on the street to this day. Sitting atop gray cement posts with decorative turnings, the glass fixtures covering the incandescent bulbs were elongated like the shape of a flame, only slightly rounder. The streetlights coming on automatically at dusk signaled the end of the day for most kids. "See you tomorrow," we'd yell as we took off running for home.

Those were the days when mothers came out on the street and loudly called their child's name to come home. I can remember my mother calling "S u s a n," her hands cupped around her mouth like a megaphone.

As I got older, I had the run of the neighborhood and could travel blocks away from home. Then the "certain time" rule applied. When I went out to play, Mom told me what time to come home. I often asked a friend, "Go into your house, and let me know what time it is."

A German hand carved wooden cuckoo clock that Mom had received as a gift from her father hung on the wall in our house. It had two weights on chains and a pendulum. The cuckoo called on the half hour and hour, so we always knew what time it was.

How handy it would have been if mothers were able to reach their children by cell phone. The phones of my childhood in the early 1940s were the black rotary models, and the number had a word prefix (ours was Crestview). It wasn't polite to linger on a call unnecessarily, because, like many Bell Telephone customers, we had a party line. We shared the line with a stranger. Stay on the phone too long, and someone might repeatedly click the receiver in our ear to indicate their impatience. The chance that someone could surreptitiously listen in on a conversation was also a possibility. Long-distance calls were expensive, so we wrote letters or sent telegrams.

Our house faced west toward the setting sun and Pacific Ocean, only eight miles away. The style was plain and symmetrical; one story with a low roofline, characteristic of contemporary homes built in the 1930s. Everything except the trim was painted white, the color of the seagulls that made their way inland every so often. Large casement windows opened outward. The front door and shutters were painted gray in contrast to the white stucco. Although the facade lacked significant architectural interest, the lot was unusual, sloping upward on the hillside. The house encompassed three separate levels, giving it character and a feeling of spaciousness.

I can't remember living in the house at the age of two when my parents rented it. However, my mother kept a few good stories alive. Dad might have been the writer in the family, but Mom was the consummate historian. Her stories about everyday life, family members, and friends were interesting and entertaining. I was intrigued and a good listener.

Mom told me this story. "One morning, I took you with me to the camera store in Beverly Hills. I was busy at the counter and didn't notice you'd left my side. When I turned around, I saw you sitting on a man's lap, looking at his photographs." The man just happened to be Van Johnson, one of the biggest movie stars of the day. "I was a bit starstruck," Mom said, "but he was very nice."

That was around the time my acting career started. I went for an audition at MGM studios, and Mom said the casting director liked my looks and curly blond hair. It seemed that I had the part, but then the director had a moment of doubt. "He is a boy, isn't he?"

With that, my acting career ended.

Before we moved into the house in August of 1943, my parents spent several weekends working in the front yard. Nanny helped out as she usually did whenever we moved. She lined the kitchen shelves with fresh paper, scrubbed down the bathrooms, and took care of Sally. It was an exciting time for me. The house felt enormous and intriguing from my perspective. The newly waxed hardwood floors smelled of lemonwood. The odor of fresh paint drifted from the bedrooms. There were nooks and crannies to explore. I had my own backyard filled with interesting plants and creepy crawlers. There were prospective friends to meet. I felt a heightened sense of adventure.

One day, the weather was exceptionally hot with no cooling breeze off the ocean. The row of stately poplar trees lining the parkway provided nice shade. Forgoing the shade, I played in the sun while my parents were preoccupied with digging out the purple lantana that had overtaken the ivy on the front slope. After a while, Mom noticed that I was sitting on the front steps with my head slumped forward. "What's wrong?" she said, rushing to my side.

I vomited before I could answer. That was my first and only encounter with heat exhaustion. The next day, I was feeling fine, but Mom wasn't. She'd been sitting in the lantana wearing shorts. An acute rash had erupted between her legs that burned and itched like poison ivy. Her instructions after that were clear: "Don't ever sit in lantana."

Train Trip

With my father's job requiring long hours, Mom decided to take us on a vacation without him, and Nanny came along. Sally was three, and I was seven. We traveled by train from Union Station in Los Angeles to San Diego.

The train was filled with sailors. Many of them had to stand the entire way because there weren't enough seats. Sally, being cute with her mop of curly hair, was a big attraction. She entertained some of the sailors, talking and telling stories like little kids do. As we neared San Diego, I saw that the shipyards and manufacturing buildings were covered in camouflage for blocks and blocks. Seeing this from the windows of the train was a chilling reminder that the friendly young sailors laughing and talking with us were on their way to board ships and fight in the war.

Our final destination was La Jolla, where we planned to enjoy the seaside town and see a cave that once was a hiding place for pirates. To get to the cave after going through a gift shop, we had to go down 145 stairs (the exact number was posted on a sign). I couldn't wait to see the pirates' cave. My poor grandmother huffed and puffed climbing back up those stairs.

We stayed in a hotel overlooking the ocean called the Casa de Mañana. What a spectacular view! I left my cloth doll with the red hair on the bed whenever we went sightseeing. On our return to the hotel room, my doll would be standing or sitting somewhere else or placed upside down on the bed with her foot in the air. The maid had a good sense of humor and sure knew how to make a young girl giggle.

The House

Most of the driveways along La Grange Avenue were short pull-ins because of the hill. Tinted a red adobe color, our concrete driveway swept dramatically across the front of the house, ending at the attached two-car garage. The driveway was the center of activity for Sally and me, a place where we could push our doll babies in their carriages, skip rope, play hopscotch, or ride our bicycles in tight little circles.

I loved to roller skate. Flying down the hill, I'd yell, "Look out, Sally." I'd zip onto the driveway like a pilot landing on a short runway. I had to make a quick turnaround to avoid banging into the garage door. The skates were secured to the soles of my brown leather oxfords by metal clamps. I hung the skate key around my neck on a string.

The raised front porch was just a landing with a skimpy overhang, framed by wrought iron lattice panels. We kept the milk rack from Adohr Farms there. Using Adohr's printed list of products, Mom could check off what she wanted and leave the list in the neck of an empty bottle. The milkman came on delivery day to bring milk and the things on the list such as butter, cream, cottage cheese, and buttermilk. Mom loved buttermilk and drank it straight.

A utility closet on our service porch, or laundry room as it's called today, had a small, octagon window that overlooked the driveway. Sally and I had fun playing elevator operator in the closet. Elevator operators at the May Company store on Wilshire Boulevard used finger castanets to warn customers that the doors were closing. Clucking my tongue to imitate the sound of castanets, I'd call out with authority, "Step to the rear. Going down." Sally and I would slowly squat on our heels, simulating the action of a descending elevator.

Our icebox and washing machine were kept on the service porch. My parents may have needed modern appliances, but that was out of the question. Families were stuck with their prewar purchases. As the nation concentrated on manufacturing equipment for the war effort, there were shortages of many things: automobiles, tires, shoes, clothing, meat, sugar, butter, household items, paper products, and even children's toys and bicycles. Necessities as well as luxuries were rationed. The government issued ration coupon books to everyone. Without the coupons, we couldn't buy an item no matter if it was available.

The washing machine was an old-fashioned wringer type. It had a simple on-and-off switch. Mom was careful not to get her fingers close to the rubber rollers as she fed wet clothing through them. In an emergency, the wringer function could be stopped by hitting the tension bar. I saw Mom hit the bar several times when the clothing started going through the rollers too fast.

"Stay back," Mom often said, keeping her girls at a distance if she thought we were too close when the machine was running.

Nanny helped out with the laundry when she came to visit. One day when I was at school, Mom was busy making the beds when she heard Nanny yelling, "Help, Ethel. Help me."

Mom rushed to the service porch and found my grandmother leaning over the washing machine with her head caught in the wringer. The hair at the top of her head had disappeared into the rollers, and she was being scalped alive.

"There was no time to fool with the tension bar," Mom said. "I yanked the electrical cord right out of the wall."

She wrapped Nanny's bloody head in a towel and took her to the emergency hospital. Her scalp had been pulled back maybe two inches and had to be stitched on. Once healed, the scars were light and, thankfully, hidden by her hair.

Mom cautioned Nanny about using the washing machine, but then it happened again. That time, Nanny's arm rolled up in the wringer to her shoulder. Miraculously, no bones were broken. Mom furiously told her, "This is the last time you're using the washing machine, Mama. I don't want you going near it."

I remember thinking that Nanny should have been more careful, that maybe Mom was smarter than her mother. No matter, as Nanny was the kindest person I knew. All she wanted to do was help.

Our icebox wasn't very large. The upper section held a block of ice, and the food went in a separate section below. The iceman came once a week. With arms as strong as Popeye's, he single-handedly toted the ice from his truck, securing it with heavy-duty steel hooks that hinged in the middle like giant salad tongs. A telltale drip line marked his path across the driveway, around the side of the house to the backyard, and into the service porch.

I looked forward to those weekly ice deliveries. When the iceman left his truck—the back end was protected by a loose-hanging, black rubber sheet—Sally and I and the kids on the block grabbed shards of ice and licked them like popsicles. On hot summer days, I slathered a piece up and down my arms, enjoying the coolness.

On his return, the deliveryman often called out, "You kids get away from the truck." He was understandably concerned that an ice block might slip off the truck and take out a few toes.

Mom had to shop for food often. She also checked regularly to make sure the ice hadn't melted down, causing food to spoil. There were many nights that she served some unusual dinner concoctions to use up the food before it spoiled. This was the way it was during the war years. People didn't waste food. In fact, they didn't waste anything.

Everything that could be repaired was fixed. I helped darn socks. Our leather shoes were resoled until they no longer fit or the topsides wore out. Even then, we had to have the required ration coupons to buy new shoes.

Next to the service porch was a small kitchen. A window over the sink overlooked the backyard. On the window sill, Mom kept a wiry twig from the backyard tree, and it was mostly there as a threat. "I'll get the switch," Mom warned us, and that was enough to keep us in line. Sally and I were good kids. We only got the switch on our legs a few times for being naughty. Mom usually used more effective punishments like making us sit in the corner or not letting us go out and play.

Around the age of nine, I developed a smart mouth. One afternoon, Mom was washing dishes in the kitchen sink, and I asked if I could go outside, knowing that it was too late in the day. "Not now," she said, with her back to me. "It's almost dinnertime."

Instead of taking no for an answer, I pushed for a change of mind. When she said no again, I sarcastically said, "Thanks a lot."

Without warning, she whipped the wet dishrag around, and it caught me square across the mouth. Whap! Her message was clear. No more sass.

We had an older Wedgewood stove that sat on tapered legs, crème colored with black trim. Mom used a match to light the gas burners and oven. A small, white table where Sally and I ate most of our meals was against the opposite wall. We rarely had dinner in the dining room with our parents. For one thing, Dad didn't get home from work until around seven, which was past dinnertime for us kids. Tired and wanting a quiet house, he didn't like us talking and fidgeting at the table. Eating in the kitchen suited me fine, because then I didn't have to worry about my table manners. There were nights when I was still sitting at the table when Dad got home from work because I hadn't finished my dinner. The rule was I had to eat everything on my plate. "Think of the poor starving children in Europe," Mom said when I refused to eat something.

Starving children or not, it didn't make me want to eat the slimy spinach or the green beans with strings that caught in my throat. Peas and carrots were okay. My favorite part of the meal was dessert, which we didn't have every day. Mom rarely baked, so there were no homemade pies, cakes, or cookies unless she made a special-occasion cake for Dad's birthday or mine. What she normally made for dessert was Jell-O, pudding, or junket, a watery gelatin-like pudding that I didn't like. However, we could count on Dad to stop at the bakery every so often and bring home a treat.

While my parents had dinner together in the dining room, Sally and I stayed quiet. No roughhousing, laughing, or running around the house allowed. I listened to the radio quietly after my homework was finished. I always had a lot of homework from Catholic school—books, papers, and supplies were carried home in a heavy, canvas book bag with a handle. From the living room, I could hear their conversation in the dining room: discussions about people at the office, scripts in progress, or maybe what was going on at my aunt's house. Bedtime was seven-thirty sharp on school nights.

Mom's days were filled with the routine of cleaning, cooking, laundry, ironing, and childcare without modern conveniences such as automatic clothes washers and dryers, fabrics that didn't need ironing, dishwashers, frozen foods, ready-cooked meals, or internet shopping. Meals were made from scratch. No instant anything. I helped Mom shell peas and squished the orange dot in the white margarine package until it turned the fake butter yellow. Meal preparation and laundry chores dominated a housewife's day. With one car in the family, Mom planned her grocery shopping and errands around Dad's schedule, taking advantage of the weekend. On the other hand, it was a slower lifestyle and perhaps less stressful. Nevertheless, I think Mom was often bored and lonely, especially when Dad was working long hours. Though Sally and I were unaware, she probably started drinking more regularly while we lived on La Grange Avenue. She liked beer.

My father had grown up with servants, and his family had a cook who prepared the meals. The cook regularly made a special spinach dish that Dad absolutely loved, and he tried to explain to Mom what it tasted like in the hope of experiencing that wonderful flavor again. My mother fixed spinach every way she could think of—creamed, pureed, chopped, with and without seasonings—but she was unable to duplicate the taste he remembered from childhood until she accidentally discovered the secret.

Dad sat down to dinner that evening and immediately noticed the spinach on his plate. He couldn't believe his eyes. It looked right. Could it be? He dug in with gusto. "My God, you've done it," he said, giddy with excitement.

Mom looked at him like he was nuts. "You're kidding me, of course."

"I'm absolutely serious. This is it. How did you do it?"

"Walter, it's out of a can. Canned spinach."

"I never knew that," he said sheepishly. They both laughed uproariously.

The house on La Grange Avenue might have been Mom's favorite, but it wasn't mine. What mattered most to me was having girlfriends my age, and the street fell miserably short in that regard.

"Sally, do you want to play?" I'd ask her when there was no one else around. She always said yes, feeling honored that her big sister wanted to play with her. I felt a little guilty knowing she was my last resort.

Sally and I still like telling one story although from different points of view. Hers illustrates the woes of growing up as my kid sister. Mine describes how I wanted to look cool without my younger sister tagging along.

Neighbor Kids

Lynn lived a few doors up the street from us. She was a grade ahead of me at Beverly Hills Catholic School and could be mean sometimes. Since there were no other girls living nearby, I put up with a lot from her just to have some companionship.

Lynn's younger brother, Fella, was adorable and likable. He and Sally attended first grade together and got along splendidly. On school mornings, Fella stopped at our house to get Sally for the bus. Occasionally, he carried a bundle of roses wrapped in newspaper for their teacher, Sister Kathleen Mary. His mother had a beautiful rose garden. Occasionally, he brought Mom a bouquet of roses too. "I picked these especially for you, Mrs. Wise," he'd say with a big grin, bringing the flowers out from behind his back.

Then there was Lynn. When she was nice to me, depending on her mood, we played jacks and hopscotch on the sidewalk, jumped rope, or traded playing cards. We kept our collection of playing cards in cardboard cigar boxes, divided by picture categories such as sailing ships, horses, dogs, cats, floral arrangements, scenic wonders, and ocean scenes. Some of the cards were more collectable and valued than others such as Thomas Gainsborough's *The Blue Boy* and Sir Lawrence's *Pinkie*. Lynn had the best of the best and often two of the most coveted cards. When it came to trading, she drove a hard bargain. "I'll take three of your cards for this one," she would say, and I usually caved in to the pressure.

Sometimes Lynn invited me to her backyard. We sat under the weeping willow and counted furry caterpillars as they slithered along the drooping, narrow leaves. With our cigar boxes in tow, we also compared trading cards. During the summer, it was refreshingly shady and cozy under the willow, and I loved being there.

One day after being invited, I happily accompanied Lynn into her backyard. I heard footsteps behind me and turned to see that Sally had followed us. Since Fella was nowhere around, I thought Sally was just being a pest. "Go home," I said, hoping she'd leave before Lynn noticed.

"I don't have to," Sally said, not budging.

Her stubbornness took me off guard. Eyes narrowed, I glared at her menacingly. "You'd better go home or else."

That threat didn't seem to faze her one bit. She stood her ground, jaw set, her face uplifted in defiance. "I'm telling Mom."

That made me mad, because Sally always told, and heaven help me if I laid a hand on her. As punishment, I might be restricted from playing outside for a whole day, but on this occasion, no physical show of strength was necessary. Without another word, Sally turned around and left the yard. She tattled on me, of course, and I received a good scolding.

"Be nice to Sally," Mom said. "You're the big sister. You need to take care of her. She's the only sister you'll ever have."

Mom always encouraged us to be loving sisters and good friends. However, on that day, I shrugged indifferently, not fully understanding how lucky I was to have a sister. Mom's words meant something, and we later became close and loving sisters, but when I was a kid and Sally tagged after me or refused to let me have my way, it was easy to retaliate and call her names. "Brat," I'd holler when I was mad, feeling a little sorry afterward but never letting on.

That incident in Lynn's backyard hurt her. To this day, she stands firm in her conviction that I could have been a whole lot kinder.

More about the House

Our backyard was different than the usual square plot of land. As the second-to-the-last property at the bottom of the hill, the backyard was a side yard. It sloped upward, sharing lot lines with three other properties on Dunkirk Avenue, the steep street behind us. An ivy-covered chain link fence separated the yards.

The inside of the house reflected the upward slope of the property, having three levels separated by several steps. The kitchen and dining room were on the lowest level. On the main level were the living room with a fireplace, my parents' bedroom and bathroom, a small den with a second fireplace, and a bonus space behind the den. The bedroom and bathroom that Sally and I shared were on the upper level.

The living room held our baby grand piano, which replaced the original one that was Mom's surprise birthday gift. Mom loved having the bigger piano and took lessons for a short time. Her favorite sheet music was "Begin the

Beguine" by Cole Porter. The sounds of her stopping and starting the piece, and occasional utterances of frustration, would often carry through the house.

Music lessons were offered at my parochial school, which my parents thought was a wonderful advantage. Initially, I played castanets in the school orchestra. In the third grade, I started piano lessons at school. While Mom enjoyed playing popular tunes, I had to learn classical music. I compared my progress to Marlene and Karen, classmates of mine. At birthday parties, if a piano was available, they played Chopin's "Polonaise" from memory with great showmanship for the enjoyment of everyone. No matter how hard I practiced every day, I never came close to playing "Polonaise," which was my favorite music. Of course, I didn't know that Marlene and Karen were unusually gifted.

The school had a piano recital one year in the ballroom at the Beverly Hills Hotel. It was a fancy affair. I was in the recital and wore a white formal dress. Though nervous, I finished my piece without a mistake while Mom and Dad looked on with pride.

Our living room wasn't particularly large. Even with the piano, there was space for a couch underneath the wide front window, a comfortable easy chair on one side of the brick fireplace, and Dad's favorite wingback chair on the other side. A stack of racing forms was always beneath his chair. We had a console Philco radio, which was our main source of home entertainment. I enjoyed listening to many good programs such as *Blondie and Dagwood*, *The Green Hornet*, *Fibber McGee and Molly*, *The Baby Snooks Show*, and *The Jack Benny Program*.

Since there was a war going on, my parents always listened to the nightly news. I sat quietly with them and listened too. The news was somber and ominous, causing me worry and a sense of foreboding. So many men killed, so many planes down and ships lost. When would it end? Would the enemy bomb us? I remember hearing Winston Churchill's iconic speech to defend Britain. It brings tears to my eyes when I hear it replayed. The war came a little closer the day we learned that Uncle Paul's brother, Joseph Clay, went down with his submarine after it was torpedoed.

The living room also held our only built-in source of heat in the house, a recessed gas wall heater. For extra warmth in the winter, sometimes Mom lit the kitchen stove and let the oven door hang open. The ceramic crossbars on the gas heater glowed red-orange from the heat of the flame. Sally and I stood in front of the heater on cold days but were careful not to get too close.

One cold Sunday morning, Sally and I were warming ourselves in front of the heater. Dad woke up in a cranky mood and started yelling at Sally when he saw she wasn't wearing slippers. He stomped his feet angrily, coming close to landing on Sally's feet, as I looked on, feeling upset and scared. Sally took it in stride and calmly went to get her slippers. She said he apologized afterward. That incident and Dad's endeavor one evening to pound the multiplication tables into my brain—a marathon session that lasted until midnight—were two painful examples of Dad's impatient nature. A sign of his German upbringing, I always thought.

His German upbringing might explain why he taught Sally and me how to curtsy as if we were members of the royal family. Perhaps it was a Hollywood thing Dad borrowed from Shirley Temple and Margaret O'Brien, the adorable child stars who charmed the public with curtsies on and off camera. Dad often asked us to curtsy for guests, and I felt silly. It impressed everyone, and that pleased him. Pleasing him was important to me, so I worked hard at mastering the art of a graceful curtsy. The ability to do so would pay off for me later on.

Sally Almost Dies

We had a cozy, knotty pine-paneled den and a second fireplace behind the living room. A delicate French provincial desk sat perpendicular to the wall next to the fireplace. It was one of my parents' favorite auction purchases before I was born. It made it through the moving van accident in Laguna Beach, except that one of its slender legs was permanently tweaked. On the opposite wall were two boxy closets with space between them and just enough room for a comfy couch. The closet doors were covered in a collage of liquor, beer, and wine labels that were glued on and shellacked for posterity as an art project by the previous homeowners.

The afternoon Sally became dangerously ill, Mom placed her on the den couch. By dinnertime, her temperature had risen so high that she had convulsions and didn't recognize me. "Sally, it's me, your sister," I told her. She only moaned and went back to sleep.

Mom made a desperate telephone call to our pediatrician, Dr. Helen Hopkins, a niece of the founder of Johns Hopkins Hospital, according to Mom. Dr. Hopkins came to the house right away and expressed great worry after examining Sally. The diagnosis was strep throat. Since penicillin was just being developed, she gave my sister a new drug called sulfa, although its effectiveness against the bacterial infection was uncertain. Sally was given alcohol rubdowns to reduce the fever. As it neared midnight, my parents went to bed while the doctor kept watch over Sally, dozing off and on in a chair next to her. By early morning, the fever had broken. The sulfa miraculously worked. Sally was herself again and knew who I was. Dr. Hopkins saved my sister's life.

Childhood illnesses were a big scare when I was young, because there were no antibiotics. I had a friend named Alexis who lived a few blocks away and went to the public school. Our friendship was going well until the day I found an official-looking printed notice tacked to her front door. I didn't knock because it read "Quarantine. Do not enter. Scarlet fever." After that, I never saw Alexis again and didn't know what happened to her.

Master Bedroom

My parents' bedroom was in a separate wing of the house, near the entry hall and main bathroom. It was a large room with windows on both sides that let in plenty of natural light. Mom loved the French provincial bedroom furniture that was purchased along with a dining room set from her father's life insurance money after his death. There was a highboy chest-on-chest, a dressing table with drawers, bedside tables, and a four-poster double bed.

I was fascinated watching Mom get dressed for a night out with my father to have dinner at a restaurant or maybe play bridge with friends. Those were the nights that Sally and I had a babysitter such as Mrs. Frank or Mrs. Powers' daughter, Patty. If Nanny was visiting, she was our babysitter. Nanny was gullible, and one time I took advantage, asking if Sally and I could go outside and play after dinner. Nanny didn't know better, so she said okay. Feeling guilty as the sky darkened, I came back in with Sally and said, "I fooled you, Nanny. We're not allowed to go out after dinner."

Nanny smiled and said, "Well, I'm glad you girls came back in."

My mother was slim and attractive, and she always looked good in her clothes. Pinafores for children were popular, and Sally and I had several—even matching ones. They were worn over dresses like aprons and were cute with ruffles over the shoulders. Mom had a wool, small-checkered plaid jumper dress in muted colors of gold, hunter green, and tan that reminded me of a pinafore because of the small ruffles over the shoulders. I thought the jumper made her look younger and prettier than ever. Sometimes she dressed up in her black sheath dress and wore a little black hat with a veil. On her left hand, she wore a small, diamond engagement ring and wedding band, and on the right hand, a large silver ring that held a black onyx stone that always caught my eye.

Watching Mom apply her makeup as she sat at her dressing table intrigued me. A round, decorated container held her powder and puff. The black eye shadow was hard and came in a tiny box. She spit on a lash brush to moisten the shadow before applying it on her eyelashes. Using her pinkie finger, she put on red lipstick and rubbed some lipstick on her cheeks for color. Finished, she looked at me in the mirror and smiled. "I'm ready to go."

One morning, Mom was getting dressed in the bedroom while six-year-old Sally and her friend David, whose mother was big chested, were playing in the house. They ran into the bedroom, catching Mom naked from the waist up. David's eyes widened with alarm as he looked at my mother's petite figure. "Mrs. Wise," he said, "where are your breasts?"

Nanny's Room

The second bedroom and bathroom that Sally and I shared was an addition to the house before we bought it. The added square footage turned the den into a corridor room leading to our bedroom. Between the den and the steps leading to our bedroom was a small alcove with a high, narrow window and cement floor painted blue. In winter, the cement chilled my bare feet, and in the warm summer months, it felt cool and nice. That space was just big enough to hold an extra bed for Nanny. She slept in the alcove when she came to visit us, which was usually one week out of every month. This was the space that was advertised as a sewing room when the house was listed for sale.

Nanny had little privacy in the alcove, but she didn't complain. She never made demands. It wasn't her nature. She preferred giving to others, which she did abundantly. "Nanny is a loving soul," Dad always said, and everyone who knew her agreed.

For as long as I can remember, Nanny came regularly no matter where we lived to visit and help Mom with the household chores. She traveled from my aunt's house in Eagle Rock, working her way across the city using transfers from one bus or streetcar to another. The journey took several hours, but she enjoyed the trip, making friends with seatmates along the way. She arrived at our house full of stories from her trip about the lives and problems of the people she met along the way.

"I suppose you told the stranger about *our* personal business," Mom grumbled after one of Nanny's lady-on-the-bus stories.

"Just a little," Nanny said. We all knew that Nanny didn't keep any secrets.

Come time for Nanny's visit, the deep wicker laundry basket was full of Dad's white cotton shirts and everything else that needed ironing. She did all the ironing, and it took her many days to finish. There was no such thing as permanent press or wash-and-wear fabrics. We didn't have a steam iron. She sprinkled the garments with water and rolled them up tightly in towels until, she said, they "had a chance to cure." Leave them rolled up too long, and green mildew spots formed, a sure sign the clothing was on its way to ruin. A handy hint of the day suggested using a glass soda bottle and punching nail holes in the cap as a water shaker to wet down the ironing. Nanny preferred to dip her hand into a bowl of water and shake it gently over the clothing. Sometimes she even pressed our sheets and pillowcases by hand.

Sally and I always looked forward to Nanny's visits, and she worked hard helping Mom with the household chores. In the afternoon, she usually stretched out on her bed in the alcove for a short nap. She covered herself with a brown afghan decorated with orange, green, and yellow flowers that was a family heirloom of sorts. Mom had crocheted it while she was pregnant with me as a way to keep busy during her months of bed confinement. The afghan was around at least until I finished high school, warming Sally and me as we recovered from childhood illnesses.

Before going to sleep, Nanny placed her flowered cotton housedress at the end of the bed so it wouldn't get wrinkled. Her black Sears and Roebuck orthopedic shoes fit neatly under the bed frame with only the sturdy heels poking out. She kept her wire-rimmed spectacles and the earpiece to her hearing aid next to the pillow. When she was wearing the hearing aid, Sally and I couldn't help but notice the wires running from the earpiece to a pocket hidden in her flesh-colored undershirt where the control box was kept. It took some doing to get the sound just right. Sometimes the hearing aid made a high-pitched squawking noise that made her jump, and she'd reach inside of her shirt to lower the volume. "Sorry, dear," she'd say apologetically. "This contraption has a mind of its own."

At night, Nanny kept her teeth in a glass of water on the bathroom sink. One time when I was small, Mom came into the bathroom and found me trying to pull out my teeth. "They won't come out," I whined. That gave Mom a good laugh, and that's when I learned about false teeth.

All of Nanny's special stuff was intriguing paraphernalia to the prying eyes of two small children. So far as Sally and I knew, all grandmothers came with glasses, false teeth, and hearing aids. The hearing aid was probably the most useful item. By twisting a knob, Nanny could bring conversations to life or turn everyone off, especially when things got too noisy around the house. With it off, she heard nothing. During those times, she'd sit in her chair, wearing a sweet smile.

While Nanny slept, the hearing aid was always turned off, and she looked peaceful. Nanny was often still asleep when I came home from school. Disappointed, I couldn't wait for her to wake up. "Don't touch her or jiggle the bed," Mom said.

Sometimes, I stood next to the bed and stared at Nanny—not touching—and then to my delight, her eyes popped open as if she hadn't been asleep at all. "I'm awake, darling," she'd say, smiling.

Although Nanny never went beyond the sixth grade, her lack of education didn't stop her from becoming an avid reader. She also had a good imagination. I preferred her creative, made-up stories to any story that she read to me from a book, especially her takeoff on *Beauty and the Beast*. Her stories continued from one night to the next like the serial cowboy movies at the Hitching Post Theater in Beverly Hills where Sally and I went for an occasional Saturday or Sunday matinee. The theater was packed with noisy kids, some of them wearing cowboy outfits and toting cap pistols, who, like us, loved seeing our favorite cowboy stars on the movie screen.

Children's Bedroom

To get to the bedroom and bathroom that we shared, Sally and I had to walk up two steps from Nanny's alcove to a landing, turn left, and walk up four more steps. A single French door on the landing led to a shady spot outside. A retainer wall of broken concrete pieces held the slope secure where, in summer, yellow and orange nasturtiums bloomed under a handsome sycamore.

Even with our maple twin beds, dresser, and an assortment of doll furniture and toys, the bedroom was roomy. There was good light from the window over our beds and the French doors with screens that led to a U-shaped, grass-covered space outside. Mom planted a jacaranda tree there for shade and the pretty lavender flowers that bloomed in June. We kept the doors closed and locked except maybe during a summer heatwave. The outside space separated the children's room from the master bedroom. If the French doors were open, Sally and I could call out, and our parents would hear us through their open windows. Otherwise, we were rather isolated, because it was a long trek to reach their room through the inside of the house. It was an especially scary journey after having a bad dream.

My nightmares were plentiful and often about lions and tigers. Sometimes one or the other leaped out of the unknown and took chase. In my sleep, I ran wildly in terror, my legs twitching involuntarily under the covers. In that instant before waking up, I turned courageously to face the inevitable and defeated the wild beast in a frenzy of fists and kicks. My eyes popped open to reveal my surroundings, and I sat up abruptly in bed like a jack-in-the box toy, jerked from another world, a silent scream in my throat and my heart pounding.

I got out of bed and headed for my parents' room, walking rapidly and then breaking into a run about halfway through the darkened house. Still barely out of the dream state, my body trembled from the terrifying thought that a lion or tiger could be lurking in the shadows, ready to pounce on me. It seemed like forever until I reached their bedroom and safety. Once there, however, it was nearly impossible to wake them. Their snores sounded like bullfrogs on a summer night. "I'm scared," I'd whisper, out of breath, shaking the bed to wake them. "I had a bad dream."

No matter who woke up, the reply was the same. "Everything is okay. Go back to bed."

I never was allowed to crawl into bed with my parents, so back through the spooky house I went, trembling all the way.

What frightened me most in the middle of the night was hearing the neighborhood cats fight under our bedroom window. Their screeching and yowling always woke me up. My hair almost stood on end, and I was sure that a lion or tiger would come crashing through the French doors. I was too scared to get out of bed or call for help, so I curled up in a ball with the covers over my head until the jungle night became silent. Sally usually woke up too, and we talked to each other from under the covers. One of us finally got up and turned on the light, which was left on until morning.

Sometimes the sounds that woke us up in the night came from the inside of the house. Those were the times when angry voices drifted up from my parents' bedroom. There were nights when their fighting went on for quite a while before I heard the crickets again. I felt anxious and scared. Nightmares followed, and I developed a bad habit of biting my nails.

Our bedroom was an ideal setup for children. With easy-care linoleum on the floor, we played hard, danced, or painted with watercolors without worrying about damaging the floor. A portable gas heater kept us warm in the winter. Once, Sally and I got into a tussle while we were getting dressed in the morning, and she pushed me into the heater. It burned like heck. I can't remember what got us going, but with all the shoving and pushing, we almost knocked the heater over. The unvented heaters were dangerous, and a downed heater could start a fire. I carried a double burn scar on my upper thigh that looked like railroad tracks for years as a reminder of our scuffle.

We had a closet in our bedroom with double doors. One day, I stepped into the closet to get my clothes. Without warning, the floor gave way, and I fell into a dark hole. "Help," I screamed, and Mom came running. The sight of me standing in the closet with the lower part of my legs missing was disconcerting but funny, and she had to laugh.

The verdict was termites. When the bedroom and bathroom were added to the house, the builder left scraps of lumber in the crawl space, and that attracted the termites.

It cost nearly $1,000 to rebuild the closet floor and replace the infected support beams in the bedroom. That was a lot of money in those days and certainly no laughing matter. Nor did Mom think it was funny when shortly thereafter I used my bed as a trampoline and broke the slats that supported the mattress.

Backyard and Clothesline

Because the house's irregular shape conformed to the uphill slope, the backyard had separate areas. The largest space was visible from the kitchen and dining room windows. There, the clothesline stretched between two metal poles, showing off the family laundry as it undulated in the coastal breeze. Hung out to dry during the week, secured by wooden clothespins, were my father's long-sleeved cotton dress shirts that had been starched in readiness for Nanny's skillful ironing. Sheets, towels, blue school uniforms, dresses, blue jeans, blouses, underwear, and socks—lots of socks—were also on the line.

Sometimes I helped Mom hang out the laundry. I had a system. I tossed an item over the line and stepped up on a wooden footstool so I could reach and secure it with a clothespin. The clothespins were kept in a cloth bag with a hanger that hooked over the clothesline. The bag had a habit of getting away from me and sliding down the metal line. Mom taught me the trick of stuffing some clothespins in my pocket and gripping a few in my mouth before starting the job. By the time I was old enough to be good at hanging out the laundry, I had outgrown the stage of wanting to be helpful. Thank goodness the electric dryer would soon be on the market.

Grumpy and Baby Dog

Besides this being our clothesline area, it was also the place where our honey-colored coonhound named Grumpy hung out. One day, my father surprised us by bringing home this enormous dog with long, floppy ears, a wrinkled brow, and the saddest dark eyes we'd ever seen. Dad loved dogs, and we'd been without one for a while. Grumpy was full of love and energy with a deep bark like a trumpet horn. His soulful howling at the sound of sirens from fire engines or ambulances always made us laugh. The poor thing had to stay tethered to his doghouse because there was no fence next to the garage that would have closed in the yard. Sometimes when the clothesline was free, Mom attached him to the line by a rope so he could run back and forth for exercise.

Boy did Grumpy love to run. That's why he didn't last long in confinement. He was an escape artist. Dragging his doghouse with him, he'd charge down the front slope in hot pursuit of another dog off leash and on the loose. Nose held high, voluminous ears flapping, the doghouse bumping along behind him, Grumpy resembled a cartoon character from the Sunday funny papers. Even though Mom saw the humor in it, she was more than frustrated with his numerous bolts at freedom.

One day when the rope broke, setting him free from the doghouse, Grumpy disappeared, and we couldn't find him anywhere. We thought he was gone for good, and Mom undoubtedly hoped he was. However, several weeks later, while we were eating dinner, Grumpy surprised us by barking at the front door.

"Grumpy!" Sally squealed, throwing her arms around his neck. "Where have you been?"

Later, we learned that Grumpy had been living the good life at someone else's house. A lady who lived about a mile away explained this to us when she came to our door and asked if we wanted to see Grumpy's puppies. We were sure surprised. On one of his earlier breakaway jaunts, Grumpy had apparently fathered a litter. The lady wanted to keep Grumpy permanently, and my parents were more than agreeable. Sally and I had to reluctantly kiss our Grumpy goodbye.

About this time, a gray-striped kitten wandered into our yard, and Mom let us keep her. We named her Petunia. Later on, we discovered that Petunia was a male, but he kept his name. We had Petunia for quite a few years and took him with us to our next house when we moved.

The people living two doors up from us were a couple whose daughter and grandchild came to live with them when their son-in-law went off to war. They had Baby Dog, an older white poodle. After Grumpy left us, I tried to engage Baby Dog in some playful fun, but he didn't have much get-up-and-go. Sally, on the other hand, told me that she and Baby Dog were good friends.

As the war was ending, I saw a man trudging down the hill in his military uniform with a large duffel bag slung over his shoulder one day. I didn't know who he was. A neighbor woman who was outside at the time started yelling her head off for the lady who owned Baby Dog. A few minutes later, a woman came running out of the house, followed by her parents. Oh, that was an emotional sight that day as the couple came together on the sidewalk, hugging and kissing. Everyone was so happy. I watched the whole scene unfold, wide eyed, as if I were watching a movie. Mom explained later that the family had no idea their soldier was coming home.

Vacant Lot and Indian Village

Next to our house was a vacant lot. No one built on it for several years, and during that time, it belonged to the neighborhood kids. In springtime, the wild grasses and mustard plants grew nearly as tall as any of us. At dusk, we could hear the insects having a party. For hours on end, Sally and I and the other kids dragged pieces of cardboard boxes around the lot, flattening the grass into rooms and pathways. The maze became a fort, a hideout, or a make-believe house. When we sat down, the grass hid us from view and the prying eyes of grownups.

One afternoon in late summer, after the weeds had turned brown and brittle, Sally, Mom and I were taking a nap when an unmistakable crackling noise woke Mom up and she shouted, "Wake up! There's a fire!"

I opened my eyes and saw the orange flames reflected in the bedroom window. We ran out the front door as the giant hook-and-ladder truck pulled up with its siren blaring. Neighbors rushed out of their homes as the firemen worked quickly to put out the blaze. No one knew how the fire started.

"Don't ever play with matches," Mom said, using the fire as an example of the danger.

The vacant lot was sold, and construction started on a new home. After the workmen left at the end of the day, Sally and I scavenged bricks, wood, and odd pieces of construction stuff, dragging our stash to the dirt area behind our bedroom. I wanted to build an Indian village, and Sally was all for it. Using a shovel and tools from the garage, we dug out as much dirt as we could. We carved shelves into the sides to hold things. Realistically, our Indian village looked more like a large planting hole. Nevertheless, we eagerly mixed dirt with water to make bowls and plates for our make-believe kitchen. We placed our dinnerware in the sun to dry and were disappointed when it cracked and fell apart. The Indian village kept us happily occupied for hours on end. The winter rains came and washed away our hard work.

Dad's Boss and Work

Dad's boss, Shirley Burden, was a philanthropist, promoter of the arts, and an affable and talented man of many interests including filmmaking and fine art photography. Shirley was the great-great grandson of the nineteenth-century entrepreneur Cornelius Vanderbilt and was married to Flobelle, who was the niece of Douglas Fairbanks, Sr. They had two children with cute childhood nicknames: Muff and Winks. Shirley was wealthy but not a bit pretentious—a kind, down-to-earth man who my father liked immensely.

After the war ended and the contracts were cancelled, Tradefilms went out of business. Dad found a new writing job. With his photographer friend Hal Walker, Shirley opened a photography studio in Beverly Hills for advertising and architectural clientele that was very successful.

One of the training films Dad wrote while working at Tradefilms was used to teach military pilots how to fly even though Dad himself had never been in a cockpit. His gift was learning about a difficult or complicated subject and explaining it in an easy and understandable way. He did this extremely well.

He talked about a visual they used for safety training to demonstrate what happens when pilots go above a certain altitude and fail to put on their oxygen mask. They black out without warning. This was demonstrated by having a pilot use lipstick, which was a good example on film. Starting out, the pilot applies lipstick to his lips perfectly. As the air thins, the pilot is unable to control the application of the lipstick and starts rubbing it all over his face, unaware that he's doing it.

Once Dad was in the cockpit with a pilot when they were ready to land at Lockheed Airport in Burbank. An alarm went off, indicating the landing gear had failed to come down, and the landing was aborted. The pilot circled the field while the tower operator used binoculars to determine if the landing gear was up or down. Dad said later, "Thankfully it was just an alarm malfunction, but I had some very tense moments before we landed safely."

My father was a stickler for manners. Having class was a trait that he admired and valued. He taught that loud and clear as my sister and I were growing up by using the example of Shirley's wife, Flobelle. Dad described a dinner party that he and Mom attended at the Burden's home in Holmby Hills along with his coworker Hal Walker and his new fiancé, Betty. As Betty proudly showed off her engagement ring with a tiny diamond, Flobelle turned the stone of her ring to the palm of her hand.

"That is class," Dad said, and we couldn't disagree.

Playhouse

When Dad was out of town for work, life was more relaxed. Mom had the car to herself, and she didn't have to fix a big dinner. Sally and I were usually allowed to stay up later, and it was fun having Mom all to ourselves.

Mom knew that I wanted a backyard playhouse and decided to take on the project during one of Dad's business trips. I envisioned a one-room cottage with decorated walls, a shingled roof, a Dutch door, and real glass windows with ruffled curtains. Sally wanted a playhouse too, but she was too young to care what it looked like. Mom told me her plans, and I was thrilled at the thought of helping her.

We went to the brickyard in Sawtelle and piled as many used bricks in the small trunk of our Plymouth coupe as it could safely carry. The bricks were for the floor of the playhouse. No chipped or cracked bricks allowed. It was tough work, and my hands became chafed as I carried a brick in each hand from the stockpile to the trunk of the Plymouth. Sally helped too. It took quite a few trips to the brickyard before we had enough bricks. It was risky of Mom to use the car in that way. Gasoline was rationed, and we couldn't buy new tires if the heavy loads damaged them, but we got all the bricks home without a problem.

The area outside of the kitchen window between the clothesline and the chain link fence was chosen as the ideal location for the playhouse. The ground needed leveling, and Sally and I worked together to dig out stones with our bare hands. We used a rake to smooth the ground. Mom placed four boards on the ground to define the square space. She filled the area with a foundation of sand and laid the bricks end to end to create the floor. Of course, this took several weeks. Later, posts were placed at each of the four corners, and they were anchored with cement for structural support. Mom hired a handyman to do that work. The handyman also built and installed the roof, which was nothing more than a square frame with crossbeams set about a foot apart.

Disappointed, I was beginning to have doubts. "Is this going to have walls and a front door?" I wanted to know.

Mom reassured me. "I promise you'll like the playhouse once it's finished. Just wait and see." She explained about the shortage of building materials. Supplies were hard to get, and money was tight. There was a war on.

I fortunately grew up in America where I was protected from the horrors of the war being fought overseas. However, I was aware that my parents were anxious and worried at times. They talked about the war privately in hushed tones. When we gathered around the radio after dinner and listened to the nightly news, I heard the war reports. I was a sensitive, intuitive child. That day when we were building the playhouse, I studied Mom's face carefully, focused on her eyes—dark, sad, fleeting emotions caught there—thinking they were saying something to me. What? This was one of those times I couldn't read her expression, but then she smiled like nothing was wrong. She said, "Sometimes, Susan, you just have to be a little creative when you want something. Do the best you can with what you've got."

Since Mom planned to handle most of the playhouse construction herself and on a shoestring budget, she intended to keep the design simple and use her talent and ingenuity. This was a powerful lesson that I learned from her, and it made a strong impact on my life. She had lived through the Depression years. She had experienced disappointment and sadness the year her parents divorced when all she received for Christmas was a few yards of blue serge so she could make herself a dress. She had seen hard times and survived. She was tough and resourceful and wanted me to be strong too.

Once the lattice roof structure of the playhouse had been secured, several boards were nailed to the three sides running from post to post. The front remained open. Mom installed wooden fruit crates on the inside for kitchen cupboards and lined them with shiny oilcloth to hold our metal play dishes, pots, and pans. Hooks held cups and other handy utensils suitable for hanging. Mom painted the wood white and planted variegated ivy at each post. The ivy took hold quickly and eventually covered the structure, creating a shady retreat. Later, a brick entrance path was added with flowerbeds where we grew petunias, geraniums, and sweet william in jewel colors in the summer.

After it was finished, Sally and I played for hours in our playhouse. We pretended we were mothers busy at our tasks of cleaning, cooking, and taking care of our doll babies. We often ate our lunch in the playhouse, sitting on wooden chairs at a little round table. The neighborhood children visited, and we were the charming hostesses. We had tea parties with cookies and real tea diluted with milk and sugar. Sometimes we cut up pieces of ice plant, which grew next to the playhouse, and served the watery succulent on plates to our guests as make-believe food. Although this wasn't exactly the playhouse of my dreams, it was unique and charming, like an outdoor room in the Italian countryside if you thought about it. More importantly, our Mom built it with love and ingenuity especially for Sally and me.

Playhouse.

The Day I Became Jewish

My passion for tea parties led to a traumatic, life-altering experience. It happened during the Easter season at Catholic school. I was eight and in the third grade. You have to know that most of the nuns at the school were kind and dedicated educators who encouraged students to excel in their studies. However, a few were imposing authority figures, especially when it came to religious principles. Catechism studies were a regular part of our curriculum. We learned about Jesus, God's love, and Catholicism.

Sister Pascalita taught third grade, and unfortunately, she was one of those nuns who children feared and disliked. She was a strict disciplinarian who allowed no talking or laughing in her classroom. She punished overzealous boys with finger thrashings using a wooden ruler.

Kids who were caught talking in class were punished by

having to write "I will not talk in class" either five hundred or one thousand times. This was in addition to the regularly assigned homework, which took several hours. I had to write those papers a couple of times before I learned to keep my mouth shut. When students returned their punishment paper the next day, they had to stand in front of the class while Sister ceremoniously tore up the paper and threw it into the trash basket. This was a strong lesson to other would-be talkers. I remember feeling embarrassed when it happened to me, which was a mild reaction compared to what was coming next.

It was the Monday before Good Friday, and morning recess had just ended. Our class was standing in line on the playground, ready to return to the classroom. Sister Pascalita approached me, her prayer beads rattling ominously on the outside of her black robe. "What did you hand out during recess?" she said.

"Invitations to my tea party," I politely answered.

She wanted to know when I was having the party.

"Friday afternoon," I told her.

Her expression darkened. "That's not a day off to play. We're supposed to attend mass and pray on Good Friday. You need to take back your invitations and cancel the party."

Reluctantly, I agreed to do that.

Mom was surprised when I told her what Sister Pascalita had said. She decided to call a few other mothers to get their opinions. They all thought an afternoon tea party on Good Friday would be fine since it wouldn't interfere with morning mass. I went ahead with the party, and my six closest girlfriends came. We had a good time.

The first thing Monday morning, Sister Pascalita called me to the front of the classroom. "Did you have a party on

Good Friday?" she asked through clenched teeth. Her eyes were piercing as she glared at me through wire-rimmed spectacles.

I started to tremble and felt my heart racing. Everyone stared at me. How did she know? In self-defense, I muttered, "My mother said it was okay."

She glowered contemptuously. "Everyone knows you're a Jew. That gives you no right to disobey and go ahead with your party."

It was like she had struck me in the head with a hammer. The implication of her words wielded an unimaginable blow. "I'm *not* a Jew," I said, having had no religious training other than what I'd received at Catholic school.

"Yes, you are. If you don't think so, just ask your parents."

Tears slid down my cheeks as I flushed with humiliation. My classmates sat frozen, gaping at me. Not knowing what else to do, I bolted for the door.

"Come back," Sister called after me.

I didn't turn around. Crying, I ran past the statue of the Virgin Mary, her arms outreached in loving benevolence, and left through the school's main double doors. I stopped only long enough to catch my breath as I traveled over a mile, going down Wilshire Boulevard and Santa Monica Boulevard, past the sets on the back lot of Twentieth Century Fox Studios, up Fox Hills Drive, and down La Grange Avenue before finally reaching our front door. I burst into the house. "Mommy, please tell me I'm not a Jew," I cried, sweaty and exhausted.

The school had already telephoned home, and the police had been called. Mom wrapped me in her arms and tried to console me. "Yes, it's partly true," she said, searching for the right words. "Your daddy is Jewish, and I'm a Christian. That makes you half Jewish."

Growing Up Wise

"It can't be true," I wailed. "Everyone hates the Jews because they killed Jesus. I don't want to be *any* Jewish."

I can't remember everything she said—something about my parents' religion being on the enrollment application and the school accepting me knowing that my father was Jewish. Why didn't I know? Why hadn't they told me? When my father came home that evening, there was a long discussion. I told my parents, "I never want to go back to that school again."

My father said, "You have to go back. You did nothing wrong. You have to be strong. You're a Wise, and Wises are strong."

I cried and begged him to reconsider, but he held firm. "It's important for you to face this and not run away."

When I finally fell asleep that night, I had nightmares.

The next morning, instead of taking the school bus, Mom drove me to school. She had an appointment with the Mother Superior. We parked, and she headed for the principal's office while I reluctantly went to my classroom. I can't believe that I had the courage to walk into that room. I dreaded the reaction of my classmates, I was afraid to face Sister Pascalita, and my stomach was in a knot. I couldn't look anyone in the eye.

Surprisingly, the kids acted normal when they saw me like nothing had happened, but I couldn't relax. We sat there without a teacher for about thirty minutes. Finally, Sister Pascalita entered the classroom. She looked visibly shaken and addressed the class. I don't remember exactly what she said, but it was something like this: "Before God and all of you children, I want to apologize to Susan for saying what I did. I have sinned. I will need to repent and ask for God's forgiveness. I am truly sorry."

I said nothing to Sister Pascalita that I can recall. My only wish was that my classmates would forget this ever happened. I didn't know that I would have great difficulty forgetting and would, in fact, spend many years trying to overcome the trauma and shame I had experienced on that fateful day. I was a changed Susan.

From then on, I was afraid that everyone in the school would know that I was different from them—a Jew, I suppose. I didn't feel like a Jew because I didn't know anything about the Jewish religion. I had been raised Christian, actually a Catholic, even though I hadn't been baptized or taken my first communion. I believed in Jesus, prayed to him every night before going to sleep, and celebrated Christmas and Easter. I couldn't bear the thought of being considered like those murderous people who had killed Jesus. That was what I had been taught in the parochial school.

The kids in my class seemed to forget what happened. No one mentioned anything about it. I was never treated any differently and never lost any friends, but I felt different. Unfortunately, rumors spread to the kids in an upper grade. It wasn't long before some older boys started chasing me into the girls' bathroom yelling, "Let's get the Jew." Those were scary, humiliating scenes with me running like a scared rabbit into the girls' bathroom and waiting inside, not knowing when it was safe to come out.

From then on, Lynn started harassing me. When I walked by her house, she pretended to vomit and made a repulsive gagging noise. "Jews aren't allowed to walk on this side of the street," she'd jeer. To avoid her, I nervously crossed to the other side of the street. When I complained to my parents, my father responded with a lecture on how to deal with bullies and stand up for myself, but I never learned how to do that or to stop Lynn's taunting. I internalized the bad feelings and simply stopped talking about it.

It was difficult to finish the third grade in Sister Pascalita's class, but I did it. That was when I fell behind in arithmetic, which was never my best subject anyway. My mind wandered, and I wasn't going to ask for help from my teacher. The more invisible I became in her classroom, the better. As the weeks passed, I felt increasingly sad and lonely, even though I tried to wear a pleasant face. Inwardly, I suffered and felt insecure and unhappy. I worried about being accepted and liked. From then on, I protected my secret, afraid that if known, I'd be subject to another devastating surprise attack like the one Sister Pascalita had wielded. Trust became an issue. After all, if you can't trust a person of God, who can you trust?

One of Dad's jokes took on a greater meaning. Using a Yiddish accent, he told the joke this way. "A father held his son up in the air as the son pleaded to be put down. The father assured the son he wouldn't drop him, raising the boy higher and higher. Suddenly, the father let go, and the boy fell to the ground. Through his tears, he said to his father, 'You promised not to drop me.' The father said, 'Let that be a lesson. Don't trust anyone, not even your father.'"

After the incident with Sister Pascalita, I prayed a lot and even made an altar in my bedroom out of cardboard boxes covered with a white sheet. On the top box I had a crucifix, my rosary, and a statue of the Virgin Mary. After Sally fell asleep at night, I knelt in the darkness before my altar and prayed to God for help. I must have been a pretty depressed little girl.

Wilshire Boulevard and Allergy Shots

It was around this time that I woke up in the middle of the night with my heart racing as if I'd been running around the block. Frightened, I went to my parents' bedside. "My heart won't stop pounding," I said, thinking it was audible through my pajama top. I had no trouble waking up Mom and Dad, and they were alarmed. Was it a heart attack?

My heart was still racing the next morning, and Mom took me to see Dr. Hopkins at her office on Wilshire Boulevard. She examined me and ordered heart tests and allergy tests. Nothing was wrong with my heart, but I came up allergic to almost everything—pollens, animal hair, dust, mold, and so forth. The rapid heartbeat was probably an asthma attack, the doctor surmised. Allergy shots were recommended, and I took them for nearly four years. The rapid heartbeat phenomenon disappeared and never returned until I was an adult and reacted to an ingredient in something I ate. That's when I learned that I had serious food intolerances and was sensitive to gluten.

The good thing about going to the pediatrician every Saturday morning for allergy shots was the opportunity for an outing to the mid-Wilshire district where there were many stores and restaurants. Since I was crazy about shoes, a stop at the Buster Brown store was always fun. Though ration coupons were needed to buy shoes, Mom had them when it came time to replace our outgrown shoes. I remember putting my feet in the x-ray box (fluoroscope) and seeing the outline of my foot magically show up green inside the new shoes, assuring a good fit. We know now that we, and especially the salespeople who operated the fluoroscope daily, were being exposed to radiation. I tried to talk Mom into letting me get black patent leather Mary Janes with the single strap, but I usually came away with the sensible, brown leather oxfords.

We also made regular visits to the May Company department store. The window decorations, filled with clothes, toys, and many things that caught my eye, were alluring. There were no escalators, and going up and down in the elevator was fun. The elevator ladies wore tailored suits and clicked castanets held in their hands to let us know when the door was opening or closing. Just before it closed, the operator blocked the entry with a stick that looked like a cane so no more customers could get on. "This elevator is full," the operator announced, and then we were on our way.

At Christmastime, we visited Santa Claus. He sat in the May Company window, and kids lined up to sit on his lap and tell him what they wanted for Christmas.

"I want a new maroon Schwinn two-wheel bicycle with hand brakes," I told Santa Claus each December for several years. It would be a long time before I got anything close to a hand brake bike.

Christmas

Christmas was always my favorite time of the year. Driving by houses decorated for the holidays was a family tradition, and Beverly Hills had some of the best. Mom didn't decorate our house much, but she did put on the coffee table a bowl of ribbon candy and a wooden dish filled with almonds, walnuts, and Brazil nuts that we opened with a handheld nutcracker. Stockings for Sally and me were hung over the fireplace and filled with an orange in the toe, some nuts and hard candies, plus maybe some socks, barrettes for our hair, and other small things. Dad taped dollar bills together so they pulled out of our stockings in a continuous stream. The older we got, the more dollar bills there were.

We always had a large fir Christmas tree that smelled of pine, and Sally and I helped with the trimming. Tinsel was popular, and we took special care to hang each strand one by one after the ornaments were on. A wind-up choo choo train went around the bottom of the tree.

Trying to find hidden Christmas gifts was an adventure that Sally and I shared while Mom tried to outwit us each year. One time, she was in a hurry and stored some unwrapped boxes on the upper shelf of the guest closet. When she wasn't looking, I reached up to see what the boxes held, and the contents spilled out. No toys there, just a couple of white dress shirts for Dad. Mom showed up and gave me a half-hearted scolding, saying, "These aren't for you. They're for Daddy."

After Dad was settled in his chair that night, I exclaimed, "We got you a surprise for Christmas, and that means a shirt." From then on, that became a special saying in our family anytime someone was getting a gift. "We got you a surprise, and you know what that means. A shirt."

On Christmas morning, we opened our gifts. Even if money was tight, my parents made sure that we had a good Christmas and received most of the gifts on our wish list. I never did get the Schwinn bicycle I so desperately wanted. Instead, I got a used blue bicycle with balloon tires and a foot brake, but it did have a bell and a metal basket attached to the handlebars.

For as long as I can remember, Dad's cousin Bennett Cerf sent books for my parents and books for Sally and me. I can't recall getting a Christmas gift from my grandparents in New York, but they never forgot my birthday, always sending a card with money inside.

Sally and I were the recipients of some of the most beautiful Christmas gifts from the Burdens. They arrived by courier from Saks Fifth Avenue in crème-colored boxes tied with magenta or turquoise satin bows. Mom and Dad playing Santa Claus could never compete with those gifts. They were the last ones we opened on Christmas morning so we could wait and savor the enjoyment. One year, I received satin lounging pajamas. Another year, I received a gorgeous bridal doll with a white veil so long that I could wear it on my head during processions for religious ceremonies at school.

The most memorable gifts from the Burdens were our baby dolls. Sally received a large doll she named Ann. I received an even larger one, the size of a three-month-old infant, and named her Margie. I dressed my doll in real infant clothes that Mom had saved as keepsakes including a pair of knitted wool soakers worn over my diapers before the invention of plastic pants. I kept Margie throughout the years when I hoped to have a daughter. Sadly, years later when I was newly married, our German shepherd chewed Margie beyond repair during a thunderstorm.

In the afternoon, after we opened our presents, we visited Aunt June and Uncle Paul to exchange gifts and have dinner. Nanny was there since she lived with them and Ole Tvedt was also there. Nanny told me he was her husband. They were together for maybe thirteen years, but I remember seeing him only once. He disappeared from Nanny's life when I was about seven. They had a little black dog named Mickey Mouse—a Pomeranian that barked a lot and wasn't good around children.

My Dad thought Uncle Paul was a cheapskate because he waited until Christmas Eve to get a tree for free. Their tree always looked scraggly and dry, covered by hastily hung ornaments and a bunch of silver tinsel. My father never liked my uncle very much for a variety of reasons, and sometimes I could feel the tension between them, but I loved going to their house, playing with my cousin Beverly, and having a family celebration.

Playing dress-up with Beverly.

Street Vendors

For us kids, the heartbeat of our neighborhood revolved around visits from the vendors who frequented the street including the ice delivery man, milkman, and door-to-door Fuller Brush salesman.

The double toot of his whistle announced the arrival of the Helms man in his yellow truck with blue lettering.

Mom placed the blue "H" sign in the front window when she wanted the driver to stop in front of our house. When he pulled out a long drawer from the back of the truck, I drooled at the sight of the delicious bakery items. Sally and I usually chose a jelly-filled donut as a treat and devoured it right there while Mom and our neighbors bought bread, rolls, cookies, or cakes.

The vegetable man came once a week, his truck filled with fresh vegetables and fruits, though Mom preferred buying those things at the grocery store. The fish man also came, but Mom never bought fish because Dad was a beef eater. The Good Humor ice cream truck came by almost every day. At least once a week Sally and I got a popsicle or a chocolate-covered Good Humor bar.

Most unusual were the times the organ grinder man came down the street. A small spider monkey sat on his shoulder while the man played a little tune on his grinder. Hearing the music, children and their mothers hurried out on the street with fruits and coins in hand. The monkey hopped down to the sidewalk and delighted us with his antics. "Watch your fingers," Mom said as Sally and I offered him pieces of apple or banana. He held out his little red hat for coins, and we put a nickel into it.

Looking back, I find it strange that a man and his monkey came to our Westwood neighborhood. I guess everyone was doing what they could to make a buck during those hard war years.

Sick Collie

On another day, something happened on the street that was much scarier. One of the mothers who had been out front watching her children at play started yelling frantically for everyone to go inside. "Go home now," she screamed, waving her arm as if to sweep us all off the street.

It was an odd request, and though I sensed her fear and urgency, I lingered with a child's curiosity and stared up the street. I saw a large collie lumbering down the sidewalk, foaming at the mouth and shaking his head back and forth. I didn't know what was wrong, but when you see an animal like that, you know something is definitely not right.

"He'll bite you," the woman yelled. I ran like the dickens for my front door, slamming it shut behind me.

Mom heard the commotion and came into the living room. Together, we knelt on the couch and looked out the window. The frothing collie went by our house. It was a pathetic sight. "He must have rabies," Mom said sadly, explaining that it makes dogs crazy. "You can die if he bites you."

I'm sure the animal regulation people were called and came to get the collie. From then on, I was wary of dogs wandering alone in the neighborhood.

Sunday Dinners and Market Shortages

Dad was earning a good living during the war. Unlike many families, we rarely went without hard-to-get household and food items such as toilet paper, meat, and dairy products that were rationed. Even though my uncle had a good job with Lockheed, there were times when my aunt's family ran out of toilet paper and supposedly had to use an alternative like newspaper. Ouch! We never went without toilet paper. Dad had a connection—black market, I suspect—at a grocery store in Beverly Hills where he shopped on his way home from work. That was also where he purchased the cold meats, cheese, and bakery items that we enjoyed for Sunday dinners and special occasions.

We looked forward to those Sunday meals. Cold cuts were easy and saved Mom from having to cook. Dad often surprised us with chocolate éclairs for dessert, which were a real treat. His favorite thing was lean sirloin steak that the butcher ground for him. He mixed the sirloin with an egg, salt, and pepper, and we ate it raw on fresh rye bread. "That's what my family had when I was a boy," he said, reminiscing. We called the dish raw meat on rye bread. The proper name is steak tartar.

If Nanny was visiting and knew that Dad was going shopping, a worried look crossed her face. She reminded him of the shortages in the Clay household. "Poor June. She can't get enough toilet paper for the family."

It irritated Mom when Nanny did her sister's bidding, especially when she used the verbiage "poor June." It went along with Mom's annoyance that her sister didn't drive, which made her dependent on others and especially her husband. Dad was more sympathetic and usually managed to bring home a few extra rolls for my aunt.

Nanny was grateful. "The good Lord will bless you," she said. She tucked the precious toilet paper rolls into her travel luggage, which was just a brown paper shopping bag with handles.

Chocolate

We had a French provincial hutch that matched a large table and six chairs in the dining room. Mom secured our Halloween and Easter candy under lock and key in the cabinet of the hutch and doled it out sparingly. I loved chocolate. Unfortunately, around eight years old, I started putting on weight, and Mom placed me on a sensible diet. Sweets were restricted.

"You can have carrots or fruit for an afternoon snack," Mom said, while Sally slurped down a chocolate malted milk. Sally was so skinny she needed suspenders to hold up her pants and skirts. The malts were intended to fatten her up. This was my first lesson that life is not always fair. I wasn't allowed to leave the street without permission. My desire for chocolate, however, led me to break that rule. One late afternoon, I snuck away with birthday money in hand. My destination was the Glen Market at the busy intersection of Santa Monica Boulevard and Beverly Glen Boulevard. The day before, I saw a giant Hershey chocolate bar at the grocery store while shopping with Mom.

I was gone for about an hour. By the time I got home, I was nervous, thinking I was about to get in big trouble. Fortunately, Mom hadn't noticed my absence. After devouring the last bite of the chocolate bar, I left the wrapping on the front porch and continued playing on the driveway.

"What's this?" Mom asked, waving the wrapper accusatorily when she came outside to get me for dinner. I made up an excuse about how I found it. She looked me in the eyes like a skilled police interrogator, not believing my story for one second. "Where did you get the candy bar?"

There was no choice but to confess. Mom was angry that I'd eaten the candy before dinner and shocked to hear where I'd gone to get it. "I'm really disappointed in you, Susan." She always emphasized my name when she was upset. "What you did was very dangerous. I'm driving you back to the market so you can buy another candy bar. I want you to eat it, and I hope it makes you sick."

That didn't sound like a punishment to me. I'm sure my eyes widened in surprise. Her logic was that I'd have such a bellyache it would dissuade me from ever doing that again.

We drove to the market, and she bought me another giant Hershey bar. I ate it all. We had dinner, and I finished my meal. Afterward, I felt a little queasy, but I never let on.

Mother's concern for my weight gain prompted her to write a letter to Grandma Lovey in New York. "Are there any fat people on Walter's side of the family?" she asked.

I wasn't aware of the letter at the time. I would have died knowing that she'd done that. After all, I wasn't fat, just a bit chubby.

My grandmother was irritated and wrote back, "There aren't any fat people among the Wises. Look to your own side."

The terse response surprised my mother. "It was probably a bad idea to send the letter," Mom said.

Mom wasn't all about restricting candy. One time at school, I opened up my lunch box, and there was a note inside that read, "Enjoy your surprise. Love, Mom." She had put a Hershey chocolate bar between two pieces of buttered white bread. A chocolate bar sandwich! I was the envy of everyone.

Easter Bunnies

The following Easter Sunday, Sally and I each received a live bunny rabbit. I reasoned that the bunny surprise was a substitution for not getting a lot of candy in my Easter basket. I was thrilled to have the adorable, furry creature and cuddled him softly. In the afternoon, Sally and I were thinking up names for our new pets as we sat in the double-seated glider swing next to our playhouse.

"Be gentle, and don't let them fall," Mom said just minutes before Sally's bunny slipped from her hands. The fall broke its leg. Our bunnies were quickly whisked away to where children couldn't hurt them. Where they went I never knew.

Going Out for Dinner

Dad enjoyed going out to dinner, and we did our share of that, often going to some iconic places around town. Clifton's Cafeteria in downtown Los Angeles was a favorite of mine. There was a waterfall inside the restaurant and a long line of food with many choices. Dad preferred The Original Pantry with family-style meals where we sat with other eaters at long, communal tables. Sometimes we went to Chinatown for Chinese food, Olvera Street for Mexican food, or Phillippe's near Union Station for roast beef dip sandwiches. On a special occasion, we went to Musso & Frank Grill in Hollywood and afterward walked along Hollywood Boulevard. A woman had a sidewalk booth near Grauman's Chinese Theatre where she sold fresh gardenia corsages that smelled heavenly. We once went to Knott's Berry Farm in Buena Park that had a replica of an Old West ghost town, which we toured before eating in the restaurant that featured Southern fried chicken and blueberry pie.

Aunt June's House

A visit to Aunt June's house was always a treat. The Clay family lived in a rented two-story farmhouse in Eagle Rock on Rock Glen Avenue. The old farmhouse, with its large, covered front porch, sat at the rear of a property that was fronted by a double courtyard of one-bedroom rental units. The rooms of the house were large with oak hardwood floors that creaked. There was a big kitchen, and the bathroom had a claw foot tub. While visiting, I loved hearing the distant echo of a train whistle, which was something we didn't hear in Westwood. I thought the house was in the country, but it wasn't far from downtown Los Angeles. Getting to Eagle Rock was an adventure in itself and at least an hour's drive from our home on La Grange Avenue. I knew we were getting close when we passed the Mulholland Memorial Fountain on Los Feliz Boulevard at the entrance to Griffith Park.

Swimming Pools and Polio

I loved to swim and learned at an early age. The only place for me to swim in those days was at a public pool, because backyard swimming pools weren't prevalent unless you were wealthy. Going swimming could be risky, since there was no vaccine for polio.

Infantile paralysis (polio) was one of the most dreaded diseases of my childhood. It primarily attacked children, causing paralysis or death. Survivors could end up wearing heavy metal leg braces or needing a wheelchair. Those with paralyzed lungs spent the rest of their lives in an iron lung. Images of children in silver, cocoon-like capsules with only their heads visible—the machines pumping oxygen into their lungs like panting, otherworld beasts—appeared in movie newsreels, newspapers, and magazines. The pictures were frightening. When it came to polio, everyone had a good reason to feel vulnerable and afraid. No one knew exactly how polio was transmitted, and during publicized outbreaks, doctors warned parents to keep their children away from crowded places, especially swimming pools.

There was a huge outdoor public pool nearby called the La Cienega Plunge. I begged Mom to take me there when it was open, and a few times, she did. Once I brought a friend with me. Otherwise, I swam by myself like a happy tadpole while Mom watched from the sidelines. Before I could enter the pool area, I had to step into a basin filled with a foul-smelling bleach solution. I thought it was intended to ward off polio, but it was for athlete's foot.

The indoor swimming pool at Beverly Hills High School was another place to swim. However, it was noisy and always crowded. The voices of kids yelling to one another reverberated off of the gymnasium walls, and the smell of chlorine was pungent. I went there sometimes and had to dance around on my tiptoes so I could keep my chin above water in the shallow end. Mom told me there was a retractable lid that closed over the pool to create the floor of a basketball court. It was a little spooky swimming in the pool. Even though Mom assured me it wouldn't happen, I had the uneasy feeling that the basketball floor might suddenly spring out of its hiding place and cover everyone.

When Sally was old enough for swimming lessons, we went to an official swim school with an outdoor pool. While she learned the basics, I learned more advanced strokes. It was fun, but my time in the water was never long enough.

When I was about ten, I met some friendly boys in the neighborhood one hot summer afternoon. They were on their way to a buddy's house to go swimming and invited me to tag along. Mom said okay because I was a good swimmer, but she wouldn't have allowed me to go had she'd known there was no sign of parental supervision.

The pool was military issue and sold at war surplus stores. It was round, about four feet deep, made of heavy green canvas, and installed above ground on a hillside. It had no filter system, and by the time I got there, it was dirty with leaves and grass floating on top. The boys jumped in and got rowdy. A towering shade tree with wooden slats nailed into the trunk for steps served as a makeshift jumping tower. I did it several times; climbed up, reached a limb, and from a good height, dropped into the pool. The boys did it over and over again. It was hard to keep up with them.

After a while, I began to feel uneasy and unsafe, so wisely I said, "Thanks for the swim," and headed for home.

The War Ends

September 2, 1945 was remarkable even for a nine-year-old. The radio was on as I rested in my parents' four-poster double bed, sick with chickenpox. Mom's white typewriter table was spread over the bed, with feet that touched the floor on both sides, and it held my coloring books and paper dolls. News of the Japanese delegation signing the surrender document aboard the USS *Missouri* in Tokyo Harbor was being broadcast throughout the world. Though I missed listening to my favorite radio programs, I knew this was an important moment in history. The war was officially over.

I remember the announcer saying, "They signed. No, they didn't sign yet." This went back and forth a few times, and then the announcement that the treaty had been signed was made. I heard the sounds of jubilation being broadcast from the streets of our major cities where people were celebrating. It was a joyful day indeed.

Sunday Drives and Trips to the Mountains

When the war was over, gasoline rationing ended, and we started taking family drives on the weekends. I remember going to Manhattan Beach and Redondo Beach, traveling south on Sepulveda Boulevard. With no tall buildings to restrict the view looking west, I could sometimes see the ocean shimmering in the distance. The open land along Sepulveda Boulevard had been vegetable fields and farms that Japanese Americans owned before the war.

My favorite drives were to the San Fernando Valley going through the Sepulveda Pass on a winding, two-lane road. The Valley was always sunny and warm. Traveling along Ventura Boulevard, we drove by the ghost town of Gerard (now Woodland Hills) where the small, wood-framed buildings had been abandoned and boarded up after the real estate developers left. There were no buyers for country lots during the war. This was the last stop before going over the hills toward Ventura where the Burma Shave signs along the highway were fun to read. "No lady likes to snuggle or dine accompanied by a porcupine…Burma Shave."

On the opposite side of the San Fernando Valley, Devonshire Street bordered the northern foothills where there were no houses, only beautiful ranches. Some of the ranches were surrounded by white, split-rail fencing that enclosed green pastures where retired race horses grazed. Sally and I brought carrots along to feed the horses.

The town of Chatsworth was at the end of Devonshire Street near Rocky Peak and the Santa Susana Mountains. Sally and I loved going there because it looked like the Old West. The dirt road had just a few stores on it with hitching posts out front. Many of the people in the area had horses and rode them to town. The Peterson Dairy Farm was on Devonshire Street. We stopped there, and Sally and I experienced drinking fresh milk and cream.

One January morning before dawn, Mom and Dad woke us girls up from a deep sleep. They were great at initiating surprises, and this was a big one. "We're going to the snow," they said with enthusiasm.

Sally and I had never seen snow. Not believing this could be true, we realized it was for real when we saw our packed suitcases with snow clothes that Mom had collected from used clothing stores. We piled into the Plymouth coupe, and off we went, stopping for breakfast at the famous Brown Derby in Beverly Hills. Dad's coworker, Hal Walker, and his wife, Betty, met us at the June Lake Lodge in the High Sierras where we stayed for a long weekend. Sally and I had fun playing in the snow. I brought my ice skates along and skated on June Lake, though it was bumpy and not good for skating.

Our next trip, during the summer, was to Twin Lakes in the same Mammoth Lakes area. This was a week-long trip, and Nanny came with us. How breathtaking it was to see my first sunrise at dawn as we headed north through the Mojave Desert. With the windows of the Plymouth cracked open, I smelled the pungent fragrance of sagebrush. We rented a small cabin at the Tamarack Lodge and Resort that had a wood stove for cooking our meals, which took a long time. There was no indoor bathroom. We had to use an outhouse, though Nanny kept a chamber pot under her bed.

Mom liked the outhouse. She said, "I open the door and sit there enjoying the scenery with my morning cigarette." Once, a man walked by and saw her doing just that. She was unable to close the door in time. She shrugged, telling us, "I just waved and said hello to him."

I loved the beauty of the mountains—the wind rustling through the towering pine trees, clear air, a crystal blue sky, and huge granite boulders that were perfect for climbing. Sally and I played under the trees and took walks in the woods with Mom and Nanny while Dad, who had become an avid fishing enthusiast, went fishing. Sally and I forgot to bring our dolls, so Mom made each of us one out of socks stuffed with newspaper, the happy faces drawn on with a pen.

On Sunday morning while Dad went fishing, the rest of us went to the nondenominational church service held in the open under the pine trees where we sat on logs. That was the first time I heard "America the Beautiful" as it was sung while we gazed at the majestic mountain peaks in the distance. It made quite an impression on me.

We went sightseeing in the mountains, visited a natural hot spring, and sidestepped cow patties along the Owens River while Dad fished. We even tried to drive up the road to the summit of Mount Whitney, but the old Plymouth's radiator boiled over, and we had to let it cool before turning around.

Coming back from one excursion, I ran ahead of the family to our cabin and was first to notice the side of the cabin next to ours on fire. Someone had cleaned out the coals of their wood stove, put what they thought were dead coals into a cardboard box, and then put the box under the eaves of the cabin. I ran as fast as I could to the lodge to report the fire. The lodge workers put out the fire right away, and I got a candy bar as a reward.

Going home from Twin Lakes, we had an unplanned overnight stay in the town of Lone Pine. The desert wind blew so hard that Dad couldn't drive any farther through the sandstorm.

Our next trip was to Convict Lake for a few days—a serious fishing destination in the same Mammoth Lakes area. As we arrived and were walking to our small cabin, we noticed a metal chimney stack resting on the ground, obviously from the roof of one of the cabins. Dad made the comment, "Someone's in for a surprise." When he lit a fire in our wood stove for heat, smoke poured into the room. Surprise—it was our chimney stack laying on the ground.

At Convict Lake, Sally and I had our first experience fishing for trout. Dad brought some fishing gear for himself and set Sally and I up with drop lines attached to a piece of wood. He left Mom, Sally, and I on the sandy beach with our drop lines while he went to the other side of the lake. There was another man fishing near him, and neither of them had caught anything when I got a bite. Not having a reel, I ran up on the beach, pulling the trout on a string behind me. I yelled loudly, "I got a fish. I got a fish," my voice echoing across the quiet lake.

Dad came hustling over to me. He seemed perturbed, maybe jealous. "You can't yell like that when you get a fish," he said, and my excitement over the catch diminished.

Aunt Delphine Visits

I was excited to meet my father's sister and her family when Aunt Delphine, Uncle Ralph, and my cousin Susan came from New York for a visit. They stayed at the Hotel Bel-Air in Beverly Hills and rented a convertible to take advantage of the California sunshine. We went with them on tours of the local sights in their car with the top down, and it was fun. Susan was about fifteen. She taught Sally and me the song "She'll Be Coming 'Round the Mountain," which we sang with gusto as we toured the streets of Hollywood.

Susan and Aunt Delphine

The Hotel Bel-Air was ritzy and beautiful, nestled against a hillside, but Aunt Delphine complained of the crickets. She was accustomed to the Manhattan traffic noise, and the sound of the crickets kept her awake at night. While

Susan was outgoing and Uncle Ralph was a good talker, Aunt Delphine seemed aloof. I wish I could have known her better, but that wasn't possible. She passed away at the young age of fifty-three, and I wouldn't see Susan again for a long time.

Delphine

More about Catholic School

I attended Beverly Hills Catholic School for five years from the first through the fifth grade. Given my Protestant and Jewish background, it seems odd to me now that my parents sent me to a parochial school. I suppose they wanted the educational advantages the school offered, and at the time, their decision seemed a good one. Of course, I knew no difference until we moved and I entered the public school system in the sixth grade. Sally only went to Catholic school for one year, so her experience in elementary school was different than mine.

At the Catholic school, the girls wore blue uniforms, and the boys wore blue shirts with long pants. Our desks were attached by runners on the floor, one after the other. We had inkwells in our desks and used fountain pens for writing that needed to be refilled with ink. The inevitable drips from the ink stained our desks. Many of the girls wore pigtails tied with ribbons, me included, and sometimes a mischievous boy would dip the tip of a girl's braid into an inkwell. Fortunately, that never happened to me.

The number of students in each class, offered from first through eighth grade, was relatively small. There were no students in any of my classes who had special needs, learning difficulties, or behavioral problems. It was a one-size-fits-all education, each class taught by a nun requiring strict adherence to manners and rules and giving lots of homework. The affiliate Church of the Good Shepherd in Beverly Hills was within walking distance. It was the church of local movie stars and celebrities of the Catholic faith, and some of their children attended my school. The education was top notch, and I did well with the exception of third grade in Sister Pascalita's class.

Besides music lessons, recitals, an orchestra, and an annual spelling bee, the school had fall festivals for the children and their parents. Game booths and food booths with roofs made from palm leaves were set up on the playground, and we looked forward to the festivals.

We also celebrated May Day when the girls were allowed to wear pretty dresses to school instead of uniforms. We put flower garlands in our hair and danced around the decorated maypole.

Throughout the war years, the school had tin can and newspaper drives to earn money for the war effort. I took my red wagon and went from house to house and street to street in my neighborhood, collecting newspapers. I made stacks of the newspapers in our garage and tied them with twine for my parents to drop off at school. With the piles of newspapers accumulating on the playground, the school looked like a recycling center. The student who brought in the most weight in newspapers received a prize. I never won, although I was tenacious in my effort to try for the win.

On special church holidays such as Ash Wednesday, we had processions. The students walked two by two along the sidewalk from the school on Linden Drive to the Church of the Good Shepherd on Santa Monica Boulevard. The procession continued inside the church as the children filed into the pews, hands folded together in silent prayer. The girls wore veils on their heads, and I wore the veil that belonged to my bridal doll since it was long enough for that purpose.

The first time I attended mass, or a church service of any kind for that matter, was at age six when I was in the first grade. The parents of a classmate of mine took me with their daughter to the Church of the Good Shepherd. When I returned home, Mom asked, "How was the service?"

I said, "Father Concannon wore something like a nightgown and spoke in a language that no one could understand. Everyone got so tired they fell down on their knees."

Several of the nuns asked if I would like to convert to Catholicism and have my first communion. During mass, when the other kids took communion, I had to remain in the pew, but after my experience with Sister Pascalita, I knew I would never become a Catholic.

Since the classes were small, the girls formed a tight-knit group, and most of them were classmates of mine from year to year. There were many birthday parties, and they were the highlight of my youthful social life. Gifts received and given included toys such as a jump rope, spinning top, checkers, pick-up sticks, tiddlywinks, jacks, paper dolls, books, watercolor paints, crayons, or one of the many charming storybook dolls.

My friend Ellen from school invited me on an outing to her ranch in the San Fernando Valley one Saturday. It was on Balboa Boulevard near the railroad tracks not far from what is now Van Nuys Airport. A ranch house sat sideways on the property that held row after row of walnut trees. There were no other structures in sight, just farm fields and the Santa Monica Mountains looming in the distance. We played under the walnut trees where the wild grass was tall from a recent spring rain. The rear of the property stopped at an irrigation channel.

Dolores, another friend from school, invited me to come home with her after school. The Mother Superior called my home, and Mom gave her permission. Dolores lived in Sherman Oaks in the San Fernando Valley, some distance away. Her mother picked us up from school and drove me home after dinner.

Recapping my visit to Delores' house, I told Mom, "Her father plays the piano and better than you do." Her father happened to be Carmen Cavallaro, the popular pianist of the day who was featured on the radio and in movies.

Lourdes from Mexico went to my school for a short time. Her mother was a gourmet cook. She was brought to the United States by Joseph Schenck, cofounder and chairman of the board of Twentieth Century-Fox Studios, after being discovered on one of his trips to Mexico. The other girls made remarks about Lourdes looking foreign and being different. She had an accent when speaking English and wore a wool plaid cape on winter days instead of a regular coat. I liked her exactly because she was different. She was unique, fun, and smart. We played imaginative games together during lunchtime on the playground. She taught me words in Spanish, and my interest in learning Spanish blossomed. For lunch, her mother made huge sandwiches of bologna and cheese or ham and cheese on thick bakery bread, which Lourdes sometimes shared with me. Knowing I liked the sandwiches, her mother started including a second delicious sandwich just for me in Lourdes' lunch box. That's when the other girls had second thoughts about Lourdes and thought they too would like to be her special friend.

One day, Lourdes' mother telephoned our house, sounding upset. "Mrs. Wise, do you know anyone who needs a cook? I've lost my job." Apparently, Mr. Schenck had fallen out of favor with her cooking and hired someone else. Without work, she would have to return to Mexico. Mom did our cooking, and she didn't know of anyone who needed a cook. A few days later, there was an empty desk in my classroom. Sadly, my friend Lourdes was gone.

I had three special friends while living on La Grange Avenue, and I have unique, in-depth stories about my friendship with each one of them.

Barbara

I met Barbara on the school bus. She was seven, and I was eight and a grade ahead of her. She lived in a Spanish-style house on Calvin Avenue, which was an easy bike ride from my house, and we became instant friends.

She was a pretty child with impeccable manners, impressive dark eyes, and cute dimples. She wore her long, brown hair in fancy French braids like the child actress, Margaret O'Brien. In school, we had to wear our blue uniforms, but out of school, Barbara wore lovely dresses that were often gifts from her father's wealthy business associates.

One day, I was visiting Barbara, and she took me into her parents' bedroom. On top of the dresser in a silver frame was a black-and-white photograph of an attractive woman with dark hair and eyes. "This is my real mother," she said sadly. "She died when my brother John was born. Isn't she beautiful?"

I was surprised and honored that she trusted me with such personal information. She was the first person I knew who had a stepmother.

Another day when I was visiting Barbara, her father said he was going to butcher a chicken for dinner. He asked, "Would you girls like to watch?"

We said yes, but I didn't know what was about to happen. From behind the garage, he brought out a squawking, red-feathered bird, holding it tightly by the neck. I have no idea where he would have bought a live chicken in our urban area. He put the chicken's head on a block of wood and chopped it off with a hatchet. Blood spattered everywhere, making me nauseous. He put the headless chicken down on the grass, and it started walking around in a circle. I yelled and jumped back, frightened it was going to run into me.

Barbara laughed and said, "Don't be scared. The chicken's not alive. It's just an automatic reflex." Obviously, she'd been to other chicken executions.

Barbara's father put the chicken in a pot of boiling water that had been set on a table in the yard and started pulling out the feathers. After that, I thought twice about where chicken drumsticks came from when Mom served them for dinner.

I wondered if Barbara's father grew up on a farm. He sure knew how to prepare fresh chicken for the cook's pan, but this was a far cry from his regular job. He was the personal secretary to film mogul Joseph Schenck. It was an important and trusted position in the business of making movies in Hollywood.

He often worked at Schenck's home in Beverly Hills on Canon Drive. Sometimes he brought Barbara with him, and occasionally she asked me to come along. Going to his estate turned out to be one of the most exciting adventures of my childhood. Mr. Schenck's home was far more palatial on the inside than the exterior revealed. Mediterranean in style, it sat on a wide lot and was visible from the street without a privacy wall or security gate, which was the norm in those days. A center walkway led to a massive front door. The driveway on the north side had a portico next to the kitchen. That's where we parked the car and entered the house, using the cook's door.

At first glance, I was amazed at the hugeness and grandeur of the house with its multiple levels, massive rooms, high ceilings, arched windows, and the most elegant furnishings I had ever seen. The unique doorbell was actually a row of chimes in the entry hall that played a melody up and down the musical scale. Barbara and I played a game to see who could get the farthest from the front door before the chiming stopped. The servants didn't seem to mind the commotion of two little girls running madly through the house, our shoes clomping on the polished hardwood floors and sounding like a herd of antelope.

An alcove next to the front door held a large pipe organ with floor-to-ceiling golden pipes like you'd see in a church. A decorative iron gate with a padlock enclosed the organ.

The step-down living room with plush furniture and heavy drapes was fronted by a two-tiered water fountain gilded in gold. It reminded me of a hotel lobby. Barbara and I played king and queen in this room.

Off the entry hall was a curving staircase and an elevator. Nearby, the formal dining room seated maybe sixteen guests. We met up with the servants in the kitchen where we were offered anything we wanted for a snack. Fresh-baked cookies were on the counter for the taking.

On one visit, Barbara and I heard voices drifting from Mr. Schenck's office on the first floor at the back of the house. We stuck our heads in the doorway. Mr. Schenck was seated at his desk, and a few other businessmen were sitting in comfortable leather chairs, including Barbara's father. The office had thick carpeting, dark paneling, and bookcases filled with books.

"Hello girls," Mr. Schenck said. "Come on in. Would you like a drink?"

We giggled, said yes, and Barbara's father didn't object. Mr. Schenck gave us a sip from his own glass. "Scotch on the rocks," he said with a broad smile.

It was my first taste of liquor. Barbara and I thought we were something else.

Among the numerous guest bedrooms on the second floor, one stood out from the rest as our favorite. Barbara and I called it "the Princess Room." Romantic elegance best describes it. Satin fabrics the color of soft, pink rose petals were used for the bedspread, draperies, dressing table skirt, and a Victorian fainting couch. For two little girls, this was pink princess heaven.

We'd stretch out on the pink satin bed—carefully, with our shoes off—and let our heads sink into the plush pillows as we pretended to be princesses. "You may draw our bawth," we'd tell our make-believe handmaidens in a feigned British accent. "We'd like tea and crumpets now."

A pass-through dressing room connected the adjoining bathroom. Two mirrored wardrobe closets faced each other and were filled with flowing evening gowns and lingerie. There was no playing dress-up, though we wanted to. Who did the clothing belong to? She was surely beautiful, we thought, deciding the gowns and lingerie must belong to a movie star, because Mr. Schenck knew many.

The bathroom was also elegant. Barbara said, "Do you know what that is?" There were two toilets, but the one she pointed to looked peculiar with no lid. I had no idea what it was. "It's a bidet." She giggled. "It washes your behind for you."

Barbara took me swimming at Mr. Schenck's house several times. What a treat! The big rectangular pool sat in the middle of a manicured green lawn, a good distance from the two-story servants' cottage. Adjacent to the pool, a cabana provided cover for an outside bar and patio tables. I noticed some guests relaxing in the shade while others were stretched out on padded chaise lounges poolside, working on their tans—glamorous women with good figures wearing fashionable one-piece swimsuits and dark sunglasses. They were sipping cocktails and chatting. A few of them talked with drinks in their hands, arms eagerly in motion to illustrate a point, and the ice cubes hit the sides of their beverage glasses, making tinkling noises like distant wind chimes.

I came home after one pool outing complaining about a couple of kids, a brother and sister, who had rubber inner tubes and no intention of sharing them. They had such a good time: tubes bouncing, water spurting, tan bodies leaping from deck to tube, rolling upside down, hanging from the donut center, and swirling furiously in circles like a washing machine. The girl was named Ellen and her mother, who lounged beside the pool, was introduced to me as Joan. Ellen was my age and hardly talked to us, and her brother ignored us altogether. Barbara and I didn't know how to negotiate a turn on the pool toys, so we played in the water by ourselves.

"I don't like Joan's daughter. She didn't let us have a turn on the inner tube." That was my grumbled recap of the day. I had no idea that many of the women sitting around the pool were movie stars.

Of course, Mom suspected otherwise. "Joan who?" she said, her eyes lighting up with curiosity. Joan Crawford was Mom's favorite actress.

I didn't know at the time, but later I learned it was Joan Blondell, a big star and the leading lady of some eighty films.

There were several more places in Mr. Schenck's house worth mentioning, starting with the rooftop terrace paved in Mexican red clay tiles where a steam cabinet was kept.

The portable steam room on wheels looked like a movable outhouse or a circus prop. I could imagine clowns with silly faces and frizzy hair popping out of it.

Barbara and I ran around the roof terrace and acted silly. We made up vivacious tap dances while pretending to be Hollywood showgirls, our feet drumming and arms swinging. Part of the fun was getting to the terrace in the elevator, a small lift that hummed softly as it crept from floor to floor. Naturally, we played elevator operator.

Underneath the house, accessible by the elevator, a huge basement awaited our inspection. One section housed a workout room with a treadmill, strength-training apparatus, an exercise bicycle, a pummel horse, and a boxy machine with rollers. "The rollers loosen your fat, and it melts away," Barbara told me. We turned on the electric switch and backed into the contraption, leading with our bottoms. It bumped and thumped, and we giggled.

We rode the stationary bicycle, but the biggest attraction was a mechanical horse that stood in the center of the room. Riding the bronco was off limits. "We're not supposed to," Barbara said. "It's dangerous."

Who could resist? We decided to go for it. Thankfully, no one heard us laughing as we bucked and bounced away.

A full-size movie theater occupied the largest portion of the basement with rows of upholstered, rose-red seats like those in a regular movie theater. This is where Mr. Schenck held private film viewings for friends and business associates. Beyond the theater, an underground passageway supposedly led to somewhere within the town center of Beverly Hills. "It's an escape tunnel," Barbara told me in strictest confidence. "No one's supposed to know." That sounded reasonable to me, given the war.

When Barbara turned eight, she celebrated with a catered luncheon held at a family friend's estate in Beverly Hills. My concern was what to wear. Since Barbara always dressed beautifully, I wanted to look my best, but rather than buying something new, Mom talked me into wearing an organdy dress that I had almost outgrown. It was too short. Many of the girls wore expensive-looking dresses and fancy hairdos. I felt self-conscious and unhappy about my appearance. Feeling out of place and trying to act pleasant in a gathering of children I didn't know was a first for me. Rich children, I assumed.

The party tables were set up on the second floor in the solarium. Lunch was creamed chicken over a biscuit, which was a dish most children liked. Of course, I liked the cake and ice cream best. A few mothers—well-dressed, classy women—accompanied their children and helped out the hostess. Barbara told me that some of the ladies were actresses.

I was on my best behavior. I felt shy not knowing anyone except Barbara and not liking my dress. However, Barbara made me feel special when she asked me to stand next to her for the group photograph. We posed on an outside staircase, the architectural curve of the stairs linking the solarium to the garden. Each of us stood on an individual step from ground level to the second floor, our hands positioned gracefully on the decorative iron railing.

Barbara (third from top) next to Susan

While the party was nice, I was glad to get home where I could relax in my play clothes, go outside and have fun, and not have to worry about being with kids I didn't know.

Childhood friendships have a unique way of achieving instant closeness. Stories and secrets are exchanged. Laughter comes effortlessly. There's an easiness like being with a sister. Barbara and I were good friends just like that. We always had fun together, and although our friendship lasted only a few short years, the memory has endured a lifetime.

Bradley Munn

I met Bradley Munn on the street when I was in the second grade. He was my age, an only child, went to public school, and lived a block away on Comstock Avenue. Bradley had a pleasing, outgoing personality and, best of all, was willing to play with me, a girl. One of his eyes wandered inward, a crossed eye, which caused him to look at me with his head cocked slightly to one side. No matter. I noticed most the happy grin on his face.

Bradley and I played games, rode our bicycles together, and sometimes just sat on the curb and talked. When Sally and I put on puppet shows in the garage for the neighborhood kids—an idea of Mom's to keep us busy during the summer—Bradley was first to buy a ticket for five cents. Sally and I wrote scripts and made hand puppets to go along with the string puppets we had received as gifts for Christmas. The stage curtain was made of bedsheets. We fashioned costumes for the puppets out of our mother's leftover fabric scraps.

Bradley also helped with my entrepreneurial ventures such as when I set up a curbside stand in front of the house and sold iced lemonade to the neighborhood kids. One time, I purchased fruits and vegetables at the grocery store to resell. Mom was a silent partner in my businesses, providing seed money and transportation to buy the groceries.

I liked to play house, and Bradley was willing to go along, though normally it was considered a girl's activity. The playhouse in our backyard was the perfect make-believe house, which is where we often played, though occasionally we played in the shed beneath the rear stairway of his duplex. My red wagon was our car, which he pulled as the driver and I sat in as the passenger.

"Will you marry me?" Bradley asked one day. I must have said yes, because he gave me a ring with a big, red stone that he bought at the five-and-dime store. I wore the ring with white tape wrapped around it to hold it on my finger.

One day, Bradley's father took us on an outing to a park in Beverly Hills. "See those fish," Bradley said, directing my attention to a large pond. "They aren't regular goldfish, Susan. They're koi fish." Bradley was an inquisitive and intelligent boy, and he enjoyed explaining things to me. Until he told me differently, I thought they were well-fed goldfish like the kind you could win at the Beverly Amusement Center.

Our family often went there on Sunday so Sally and I could ride the ponies and go on the swings that went around high in the air.

I saw Bradley's mother just once when he took me into her bedroom. The shades were drawn against the afternoon sun, and she was in bed when he introduced me. "Mom, this is my friend, Susan."

"Hello," she replied in a weak voice. "What are you children doing?"

We talked to her for a few minutes, and then she put her head back down on the pillow. I knew something was wrong even if I couldn't understand what it was.

About a year later, Bradley's father, a liquor salesman, had to go out of town on business. His wife was in the hospital, and Bradley needed to stay in school.

It was exciting to have Bradley stay with us for a few weeks. Mom made up a bed for him on the couch in the den. After getting ready for bed that first night, Bradley had a big grin on his face as he announced, "These are my new pajamas." He was proud of his spiffy new bedtime attire.

Bradley and my cousin Gary were the only boys at my eighth birthday party. The photo taken in front of our house shows Bradley standing in the back smiling broadly with his head tilted slightly to one side. I'm standing in front wearing uncomfortable, new brown-and-white oxfords and a mauve corduroy jacket and skirt showing my round belly. Sally is standing in front of me with her knobby knees, wearing a skirt held up by suspenders.

Front Row: Cousin Gary, Sally. Middle Row: Bradley, Martha, Barbara, Susan, Marlene, Mary Lou, Suzette. Back Row: Cousin Beverly, Patricia, Karen, Mary Jo

My birthday gift that year was another one of my parents' notorious surprises. They took me for an evening of ice-skating at the Sonja Henie Ice Palace in Westwood Village. I had just put on my ice-skates when a young man skated over and asked me to skate. I was confused and pulled back. I noticed my parents smiling and giving me a go-ahead nod. It was part of my birthday surprise, the first of a series of ice-skating lessons.

After that, I started ice-skating on a regular basis and loved it. Mom dropped me off at the ice rink on many Saturday afternoons. Though I went by myself, there were plenty of other girls who also came regularly. I made friends, and we practiced our twirls and bunny hops together to live organ music provided by a local organist.

Bradley and I were good friends for the four years we lived on La Grange Avenue. Many years later, after I married someone else, Mom said, "You should have married Bradley Munn." She always liked him.

The unimaginable happened. About 1980, I was working in the journalism department at California State University Northridge (CSUN) and finishing my degree in journalism. I discovered there was a journalism professor named Bradley Munn working at the University of Nebraska. Along with his bill for the *Journalism & Mass Communication Quarterly*, I sent him a brief note that resulted in a phone call from him and the rekindling of our friendship. Through subsequent letters, phone calls, and get-togethers, Bradley and I remained close friends until his untimely death in 2005.

Teresa

Newspapers around the world carried the tragic news of Maria Iturbi's suicide. She was the daughter of José Iturbi, celebrated Spanish pianist and conductor whose music ranged from classical to popular and included a Hollywood screen career appearing as himself in movies. Maria was divorced and living in her father's home in Beverly Hills with her daughters, Teresa and Antonia. Mr. Iturbi was practicing the piano downstairs when he heard the shot and discovered his daughter in her room, mortally wounded.

Nothing about Maria Iturbi's death was apparent to me (or my parents) when her daughter, Teresa, and I became friends in the fifth grade. It was about five months after her mother's death. Teresa was sweet and fun, and she invited me to go home with her after school for a visit, which had to be prearranged. Her younger sister, Antonia, was a grade behind us in school. The children had a nanny and a maid who also lived in the home.

Having Teresa as a friend and visiting Mr. Iturbi's home on Bedford Drive in Beverly Hills was a memorable experience. After arriving at the house, Teresa and I went into the backyard next to the swimming pool where she schooled me in the proper way to meet her conservative Spanish grandfather. I practiced my curtsy and what she wanted me to say. I was nervous but ready when he walked into the yard to say hello. "How do you do, Mr. Iturbi," I said with a deep curtsy. I extended my right hand to shake his. "It's so nice to make your acquaintance."

After the introduction, Teresa and I were free to play but only inside the house. It was a two-story, Mediterranean-style villa with tiled flooring downstairs. Upstairs in the girls' bedroom, I was surprised to see iron bars on the outside of the windows. Certainly, this was not a cozy home like mine. I stayed for a few hours, and we played.

The next time I went home with Teresa, I stayed for dinner. Teresa, Antonia, and I joined their grandfather in the large dining room. We sat at one end of the long table that seated perhaps twelve people. I was on my good behavior and used my best manners. Mr. Iturbi seemed to like me, which I attributed to my well-done curtsy and proper initial greeting. He had a black telephone sitting on the table. After we finished the main meal and were waiting for dessert, he played a telephone game with us. Teresa said he was very strict, but that evening he was friendly and talkative.

After dinner, we went into the living room where Mr. Iturbi had two grand pianos back to back. I told him that I was taking piano lessons, and he asked me to play something for him, which I did on the piano that had a mirror above the keys. I asked him to play Chopin's "Polonaise." What a treat it was to sit on the piano bench right next to a famous pianist playing my favorite classical music. When he finished, I asked him to play it again, and he did.

Teresa turned ten in February, and I was invited to her birthday party. It was an evening gathering with a select number of children. Her gift, a maroon Schwinn bicycle with hand brakes, something that I had long wanted, sat at the bottom of the stairs by the front door. Margaret O'Brien, the most famous child actress of the day, was a guest at the party, and I was excited to meet her. Mr. Iturbi had worked with her in a film. After the festivities, we watched *The Canterville Ghost*, starring Margaret O'Brien.

I invited Teresa and Antonia to visit my house for a Saturday afternoon of play. Mom made the arrangements through the girls' nanny. They would be allowed to stay for only one hour. Before they arrived, Mom said, "You have to play in the backyard. Absolutely do not take the girls out front." I knew there was concern for their safety because of their famous grandfather, and I promised to obey the rules.

When the girls arrived, they were driven by Mr. Iturbi himself. He walked Teresa and Antonia to our front door where Mom and I greeted them. I was in my play clothes, and they were wearing dresses and Mary Jane shoes.

He told my mother, "I'll be back in an hour," apparently planning to drive around the area until the time was up. The hour went by quickly, but we made the most of it as we played in the backyard playhouse. "We had fun," the girls said when they left.

At the end of the school year, Teresa and Antonia moved back to New York to live with their father. I didn't know they were leaving, so I wasn't able to say goodbye.

It seems that moving was on the horizon for my family as well. Dad had been out of work for a while and was living off his savings after Tradefilms went out of business. Mom said he needed to take any job he could get, even if it meant working in a gas station. "I'm a writer, not a gas jockey," Dad said.

It was time to downsize, and the house on La Grange Avenue went up for sale.

CHAPTER 9

Stanton Avenue

In the summer of 1947, Dad found a job at a Polish radio station in Glendale. He wrote commercials in English for their air freshener product, a liquid that became fragrant when poured into a ringed holder placed on a warm light bulb. This was the least creative writing assignment he ever had, but he made the most of it. Around dinnertime, we tuned in and heard him on the radio as he read the commercials using his deepest professional voice. We had lots of those little air fresheners in the house, making the air smell sweet.

My parents wanted to move closer to Dad's work, and soon we were house hunting in Glendale. I loved looking at houses and imagined myself living in every one of them. We saw some nice ones along tree-lined streets in the foothills of the Verdugo Mountains, but they were all too expensive. One day, the real estate agent took us to a house on Stanton Avenue near Griffith Park in an equestrian community known as the Riverside Ranchos.

"I see horses," Sally squealed. Sure enough, a couple of horses and their riders ambled down the street, leaving a trail of dusty hoof prints and fresh manure on the blacktop.

We parked across the street from the house under a weeping pepper tree for shade. That morning the sun was brilliant in an intense, blue sky. The air was hot and dry, and not a leaf fluttered. Insects hiding in the grass made sizzling noises. A rooster crowed from someone's backyard, and the echo of a train whistle sounded in the distance. It felt rural like we were out in the country.

The white stucco house was cute and looked cozy, like home. Ivy entwined the posts of the wide, covered front porch, and a low, white picket fence enclosed the small yard. Although my parents said the house was too small with just one bedroom, I didn't care. This is where the horses lived! This is where I wanted to be!

Dad saw the possibilities, and the house was affordable. He bubbled with enthusiasm as he said, "We can add a second bedroom. Let the kids have the master bedroom temporarily, and we'll sleep on the pulldown bed in the living room."

Mom was concerned about the construction cost and how long "temporarily" might last. At least the Murphy bed in the living room was already there, she observed. They came to a quick decision to buy the house, and my sister and I were overjoyed.

House on Stanton Avenue.

Just four blocks long, Stanton Avenue was located between Western Avenue and Irving Street, one block north of Riverside Drive near the Burbank city line. It was also a short half-block from Irving Street, a dirt road where a public horse stable was located next to the flood control channel. Across from the stable were a few homes on large lots. One of them looked spooky with a pointed, shingled roof, tiny, irregular-shaped windows, and overgrown shrubbery. My friends and I called it "the witch's house." On Halloween, we dared each other to ring the doorbell, but no one got up the nerve.

    Fronting Riverside drive, directly behind our house, was a large, ranch-style home on a double-wide lot. We didn't know the owners. They had a swimming pool and hosted pool parties during the summer. The first time blackout material was installed above our back wall, Mom told us, "Don't look over. They're swimming naked." Sally and I never peeked, but we sure talked about it.

Going west on Riverside Drive into Burbank, there were lots of horse stables, one after the other in a dusty row, providing boarding facilities, riding lessons, and horses for rent. There were also feed and tack stores, a few Western bars, and a cafe fronted by a hitching post. Miles of open terrain for horseback riding bordered the Los Angeles River nearby. Beyond the river, horseback riders had easy access to the trails in Griffith Park. Sally and I loved the expanse of open space for hiking and exploring and later took horseback riding lessons at one of the stables.

Thompson Avenue ran perpendicular to Stanton Avenue and dead-ended in front of the house where we lived. Looking up the street, we had an unstoppable view. On one corner, across the street from us, was a ranch house painted white with red window shutters and a red, Dutch-style front door. The house sat far back from the street on about an acre of land with a swimming pool, small corral, and a covered walk-in shed for their horse. White, split-rail fencing and a row of California pepper trees surrounded the picturesque property. There were no sidewalks.

Bruce lived in the ranch house and was a few years older than me. He was built like a football player and a bully. Seeing kids playing on our lawn, he'd come over and get rowdy. Sometimes he'd pounce on one of the younger boys and hold him down until the kid cried uncle. Bruce's father was a dentist, and the family wasn't friendly like the other neighbors.

The Stanton family (same last name as the street) lived on the opposite corner. A couple of huge sycamores shaded their front lawn. That side of Thompson Avenue had sidewalks and small homes on regular-sized lots. Susan lived on the corner and was a grade ahead of Sally in school. She had long, red hair, a face full of freckles like her father, and a winning personality. Susan's mother, Irene, was a little spitfire of a woman with a witty sense of humor.

Sally, Taffy, Susan

On move-in day, the giant Bekins van sat in front of our house for most of the afternoon. Kids from the neighborhood circled on their bikes to see who was moving in. Terry and Bobby lived in the house next to ours. They watched from their front porch as the movers carried cardboard boxes and furniture into our house, including the cumbersome baby grand piano. Sally and I met the boys that day. Terry was about two years younger than me, and Bobby was a few years younger than his brother.

"We have a swimming pool," Terry said. "Wanna come swimming some time?"

"Sure," I said. Horses, swimming pools, and kids; I thought I'd died and gone to heaven.

Before long, my sister and I knew every kid in the neighborhood. About half were my age, and the rest were Sally's, and everyone got along great. Myrtle and Jimmy lived a few houses away on Thompson Avenue. Butch (real name Jesse) and Glenna lived across the street from them. Beverly and Patti lived two doors up from Myrtle and Jimmy. Around the block on Jesse Avenue lived Marlene, Rene, and Victor (they had an older brother in high school named Billy). Bonnie lived next door to them. Roger and Evie moved to Stanton Avenue a short time later.

The two streets coming together—Stanton and Thompson—created a wide place on the blacktop in front of our house where we played Hit the Bat. Since most families had only one car, the streets were usually empty of parked cars, and that meant no broken windshields. Playing baseball was a popular pastime and kept us happily occupied when we weren't in school. Sometimes we'd change things a bit—boys against the girls. Terry was the self-appointed captain of the boys' team. "Susan's on our team," he'd say authoritatively, knowing I was a strong hitter. I was the only girl allowed to play on the boys' team.

School

Come September, my sister and I enrolled in Benjamin Franklin Elementary School on Lake Street within walking or biking distance. Sally was in the second grade, and I was in Mrs. Marjorie Crane's sixth-grade class. Mrs. Crane was young, pretty, and had an infectious smile. Her shoulder-length, brunette curls bounced as she walked around the room. My eyes were drawn to her red lipstick as she spoke. Learning was fun in her classroom unlike my experience at Catholic school.

One day, Mrs. Crane was writing on the blackboard and heard the kids chattering behind her. Next thing, the eraser flew at us from over her head. We howled with laughter. I loved her. What an improvement she was over those strict nuns who had no sense of humor.

Coming from a parochial school, I was ahead of the class and took full advantage by skipping homework. It wasn't long before Mom got a call. "Susan's falling behind," Mrs. Crane said, and that was the end of my easy ride.

We had a special visitor that year. A lady who was blind, deaf, and couldn't speak came to one of our assemblies. Using sign language interpreted by her personal assistant, she spoke to us about becoming good citizens and overcoming challenges. I never knew who that person was, but I'm convinced it was the remarkable Miss Helen Keller.

I made lots of new friends in school. One girl, Carol Ann Wise, had the same last name as mine. Many of the kids lived near Lake Street, close to school and the railroad tracks that ran along San Fernando Road. This was an older area with clapboard bungalows sitting close to the street on small lots. Barbara became my best friend. She lived on Lake Street a few doors from school in a two-story, wood-framed house. She had a wide smile and huge dimples, and was adventuresome like me. We remained close friends for the next forty years.

Barbara

"You look just like your mom," I said the first time I went home with Barbara after school.

"We're not related," she said, and told me about her sad start in life as an orphan.

"My mother died when I was born, and right after that, my father fell off the Golden Gate Bridge," she said matter-of-factly.

Whether it was a deadly work-related accident or her father had jumped, she didn't know. In 1936, the bridge was still under construction, and the work was extremely dangerous. Men like her father risked their lives on precarious footholds for the good money it brought. Her father's brother and his new wife adopted Barbara. A year later, they had a baby girl, and Barbara grew up with a younger sister named Donna.

Barbara was involved in her Girl Scout troop and wanted me to join. In Catholic school, I'd never heard of the Girl Scouts. I attended a few meetings and learned how to make a whistle lanyard, but I soon grew bored and stopped going. Instead, I took baton lessons, which I liked, and then horseback riding lessons with Sally at the Fred Bales Stables on Riverside Drive, which I liked even better.

The ukulele was popular among my friends, and I had one too. Mom put a couch and some chairs on our front porch, and it became a favorite gathering place to hang out or have informal jam sessions. My friends and I learned songs from each other, and Mom taught us some. She and Aunt June were still pretty good ukulele players from their youth.

For my twelfth birthday, my parents planned a special weekend trip to Palm Springs, and Barbara came with us. "You girls can go swimming when we get there," Mom said, and I could hardly wait.

Our motel had a sparkling pool, and the desert was supposed to be sunny and warm. However, gale-force winds unexpectedly blew in from the north, churning up a huge sandstorm. We couldn't see a foot in front of our faces and spent most of the time holed up in our motel room, playing board games. Dad said, "As soon as the winds let up, let's hightail it out of here." Home we went, disappointed that we never got to swim.

What initially caught my father's eye and made the Stanton Avenue house workable at all was the giant living room. The former owner had designed and built the house for his two Great Danes. While the stucco exterior appeared boxy and small, visitors stepping through the front door invariably said, "Wow. This sure is a huge living room."

The dark-green, wall-to-wall carpeting in the living room extended from the front to the back in the center of the house. The single bedroom and bathroom were on one side, and the breakfast room, kitchen, and service porch were on the other. Low windows on the backside of the living room overlooked the covered rear porch and the large backyard. The closet holding the Murphy bed was near the windows. Every morning, the bed had to be made up and stuffed into the closet, which was a hassle for Mom. Although the bed took up space, we still had plenty of room for our furniture—the baby grand piano and Dad's favorite wingback chair with the ever-present stack of racing forms sitting on the floor beside it.

Going to the Races

My father loved thoroughbred racing. Watching the thoroughbreds run was a huge thrill for him. Having taken statistics at Yale, Dad enjoyed "doping the races," as he said, as a way to relax. At six o'clock, before dinner, the recall of the daily races blared over the radio in our living room. The race caller, Joe Hernandez, is a well-remembered voice from my childhood. When the races were on, this was no time to interrupt my father or make noise. Sitting in his wingback chair, racing form spread out on his lap, he dutifully noted the results after each race. He wasn't really a gambler, but he sometimes placed low dollar bets with a bookie. For him, it was more about the odds and figuring out which horse and jockey would win, place, or show. Dad thought of himself as an expert, immersed as he was in the records of the past and present thoroughbreds and their jockeys. Mom was not so convinced, and she fussed about the stack of newspapers on the floor.

We started going to the races in season as a regular family outing, sometimes to Hollywood Park in Inglewood but more often to Santa Anita in Arcadia. We always sat in the clubhouse with a good view of the track. It was exciting to hear the bugle call announcing post time. As the horses neared the finish line, it was even more exciting how the stands exploded with noise. How we would be on our feet with everyone else, cheering wildly for our horse to win. Dad placed conservative bets and usually came out even after a day at the races. Sometimes he placed money bets on the horses that my sister and I chose (usually the most handsome one or the one with the best name).

Sally remembers picking a horse named Blue Bonnet, which was also the brand name of a margarine. "I was thrilled to learn that my horse had won the race," she told me. Many years later, it was quite a surprise when she found out that the horse didn't actually win. "Mom just wanted to make me happy," she said.

I wanted Dad to bet on the long shots, since they had the biggest payoff, but he told me, "No sense wasting the money. Long shots rarely win." He was right about that.

Between races, when it got boring for Sally and me, Mom took us to the paddock circle where we watched the parade of horses before they entered the main track. This was a close-up look at horse and jockey. My favorite winning jockeys were Johnnie Longden and Eddie Arcaro. At Santa Anita, we met the wife of jockey Alfred Robertson. She was sweet, and we became friends. We stood with her in the paddock area when her husband was racing, and that felt pretty special.

In the clubhouse, when people went to the betting windows, they saved their seat by tying a linen handkerchief to the back of their chair. At the end of the day, the handkerchiefs were often forgotten. Sally and I collected the prettiest ones (clean ones, of course), and that kept us in hankies for a good long time.

After the last race, as we made our way toward the exit, Dad had us scan the ground. "Keep your eyes on the lookout for a winning ticket," he'd say. Discarded tickets covered every square inch of the pavement. We walked along with our heads bent like seagulls hunting for sand crabs.

One time as we were leaving, my father reached down and brought up a ticket. He checked the notes in his racing form. "It's a good one," he said, grinning. We thought he was kidding, but sure enough, it was good and worth thirty-five dollars for a second-place finish. He turned the ticket in for the money, and we went out for dinner at a nice restaurant.

Dad's dream was to own a racing thoroughbred. It was a long-shot possibility, but just in case, he had already chosen the horse's name. He thought it would sound good when Joe Hernandez described the hoof-pounding push to the finish line, announcing, "And here comes Whoop Dee Doo."

Griffith Park and the Studios

Looking south from our house, the unspoiled hills of Griffith Park created a backdrop of rugged beauty. This was our extended playground. A short bicycle ride took us kids across the bridge spanning the Los Angeles River and into the park, which has changed little since those days. Encompassing 4,310 acres, it takes up the eastern end of the Santa Monica Mountain range that divides Los Angeles and Hollywood from the San Fernando Valley. There are hiking paths, horseback riding trails, picnic areas, baseball fields, golf courses, pony rides, and a miniature riding train with a conductor. Sally and I loved going to the Los Angeles

Zoo, riding the merry-go-round, having picnics in Ferndell, and visiting the Griffith Park Observatory—also attractions within the park.

My father didn't plan to remain at the Polish radio station for long but intended to find work again as a motion picture writer. Living a stone's throw from Griffith Park on the San Fernando Valley side was a convenient location for him with easy access to Hollywood through the Cahuenga Pass. Warner Brothers Studios, Universal Studios, and Republic Studios were nearby. In the early days of filmmaking, the studios gravitated to the rural San Fernando Valley for open land and sunshine, which they found in abundance. They built huge, indoor soundstages and took advantage of the vast, unspoiled landscape and encircling mountain vistas to shoot outdoor scenes and Westerns. Over the years, this area in Burbank around those studios (now Universal City) evolved into a conclave of major film, television, and music corporations including Warner Brothers Studios, Walt Disney Studios, and NBC Studios. Burbank is often billed as "the media capital of the world." Thankfully, that progress, and the congestion that came with it, didn't happen until many years after we moved from Stanton Avenue. At the beginning of the 1950s, we were able to enjoy a lifestyle that was far more unhurried, uncomplicated, and undeniably wonderful.

A Cold January

Sally and I shared the only bedroom in the house where we had privacy and plenty of room for our things. Looking out our window through venetian blinds, we also had a nice view of Griffith Park's rugged hills. A French door in the bedroom conveniently led to the rear porch and backyard.

We had a walk-in closet, which was the only real closet in the entire house. My parents hung some of their clothes on a makeshift rod behind the Murphy bed. Most of their things were kept with our clothes in the bedroom closet, including Mom's muskrat fur coat and Dad's business suits, long-sleeved dress shirts, and wool jacket with leather patches on the elbows.

One January morning, Mom came into our bedroom and switched on the light. "Rise and shine, girls," she said in a sugary voice. "It's time to get up."

Sally and I winced. It was barely light outside.

"Go look at your tree, Susan," Mom said, acting more energetic than usual for a school day. In the morning, she usually needed a cup of coffee and a cigarette to get going.

The day before, I had put our discarded Christmas tree in the middle of the back lawn and sprayed it with water from the hose to see if icicles formed overnight. On previous mornings, it had been unusually frigid. I could see my breath in the air as I walked to the bus stop for school. Lawns were covered in white frost, and so were the windshields of cars parked outside. Patches of ice sat frozen in the gutters. An Alaskan storm came down the coast, bringing cold rain.

Still half asleep, I went to the window and yanked up the venetian blinds. I couldn't believe my eyes. Everything was covered in a white blanket of snow. The hills of Griffith Park looked like a winter wonderland. "It snowed," I hollered. Sally rushed to the window to see for herself.

Mom had been awake the night before when the rain turned to snow. She got up early and set out our warm clothes, mittens, and rubber boots. "There's oatmeal and hot cocoa waiting for you in the breakfast room," she told us, all smiles. "Hurry and get dressed."

Sally and I were soon out on the street, frolicking in the snow with the rest of the kids. Joyful pandemonium describes Stanton Avenue that morning. No one went to school. Before long, the schools closed anyway. Sleds saved for trips to the mountains magically appeared. We rolled in the snow, ate it, made snowmen, had snowball fights, and threw snowballs at passing cars as smiling motorists wagged their fingers at us. Some of the kids had never seen snow before. Our cocker spaniels Taffy and Timmy never had, and Timmy lost his favorite tennis ball in the backyard. Sally and I laughed at the tunnel he made as he frantically plowed through the snow with his nose until he found it. What a day!

By noon, the bright sun had turned the snow to slush. We spent the afternoon looking for hidden pockets of the cold stuff, not wanting our snow day to end. This was a hundred-year event, I came to understand, that has never occurred since. Oh sure, we've had dustings from time to time, but never the amount of snow that fell on January 11, 1949. Every winter, I hope the conditions will be just right for it to happen again. I'm still waiting.

A Street Nearby

New Car

The year 1949 was memorable for another reason. My parents finally got rid of the prewar Plymouth coupe and bought a white Nash Ambassador. It looked brand new, but it had a few miles on the odometer. "It's a demonstrator car," Dad told us. "The dealership let their salesmen use it. I got a good deal."

This was a design change year for Nash. The new Ambassador had four doors, and the body resembled a giant turtle. Some of the neighbor kids thought it was pretty funny looking, especially Terry, who teased me about it. A shiny, new black Chevrolet sedan, which was sleeker and more conventional than the Nash with the turtle hump, sat on his driveway. The Nash had front seats that folded down into beds, and that was something to brag about. I liked the roomy upholstered backseat. However, Sally blessed it royally on our first road trip. We were headed to Sequoia Kings Canyon National Park on a winding mountain road for a short vacation where we stayed in a tent cabin. She got carsick and threw up.

Accustomed as I was to the Plymouth coupe, I didn't realize that four doors were dangerous. One Sunday, after arriving home from an afternoon drive, I got out of the backseat and slammed the rear door hard.

"Susan, open the door *now*," Mom said in a trembling voice.

I was shocked when I saw her hand wedged solidly in the doorjamb. I opened the door, and she made a beeline for the house, holding her smashed hand outstretched. I was right behind her as she went into the kitchen, thinking I'd broken her hand. "Get some ice," she said, running cold water into a bowl.

"I'm so sorry, Mama," I said, feeling awful as she dipped her hand in the water. She moaned, but she didn't cry. I thought she was very brave. Miraculously, no bones were broken, though her fingers turned the color of eggplant. "Always look before you shut the car doors," she said. To this day I'm careful.

Nat Wise

My father's cousin, Nat Wise, and his family moved from New York to California a few years before we moved to Stanton Avenue. They lived in a Spanish-style home in Beverly Hills, and we saw them off and on. Nat was the son of Arthur Wise, my grandfather's younger brother. Nat eventually took a job managing the army surplus store on Victory Boulevard in Burbank. We drove there in the new Nash several times to see him while he was working.

Nat was an affable kind of guy, warm and friendly, and his wife, Arlene, had a good sense of humor. One day, Nat, Arlene, and their son Johnny, who was a year older than me, came for a visit. Dad asked me to play the piano for everyone, which he often did, to my embarrassment, when we had company. After I finished playing, Johnny sat down at the piano and started picking out familiar songs by ear, using both hands to create the harmony. "I've never played the piano before," he said. "This is fun."

Oh brother, did I think he was faking, but his parents said it was true. Johnny had never touched the piano before that day. My piano teacher came to the house weekly for lessons, and I practiced every day after school for an hour, and here was Johnny pounding out songs like he'd been playing for years with no teacher and no practicing. It wasn't fair, but it was as it appeared. He had an unusual gift, and his newly discovered talent played out in our living room as we all watched in amazement.

The next day, I told Mom, "I don't want to take piano lessons anymore." After five years of lessons, it was clear that I would never excel at it. I quit a short time later. Johnny's folks went out and bought him a piano.

Breakfast Room and Toll Junior High

My favorite room in the house was the cheerful breakfast room with the window view up Thompson Avenue. The walls were covered in a wallpaper pattern of green ivy vines on a white background. Two corner dish cabinets, painted white with clear glass in the upper doors, sat on either side of the swinging door to the kitchen. Our French provincial dining table fit just fine, but the large matching hutch had to go in the living room. As a family, we now ate together in the breakfast room. Sally and I no longer had to eat alone in the kitchen. Mom upholstered the chairs in a vinyl material in case there were spills. She was handy when it came to projects like that.

I did my homework at the table in the breakfast room, and Dad often worked on his scripts there at night after everyone went to bed. It was there that Mom spread out pencil drawings of a uterus, ovaries, and a man's body parts for an in-depth explanation of the woman's menstrual cycle and the facts of life. She surprised me with all of this one afternoon when I arrived home from school. It was a lot to take in.

From the living room window, we had another view up Thompson Avenue. I was a "scrub," a seventh grader in my second week at Toll Junior High School on Kenneth Road in the foothills. One morning, I had a big decision: whether or not to wear my new lipstick called Natural. I reapplied it several times before leaving it on and heading off to catch the school bus on Victory Boulevard. My mother said she stood at the window and saw me stop halfway up the street, put my books down on the sidewalk, lift up my skirt over my waist, and pull down my blouse. So much for being all grown up!

With Thompson Avenue dead-ending in front of our house, the view was nice, but the location had its hazards. One Sunday, our family was eating lunch in the breakfast room and noticed a car slowly weaving down Thompson Avenue. Mom was first to realize the danger. "Oh my God, there's no driver." She gasped, bolting out of her chair. The car was headed straight for our yard. It turned slightly, careened off the curb in front of our house, and rolled to a stop. Obviously, someone had failed to set the brake.

Cookies and Ice Cream

Our kitchen was small and galley style, lacking counter space because of doorways to the dining room, living room, and service porch. We still had the old Wedgewood gas stove, but the icebox had been replaced by a used electric refrigerator with a funny-looking dome on top.

Seventh-grade girls at Toll Junior High School were required to take home economics—a semester each of cooking and sewing—to prepare for the important job of becoming a housewife. That first semester, I took cooking. The classroom had multiple mini-kitchens with a table, four chairs, sink, supply cabinet, and a full-size O'Keefe and Merritt stove with shiny chrome trim.

Barbara was my kitchen mate. Once, when the teacher wasn't looking, we got silly while washing dishes and used the spatulas to flick flour at each other. Flour got all over the place. We hurriedly cleaned it up before the teacher noticed. It wasn't until we left the classroom that we realized we had flour on our faces and in our hair. We laughed our heads off.

Cooking was becoming a real passion. I couldn't wait to recreate at home the recipes taught in class such as cinnamon sugar toast, grated orange and sugar toast, creamed tuna on toast, and baking powder biscuits.

At home, I made my favorite cookies, Toll House chocolate chip. Sometimes there wasn't much dough left for baking, because I ate it. Mom didn't bake very often, though for Dad's birthday, she usually made him a multilayer sponge cake with mocha icing that he loved. Yellow cake with chocolate icing was another of Dad's favorites. One day, I decided to make the yellow cake for him.

Mom came into the kitchen to check on my progress and found me standing on a step stool, rummaging impatiently through her spice collection in an upper cabinet. "What are you looking for?" she asked.

Annoyed, I grumbled, "You never have what I need. Where are the ingredients?"

"Oh, Susie dear," Mom said in that way of hers that let me know I'd made a childish mistake.

Ice cream has always been one of my favorite desserts. About this time, Baskin-Robbins moved its dairy to Burbank and opened an ice cream store near us on Victory Boulevard. With thirty-one flavors, it was the first of its kind. We went there often, because Dad loved ice cream as much as I did. Even with so many choices, I usually ordered the same thing: a scoop of mint chip and a scoop of coffee.

Miss White

Miss Avis White was my favorite teacher. I had her for seventh and eighth grade English, and at her urging, I took journalism under her direction in the ninth grade. Close to retirement, Miss White was a white-haired, no-nonsense teacher who could be tough and demanding. She kept the students in line and working hard, including the slack-off boys who sat in the back of the room and did as little as possible. When Miss White gave me a compliment on my writing, I knew it was well deserved. Apparently, she saw potential in me as a writer. One of the most challenging class assignments was a term paper addressing the question "Does human nature change?" Not knowing what human nature was, I did the research, handled the subject pretty well, and earned a good grade. In the journalism class, I was a roving reporter and had articles published in the school newspaper.

Dad had a thing going on with Miss White that started when she was my homeroom teacher. That was the year it snowed. "Please excuse Susan from school yesterday," Dad wrote in my excuse note. "She had a bad case of snowitis."

Miss White thought that was clever and sent him a reply. She knew he was a writer, because I told her.

Dad liked to help me with writing assignments. I was working on a difficult composition—maybe I was in the eighth grade by then—and Dad read it over and asked me to make significant changes. "That doesn't sound like me." I argued, but he imposed his style.

Sensing as much when she read it, Miss White gave me a lower grade and scribbled a note on the paper: "Let Susan do the writing next time, Mr. Wise."

He replied with a poem that made her smile.

The Backyard

I liked the idea of being a teacher. One summer, instead of pulling weeds in our yard for spending money, I decided to become a school teacher. I set up a classroom on the back porch and talked the younger neighborhood kids into coming. Cardboard boxes became makeshift desks. I gave considerable thought to the assignments and adjusted them for the different grade levels. I intended to teach the kids something they didn't already know about arithmetic, writing, geography, and reading. I was strict and assigned homework.

After a while the kids balked and didn't want to come anymore. "This is too much like real school," someone complained. That was the end of my backyard school.

We had a small service porch off of the kitchen with a door to the backyard. The porch held our new washing machine that had an automatic spin and dry cycle—no more dangerous wringer device—and a used gas dryer. The dryer was a real convenience and a huge time-saver for Mom. Clotheslines were noticeably disappearing as housewives converted to the modern dryers available after the war. Even with the dryer, we kept our backyard clothesline, because Mom thought sheets and pillow cases smelled better when they were hung out to dry.

Our grassy backyard was big and square, enclosed by high, cinderblock walls. A peach and apricot tree filled one corner, producing loads of sweet fruit during the summer. Lush dichondra grass, similar to four-leaf clover, thrived in the shade beneath the trees. The dichondra felt soft and cool on my bare feet. Sometimes Sally and I had a picnic lunch on a blanket underneath the trees.

When the peaches and apricots were at their peak of ripeness, I picked, cleaned, and bagged the best fruit, loaded the bags into Sally's red wagon, and sold them door to door. It was a good business, and I had no trouble selling the fruit. I went to Floyd's Market with the money and bought comic books, candy, and gum.

Floyd was one of our neighbors. He owned the small convenience store on Victory Boulevard that was a popular destination for the children living nearby. There was always a bicycle leaning on the wall out front, and Floyd knew everyone by name. He kept an open box of Double Bubble gum on the counter; pieces sold for a penny each. On one of her trips to the store, Mom let him know what was going on. "Floyd, the kids are coming up here and stealing gum off the counter."

He smiled and replied, "I know. I keep it there for them."

On the opposite side of the backyard, the sunniest side, we had the clothesline and a cement incinerator for burning household trash. Incinerators were an eyesore and dangerous. My mother took charge of burning our trash and always cautioned us kids to stay clear.

Terry and Bobby

Swimming in Terry's pool next door was where I wanted to be on a hot summer day. There was always a gang of kids there, and Sally and I went often. The pool was small and had a rough cement bottom with no decorative tiling around the parameter. We didn't care. It was a pool.

We had cannonball contests that sent us running across the yard to get the most speed before jumping in. With just grass and no decking around the pool, the water eventually turned into a green mess. The boys' mother, Fern, never seemed to mind. She kept an eye on us at a distance from the screened-in lanai. Mom made a point of coming over and checking on us every so often.

One day when we'd been invited to swim, I quickly put on my bathing suit and darted out of the house. Sally heard the screen door slam and knew she'd been left behind. Running in a hurry to catch up, she took a shortcut across the flower bed next to the front porch where Mom had placed red bricks on end as a decorative border. Sally's bare toes caught on the bricks, and she landed face down in the dirt. Mom heard her screams and rushed outside. Some of Sally's toenails had been ripped off, and there was lots of blood.

While I had fun swimming, poor Sally sat on the kitchen counter, whimpering in pain. Mom cleaned and bandaged her bloody toes. Afterward, she said, "It was awful. I've never nursed anything so gory. My hands shook, and I got a little woozy."

It was a while before Sally could go swimming again.

Terry was smart and fun, but his sense of humor sometimes bordered on sarcasm, and he could be bossy. Bobby was a stutterer, and Terry was not above teasing his younger brother, but Bobby had a feisty spirit and held his own. One summer day, Mom caught Bobby walking on top of our wall and helping himself to the ripened peaches and apricots. Afraid that he would fall or break some of the heavy-laden branches, she said, "Bobby, I'll be happy to give you some fruit."

Bobby grinned and stammered, "Nooope. It's more fun to swwwwipe it."

My first experience eating Mexican food was with Terry's family on his birthday. He was all laughs when I took my first bite and started snorting and coughing, overcome by the flaming hot sauce. This was long before the popularity of Mexican restaurants or take-out taco places. If you wanted Mexican food, you had to go where the Mexicans lived. We went to a cafe in downtown Los Angeles near Olvera Street.

Terry was the first boy I ever kissed. That happened during games of Spin the Bottle. Terry and I were experimenting. Besides baseball games in the street, ringing doorbells and running away, and swimming in his pool, we played Monopoly, checkers, and card games on our front porch, went bike riding, caught pollywogs in the Los Angeles River, sat on the curb and had long talks, and hung out in his garage, reading comic books from his large Superman collection. Terry was a good friend. I liked his take-charge attitude. I also liked the way he came up with ideas to interject more fun into an ordinary day.

Craigie and Laddie

Terry and Bobby had a German shepherd mix named Craigie. "He's part wolf," Terry said, trying to convince the kids in the neighborhood, but we didn't believe him.

Craigie was always out front while other dogs were kept in the backyard. During the day, he hung out on the boys' front porch or followed the boys around. He was a fearless car chaser. When a car passed by, he would seemingly come out of nowhere, barking and biting fiercely at the tires. He scared drivers half to death.

The first dog we had on Stanton Avenue was named Laddie. This was before we adopted our cocker spaniels, Taffy and Timmy. Laddie was a cute black-and-white mixed spaniel and a backyard dog. One day, our family was in the front yard doing some gardening, and Laddie, for the first time, was with us. A car came by, and Craigie took off chasing it, barking loudly. Laddie bolted from our yard and followed Craigie. In an instant, Laddie was run over. Sally was first to reach his side. "Oh Laddie," she wailed, throwing her arms around his neck. Out of his mind with pain, he bit her. It was an awful scene, and we were heartbroken when Laddie died.

The New Neighbors

Next door to us, on the opposite side from Terry's family, lived an old man and his crotchety old wife. The kids in the neighborhood hung out at the curb under the carob tree next to our driveway. We talked and laughed, oblivious that we were encroaching on the neighbors' parkway grass. The old lady sure noticed as she spied on us from her kitchen window. She'd sneak outside and turn on the sprinklers. Jumping up, not minding the unexpected shower, we'd yell, "Curbs are public, you know."

After the old folks sold the house and a young family moved in, we could sit on the curb as much as we wanted. The new owners were a doctor and his attractive, auburn-haired wife, Loretta, who stayed busy with their children: Shirley, age three, and Janice, eighteen months. Mom and Loretta became friends, though one morning Mom unwittingly insulted her. Loretta had come over early before the Murphy bed had been put away. Bedclothes were scattered around, and the breakfast dishes hadn't been done. "Excuse the mess," Mom said. "It looks like Okies live here."

In her genteel way, Loretta said, "Did you know I'm from Oklahoma?"

Mom was embarrassed and apologized. After that, she decided to substitute the word *zombie*. "If anyone claims they're a zombie, so be it," she said.

One afternoon, a partly cloudy sky turned dark, and it began to rain. Mom noticed that little Janice was still in her harness, tied to the Chinese elm on the front lawn next door where she was playing. She telephoned Loretta to say, "I think you've forgotten someone."

A surprised Loretta was the one embarrassed that time.

Living Room Invention

In our living room, we had a brick fireplace painted white, and a large mirror hung on the wall above the mantle. Mom liked to decorate the mantle with clear glass vases placed at either end, filled with sprigs of ivy from the front porch. Sometimes she put green food coloring in the water, and it matched our carpeting. During the Christmas season, she colored the water red.

Only a handful of neighbors had the newest invention, a television set, sitting in their living rooms. Not us. Dad insisted, "Let's wait and see if it gets any better." He wasn't even sure this new thing was here to stay. Some stores had displays set up in their windows that drew a crowd of curious onlookers. Television was in its infancy. "The shows are hardly fit to watch and nothing but time wasters," Dad said.

In the newness of television there was a fascination that hooked us all, even Dad eventually. Cowboy movies and live gardening shows stand out in my memory as being favored for frequent daytime programming. Soon, good entertainment shows came along in the evening using a vaudeville format. On Sunday night, our family often ate dinner in the bar at Van's restaurant on Victory Boulevard in Burbank. The bar had a television set, and we could watch *The Ed Sullivan Show*. Sometimes we had dinner at Van's on Tuesday night so we could see the *Texaco Star Theater* starring comedian Milton Berle. We didn't get our own television set for another year. When Dad finally bought one, it was a huge deal. Sally and I were thrilled, though we were limited to maybe one hour of watching a night.

Nanny

My grandmother made frequent visits to our house on Stanton Avenue, staying for a week or two. She slept on a rollaway bed in the bedroom that Sally and I shared. Aunt June's house in Eagle Rock was not too far away and required only one bus transfer. I looked forward to Nanny's visits. If she came on Saturday, I waited and watched for her. As soon as I saw her walking down Thompson Avenue from the bus stop, I ran to meet her with a big hug.

Nanny always wanted to look her best for the trip across town. She wore her newest flowered cotton housedress, sensible, black lace-up shoes, and often a small straw hat embellished with artificial flowers and crinkled netting. Most of her things were bought at the Sears and Roebuck store where she had a revolving credit plan. The wire to her hearing aid was usually visible, going from one ear to the hidden pocket in her undershirt. Unless the wind blew the skirt of her dress aside, no one could see that her nylon stockings were rolled to just below her knees and held in place by elastic bands. Pantyhose didn't exist. Women used garter belts or girdles to hold up their stockings, but my grandmother thought they were uncomfortable.

In each hand, Nanny carried a brown paper shopping bag by its handles. The bags held her clothing and personal items, maybe a store-bought coffee cake for the family and always something special for Sally and me. Arthritic knees and the weight of the bags gave her an uneven gait. Once inside the house, she looked for the nearest chair. "Give me a minute to catch my breath, dear," she'd say. "Then I'll show you what I brought."

More than presents, Nanny brought unconditional love. With tender sweetness and unending patience, she listened to my stories about school and friends as if what I had to say was the most important thing in the world. With no more than a sixth-grade education, she was instinctively wise and insightful, attributing her blessings to answered prayers and a strong Christian faith. Whenever I told her about my worries or wishes, she'd tell me, "The good Lord loves you, Susan. All you have to do is send up a prayer."

Nanny and neighbor

Warm Windy Nights and Winter Rains

Summers in this most eastern end of the San Fernando Valley were clear, hot, and dry, unlike the cooler coastal climate in Westwood. There was never any smog. Sometimes during the fall months at nightfall, a warm wind blew across the land from the Mojave Desert. Those were the Santa Ana winds that we called "the warm windy nights."

Sally described them like this: "The sun went down, and the stars came out, and the warm air felt like angel wings that could sweep you up and carry you off to wherever your imagination wanted to go." Sally was a poet at heart, as you can tell.

Those were perfect nights for playing ring-the-doorbell-and-run-away (now called ding-dong ditch). A gang of us kids from the neighborhood got together, and I was usually their leader. One night, I talked everyone into running through backyards after ringing the doorbell. Going from house to house, we climbed over fences and walls, turning the game into a difficult obstacle course. It was just good luck that we didn't run into any ferocious dogs.

I came up with another spin on the game. We attached sewing thread to a small, gold safety pin, hooked the pin to a window screen, and dragged a wet wash cloth down the thread. It made a squealing noise that sounded spooky. "Who's there?" we'd hear a frightened homeowner call out as we ran away, giggling.

During the winter in bad weather, a favorite form of entertainment was making crank calls. Mom allowed me to do this so long as the calls were harmless and not spiteful. Every kid knew the popular questions to ask. "Is your refrigerator running?" Getting a yes, we'd say, "You'd better go catch it." "Do you have Prince Albert in a can?" This referred to a popular tobacco product. If we heard yes, we'd say, "You better let him out."

I came up with a more creative idea. One afternoon it was raining hard, and my friend Patti was visiting. We looked through the phone book for addresses near the Los Angeles River. In 1938, two back-to-back storms and six continual days of pounding rain caused the river to overflow and a devastating flood. Our area was hit hard. Homes, roads, bridges, businesses, and many of the horse stables along Riverside Drive were washed away. This tragedy was the motivation for cementing the Los Angeles riverbed and building the dam at the Sepulveda basin. People still remembered that flood.

It took several calls before I found the perfect victim. In an official manner, I told the gullible resident, "This is the Girl Scouts of America calling. We want to let you know that a flood is coming your way."

The lady's voice audibly shook as she asked the question I wanted to hear. "What should I do?"

"Pick up your house, and move to Arizona," I told her, as Patti and I dissolved into fits of laughter. How wicked is that!

Summer Heat

July and August were the hottest months. No one had air conditioning in their house or car. To keep cool, we used room table fans with whirling blades and drove with the car windows rolled down and the wind wings open.

My grandmother suffered in the heat. In the middle of a hot day, she'd have to stop ironing or working in the kitchen and take a rest. She'd sit in the living room for a while and fan her face with a handheld paper fan. It could get pretty unbearable when the temperature topped one hundred degrees. Dad came home from work dripping wet around the collar and in a crabby mood. Occasionally, Mom had a picnic dinner ready. Off we'd go to the small park on Sonora Avenue, which was next to the two-lane bridge leading to Griffith Park.

One sweltering late afternoon, as we leisurely ate dinner at a picnic table under the sycamores, we heard a horrendous crash. I took off running barefoot, and Sally followed. Mom called out, "Come back, girls," but we didn't listen.

In the center of the bridge was an old, white sedan filled with Mexicans. It had been hit broadside by an Asbury bus. The occupants were slumped in odd positions and didn't seem to be moving with the exception of one woman in the back seat whose moans shook me to the core. A dead baby lay in the street and was soon covered over. It was a horrendous sight. I couldn't get out of there fast enough, picking my way through the shattered glass in my bare feet. Any time we drove over the bridge after that, I closed my eyes tightly to block out the awful memory.

Horseback Riding

Horseback riders were an everyday sight on Stanton Avenue. Plops of manure that the kids referred to as "road apples" were often left on the asphalt as the horses passed by our house. The rhythmic clip-clopping of hooves on the pavement was a pleasant reminder of our country-like surroundings. Some of the horses were stabled behind houses in the neighborhood. Others came from the stable around the corner on Irving Street. Sally and I hung out at that stable the first year we moved to Stanton Avenue, and occasionally Mom let us rent one of the horses and ride in the corral.

Sandwiched between the last house on Stanton Avenue and the flood control channel was a dirt right-of-way the kids named "the Chisholm Trail." This gave horseback riders access to Riverside Drive and Griffith Park beyond. Mostly the neighborhood girls played there, pretending to be our favorite movie heroes, Roy Rogers and Dale Evans. Sometimes we were their horses, Trigger and Buttermilk, running up and down the trail, slapping our thighs as in giddy-up and letting out high-pitched whinnies. From somewhere, I acquired a used, white leather jacket with fringes. Feeling like a real Western cowgirl, I often wore it while I was playing on the trail or going horseback riding.

The Fred Bales Stable on Riverside Drive was a short walk from our house and the closest of the many stables located along the row including Olmstead and Pickwick. Sally and I first took English saddle riding lessons and then Western saddle lessons from Fred Bales. He was a patient man, a real-life cowboy, and one of the reasons I loved hanging out at his stable. He let me brush the horses, feed them carrots, pick up manure, and rake hay. I hoped it would earn me a free ride around the corral on my favorite horse. That never happened, but I did spend many happy hours just being there.

For a few bucks from my allowance, Fred sold me a pair of worn men's boots that were gathering dust in the tack room. The boots were too big, so I stuffed rags in the toes. I wore the boots whenever I went riding or played on the Chisholm Trail.

One night, I was awakened in the wee hours by sirens and the roar of firetrucks going up Riverside Drive. I got up and headed out by myself before breakfast to see what I could find. I hadn't passed too many stables before I saw firetrucks in the street, water hoses, pickup trucks, and people standing around. One of the stables had burned and was a complete loss. The sight was ghastly. Charcoal carcasses of horses were being hauled out by chains attached to tractors. Some of the horses were still smoking, and the foul smell of horseflesh was overpowering. People were crying, and I knew they had to be the owners of the dead animals. Show horses and horses trained for the movies were often boarded at the stables along Riverside Drive. There's no telling how many were lost that night.

Roger and Evie

One day, I noticed construction underway on the corner of Jesse Avenue and Stanton Avenue, a few doors down from where we lived. I didn't know the empty lot and adjacent ranch-style house had been sold to a new owner. A small barn and fencing for a horse corral were going up. I soon discovered the barn came with a young cowpoke named Roger, and I was immediately smitten.

Roger was about fourteen, and I was a year younger. He was a pleasant-looking boy with dark, soulful eyes, a warm smile, and a take-charge attitude. Right away, I started hanging out at the corral after school and on the weekends whenever he was around. Sally came too and played with his younger sister, Evie, who was a year older than her. Roger and Evie had an older brother in high school, but he wasn't around much.

Roger's parents were divorced, and the children lived with their father. Vernon was a skilled horseman and a ruggedly handsome man. He worked as a building contractor and sometimes acted in Western movies with his horse, Boots, a quarter horse-Morgan mix. His ex-wife Daisy (the children's mother) later moved into the house, bringing three small children with her from a second marriage. "It was a trial reconciliation," Roger told me. Unfortunately, the reconciliation wouldn't last long.

Boots was well trained and a dream to ride. Roger and his older brother shared a spirited stallion named Pepper. He was hard to handle and bucked a lot. Beauty, a round-bellied, black-and-white pinto with a gentle yet stubborn nature, was added to the barn a little later. She was Evie's horse and the one that Sally and I were welcome to ride. Later, Evie got a new horse named Patches.

About a year later, Boots and Beauty gave birth to colts only days apart. The colts were adorable and hilarious as they kicked, bucked, and galloped around the corral as if on steroids. Weekends were fun as Sally and I joined others at the fence to watch Vernon work with his horses. One day the colts were gone, and I was surprised when Roger told me, "My dad sold them." I thought Vernon would keep the colts so we'd have more horses to ride.

Roger was mature and hardworking for his age and the one who usually took charge of things—watching over the horses, his sister, and the kids who played there. Besides going to school and working a part-time job at a young age, he groomed and exercised the horses, cleaned stalls, picked up manure, filled the water troughs, and loaded hay bales into the barn after the delivery truck came. Though we'd taken lessons, it was Roger who taught Sally and me the finer techniques of riding Western style.

Roger on Patches

"Can I help you with the horses?" I'd offer after arriving at the corral.

"Sure," he'd say. "Grab the pitchfork."

Picking up the manure and loading it into the wheelbarrow was a stinky job full of flies, but I didn't care. It was a way to be around Roger and the horses. Sometimes Roger and I brushed and curried the horses or moved them out of the stalls so we could pick up the manure and put down fresh hay. We rearranged the hay bales in the loft and stacked them neatly. During those times we worked together, Roger often talked about horses: what it meant when their ears were laid back, the right way to lead them, and how not to get stepped on. I was his eager student and admirer. While Sally thought of him as the brother she never had, I had a crush on him and hoped he felt the same way about me.

When there were lots of kids playing in the corral, Roger sometimes got mischievous. He'd holler, "Grab hands," and with him at the head of the line, we'd take off running, going this way and that and around the barn. When we least expected it, he touched the electric wire on top of the fence. Bzzzz. The electricity shot through his body and then ours, giving us all a good jolt and a nervous laugh.

Sally and Evie played for hours in the corral and made up all kinds of games with the horses. Sometimes they'd hang from the crossbeams of the barn or from the tree next to the corral, letting go and landing on the back of one of the horses as it passed under. Occasionally they rode standing up, side by side and holding hands. They rode bareback in the fields next to the Los Angeles River where they jumped logs, something Mom didn't learn about until well after the fact.

I looked forward to going riding with Roger. He was an excellent horseman like his father, and I felt safe with him. I rode Beauty in the corral while he rode Pepper. Other times, we rode around the neighborhood or in the open fields across Riverside Drive. Riding double on Boots was the best. Feeling like the heroine in a Western movie, I hugged Roger's waist tightly as we traversed rough terrain or crossed the Los Angeles River, which was more like a creek unless it rained.

One day, Roger and I packed a sack lunch and rode double on Boots in Griffith Park. I felt free and happy riding the trails with him, wind in my hair and the aroma of eucalyptus and mountain chaparral sweetening the air. Occasionally, he gave Boots a hard nudge with his boot heel, yelled "Yahoo," and off we went in a full-on gallop. I leaned into his back and pressed my legs hard against Boots' side to stay centered so we could ride as one. What a day!

Aunt June's House

Visits to Aunt June's house were more frequent now that we lived closer. Sally and our cousin Gary were the same age and played games of cowboys and Indians or cops and robbers. My cousin Beverly was four years older than me and in high school. We did more grown-up things such as accessorizing her clothes and modeling them, looking at fashion magazines, or riding around in her friend Nudie's Ford that had a rumble seat where I sat. Beverly was a talented artist like her mother. She entertained me for hours making colored pencil drawings of ladies wearing fancy clothing of her own design. As a young girl, she made her own paper dolls.

Nanny's bedroom was an attic room accessed by steep wooden stairs. It smelled like an antique store and was uncomfortably hot during heat spells or too cold during the winter months. A chamber pot (she called it a slop jar) was kept under her bed, as the only bathroom in the house was downstairs on the first floor. Her bedroom lacked some comforts, but she liked that it was large and private.

I loved staying overnight in the big farm house. Beverly and I shared a maple double bed in the front bedroom that was hers. We took our baths together in a claw foot tub. Before going to sleep, I listened for the sound of the train whistle. Sometimes I heard two trains go by before the sandman came.

One night when Sally and I were both sleeping over, we all gathered in Beverly's bedroom for ghost stories. Aunt June had a vivid imagination and was a wonderful storyteller. Her eyes grew wide or narrowed with emotion as she told a story, and her voice changed when she wanted to accentuate the drama. We listened to several spooky stories, and then she had this one.

> *It was a dark and stormy night. The children were alone in the house playing games in the living room while their parents were away. Suddenly they heard a voice. "It floats," the voice said.*

The children were terrified, grabbing hold of each other. No matter, they felt compelled to follow the sound of the voice. As they tiptoed into the dining room, the voice grew louder. "It floats."

The children slowly moved from room to room. In each room the voice grew louder and louder. "It floats."

The children continued to follow the sound of the voice, going upstairs even though it was dark and scary.

"IT FLOATS," the voice boomed.

The children couldn't stand it any longer. They screamed, "What floats?"

Aunt June paused as we waited breathlessly for the answer. "Ivory Soap," she said. We all laughed at the unexpected ending, and then it was time to go to sleep.

I admired Aunt June's artistic talent, especially since I had none. Her original oil paintings were displayed on the walls of her home. Several of her paintings graced the walls of our homes: one of a rolling tea table set for tea and a portrait of my father. She painted a portrait of Nanny, which I have now. Aunt June kept her easel set up in the dining room, next to two large windows for good light. It always held an oil painting in progress.

I told her, "I wish I could paint like you."

She said, "Everyone has artistic talent within them, Susan." Her eyes lit up. "I have an idea. I'm going to teach you how to paint."

Her enthusiasm made me believe she actually could, although realistically, I knew I was far from being an artist. Even my drawings of stick figures didn't look right.

After lunch, she put a blank canvas on the easel. "Let's

make a desert landscape," she said, handing me a black pencil to make peaks for the outline of distant mountains. She put a bunch of colors on a palette—earth tones, sage green, and shades of yellow, orange, and gold—and showed me how to dab my brush into the oils, mix them up, and make smudges of color on the white canvas. Standing back from the easel, those smudges actually resembled sagebrush and sand. I was proud of my painting when it was finished. It did look like a desert scene.

Sally never had one of Aunt June's painting lessons. She was making a name for herself in our household as a creative writer. Dad found her more amenable to his help and editing suggestions than me. I wanted to write things my way and felt criticized by him rather than supported.

Sally's fourth grade teacher, Mrs. O'Brien, was middle aged when she unexpectedly passed away. We never learned what illness had prematurely taken her life. The school planted a tree in her honor, and Sally wrote a poem for the planting ceremony. The poem was read at the ceremony and then printed in the *Glendale News-Press*.

> *The tree we plant now and here,*
> *Is meant for someone very dear.*
> *Since we all know what the tree is for,*
> *I need not tell you anymore,*
> *Except I do not like to hear or say,*
> *That Mrs. O'Brien has passed away.*
> *And I know that we will never forget,*
> *The sad thing our hearts have met.*
>
> By Sally Wise

For the rest of the year, Sally's class had a male substitute teacher. One day, Sally wasn't paying attention to the lesson, and the teacher caught her playing with the nickel that Mom had given her to buy milk. He took away her nickel, but Sally made it clear that he could not legally keep it. Not wanting any trouble, he told her, "Okay, call it. Heads or tails?"

Sally didn't respond, and he said, "C'mon, call it." Sally thought for a moment and replied, "Here nickel, nickel."

Laughing, he gave Sally back the nickel, and her story was retold many times around the school. My sister had proven herself to be smart, clever, and steadfast in her conviction of what was right.

Myrtle

One of Sally's best friends was Myrtle. She and her brother, Jimmy, lived a few houses up the street on Thompson Avenue in a clapboard bungalow that dated back to maybe the early twenties. It had a skimpy, covered front porch and rooms so tiny that it reminded me of a doll house. There was a red barn in the backyard, hinting that the house may have sat on farmland before the area was developed.

Myrtle was an adorable, petite child with blond hair, a flashy smile, and cute dimples. Her older brother was a nice-looking boy, but he had a habit of saying "Huh?" when you talked to him, which made him seem kind of stupid. One of his astute teachers discovered that Jimmy was hard of hearing. From then on, he wore a hearing aid and began making good grades.

Myrtle and Jimmy's mother, Emma, was a fastidious housekeeper. She routinely got up at dawn to clean the house so that she was free to enjoy the rest of her day.

She had the oldest car around, an unreliable, faded black clunker from the 1930s with weathered upholstery, but she always volunteered to drive the younger kids on outings to places in Griffith Park such as the merry-go-round or Ferndell for a picnic. Sometimes she took the kids on long bike rides in the park. She had a reputation for being the fun mom. "I wish our Mom was like Emma," Sally used to say.

That was before we knew that Emma had a drinking problem. In those days, we thought our mother was the only one who liked to drink, enjoying her beer in a tall, green glass with a white antelope embossed on the side.

Sally and I talked Mom into letting us get four bantam chicks, which are smaller than regular chickens. We made a pen in our backyard and had fun raising them. When the bantams reached adulthood, however, we discovered that one was a rooster. He started crowing loudly at dawn, waking us and the neighbors. Mom decided to give the chickens to Emma because she had the barn.

Later on, Sally asked Myrtle if she still had the chickens that we gave them. Poor Sally was so upset when Myrtle apologetically told her, "My mom cooked them for dinner."

Bonnie

Bonnie lived around the block on Jesse Avenue. She was a pretty girl with expressive, dark eyes and long lashes. Sally, Bonnie, and Myrtle were in the same class at school and played together, earning the nickname "the Three Musketeers."

Our family went out to dinner with Bonnie's parents on several occasions. Her father, Ray, was an outgoing, burly guy with a huge appetite. He found an all-you-can-eat buffet restaurant for us in Burbank, which was the perfect spot for families and big eaters like him.

Ray had a neon sign business. Despite the difference in their professions, he and my father got along well. His wife, Beulah, was soft spoken and sweet. One weekend, our families went to the mountains together and stayed overnight at a cabin in Big Bear.

Big Bear with Bonnie's Family

Beverly and Patti

My friends Beverly and Patti lived on Thompson Avenue a few doors up from Myrtle and Jimmy. Beverly was a year older than me and had a sweet, responsible, gentle nature. Patti was a year younger than me, outgoing, and strong-willed, with a reputation for flashing fiery eyes at anyone who made her angry. Both sisters were fun in their own way, and that's why I liked hanging out with them.

Beverly and Patti

Their clapboard house was small and old. It sat far back from the street on an extra-deep lawn. Wooden planks with no overhang made for a crude front porch. Running next to the house was a long blacktop driveway where their father parked his six-wheeler truck. The house had tiny rooms separated by pressboard walls thin enough to poke a finger through. Beverly and Patti shared a small bedroom with lavender-flowered wallpaper.

Like the other mothers in the neighborhood, their mother didn't work outside the home. Still, the girls had to do their share of the housecleaning chores. We all knew that on Saturday morning, Beverly and Patti couldn't come outside until their housework was done. They helped with the laundry, scrubbed floors, vacuumed, dusted, changed the beds, and cleaned the bathroom. Every week, they gave their tiny house the equivalent of a spring cleaning.

Sometimes on a Saturday morning, I went to their house early and waited in the kitchen while they finished their housework. I watched as their mother sat at her Mangle machine and pressed sheets, pillowcases, and trousers. The rollers emitted hot, hissing steam, causing beads of perspiration to appear on her forehead. I felt guilty sitting at the kitchen table doing nothing. All I had to do at home was make the bed and pick up my things. Mom did the cleaning, and Nanny did most of our ironing when she came to visit.

On the weekends, I watched cowboy movies with Beverly and Patti. Their family was the first on the block to get a television set. A magnifying glass over the screen enlarged the image.

On warm, clear nights, their backyard was a favorite hangout. A bunch of us teenagers—boys and girls—stretched out on the grass and gazed up at the stars. We looked for the Big Dipper and tried to identify other constellations in the night sky.

Marlene

Marlene and I met in Mrs. Crane's sixth grade class and became friends. She lived next door to Bonnie on Jesse Avenue. Marlene's parents were Jewish and had emigrated from Turkey. They owned Samuel's Florist at the corner of Alameda Avenue and Victory Boulevard, a Burbank landmark. Marlene was the second child of four siblings. Billy was the oldest and helped out at the florist shop until he went off to fight in the Korean War. Rene was third in line and so skinny we nicknamed her Olive Oyl after Popeye's girlfriend. The youngest, Victor, was Sally's age.

Marlene's elderly grandmother, who didn't speak English, also lived in the home. She wore black clothing, appearing austere and foreign. She was always in the kitchen when Marlene and I came in the house through the back door. As we were leaving, she would thrust out a hand with food in it and say something I didn't understand. She'd smile and point to the food, and I knew she meant "go ahead and try it. You'll like it." Her baked pastry with spinach filling was delicious.

The Neighbors

One of the best things about Stanton Avenue was knowing our neighbors well. One day, Dad didn't recognize a little girl from around the block who was about four years old. He was working in the front yard when the girl unexpectedly ran into the yard, chasing a cat and trying to grab its tail. My father, being the animal lover he was, objected loudly. "Hey, don't hurt that nice kitty."

"That's not a nice kitty," the girl shot back. "That kitty's a son of a bitch." The girl cornered the cat against the picket fence, scooped it up, and left.

My father told us, "I stood there with my mouth open and then laughed my head off."

We often had casual get-togethers with our neighbors or picnics at local parks, including Stough Canyon Park in the Burbank hills. Dad started his own Sunday tradition. He cooked up heaps of buttermilk pancakes for some of our neighbors after discovering a special technique that made the griddle cakes taste better than ever. "You have to whip the egg whites and fold them in. That's what makes the pancakes light and fluffy," he said.

I loved the Fourth of July. At dusk, the neighbors gathered in front of our house where the street was the widest. We bought firecrackers, Piccolo Petes, cherry bombs, glow worms, pinwheels, and sparklers from fireworks stands. The kids ran around with lighted punk sticks in their hands that were used to light the fireworks. Once, Sally accidently poked me in the cheek with her glowing stick. It really hurt, and I had the scar for several years.

The parents sat in folding chairs on the grass, talking and overseeing the fireworks. One time, the adults were drinking beer and having a swell time. Our neighbor, Irene, got tipsy. As the night came to an end, she swaggered across the street toward her house on the corner. Mom started singing a popular song. "Irene, good night, Irene. Irene, good night."

We all chimed in as Irene gave a little flicker wave over her head. "Good night Irene, good night, Irene. I'll see you in my dreams."

Irene's daughter, Susan, enjoyed ice-skating as much as I did. She came along whenever Mom took a carload of us girls to the Winter Garden in Pasadena for an afternoon of skating. The Winter Garden was my favorite ice-skating rink. It had a huge round fireplace with a ledge where we sat with a cup of hot chocolate and warmed ourselves in front of the fire. Susan started taking ice-skating lessons at Schramm's in North Hollywood where I took lessons a few years later. I didn't pursue ice-skating after that, but Susan went on to become a professional skater in the Ice Follies.

Sally had her struggles on those ice-skating outings. Her weak ankles bent to the ice. "Wait for me," she'd holler, trying to keep up with us.

Hercules Bike

I rode my bicycle everywhere, feeling independent and free. Once, on my way to Barbara's house, I was riding up Western Avenue and spotted a snazzy green bicycle sitting on a front porch with a "for sale" sign. It was a Hercules brand, not a coveted Schwinn. However, it was in excellent shape, and like a Schwinn, it featured gears, hand brakes, a headlight, and a nifty leather tool pouch attached to the back of the seat. What I wouldn't have given to have that bicycle instead of my old, prewar relic with the balloon tires and coaster brakes.

On my way home, I decided to ring the doorbell. "How much for the bike?" I asked tentatively.

The woman looked at mine. "Is that yours?"

I told her it was, and she said, "I've been looking for a bicycle like that. Mine is too hard to ride. Would you be interested in a trade?"

Had I heard correctly? My heart went pitter-pat. After a brief discussion, we agreed to make the exchange. First, I had to clear it with Mom. I made a beeline for home and jumped up and down with the good news. Mom went back to the house with me, talked to the lady, and approved the exchange. I rode home on my new bicycle all smiles, thinking I was one smart negotiator. After that, I enjoyed many long rides on my spiffy Hercules bicycle, sometimes spending whole days with friends riding around in Griffith Park.

I realized later that I had been the recipient of a kind gesture. That lady didn't want my bicycle. She had given me hers knowing I would enjoy it. I decided then to do something nice for someone else when I got older.

Job's Daughters

In the eighth grade, one of my classmates told me about Job's Daughters. She belonged, and I liked the idea of being in a secret club. At the dinner table, I mentioned it to my father, saying, "I don't think I can join because you need to be related to a Mason."

Dad grinned and replied, "You certainly can. Grandpa George is a Master Mason."

I had no idea. After producing an affidavit from my grandfather, I joined the Glendale Bethel of Job's Daughters with the intention of making new friends and going on fun outings. There were bimonthly Saturday meetings at the Masonic Lodge in Glendale, just a bus ride away.

As an initiate, I participated in their formal meetings. We wore floor-length, Grecian-type white robes, a symbol of purity like those that women wore during the time of Job, embellished with purple cording. The presiding officer of the bethel was called the Honored Queen. She was assisted in her duties by a Senior Princess and a Junior Princess. All of the pomp and circumstance seemed confusing and silly to me, plus the meetings were long and boring. I stuck it out for a short time before deciding to quit, and my parents didn't seem to mind.

Going Shopping

I took up the hobby of shopping. This was definitely my thing. Many Saturdays were filled with excursions to downtown Glendale, and riding the bus there cost ten cents. At the age of thirteen, I started buying my own clothes and shoes with money from Mom and instructions to "shop wisely." Sometimes I had extra money from my allowance or occasional babysitting jobs.

I was a tenacious shopper and didn't settle for just anything. In search of the perfect item of clothing or pair of shoes, I walked for blocks up and down both sides of Brand Boulevard, going in and out of every store. The millinery shops with feathered hat creations in their windows always caught my eye. Brand Boulevard was wide, and the red streetcars ran down the center. The Alex Theater, with its neon sphere and starburst on top, was a memorable landmark.

For lunch, I stopped at Woolworth's five-and-dime store and sat at the counter. I ordered the same thing every time: a grilled cheese sandwich and a cherry Coke. When I couldn't find what I was looking for on Brand Boulevard, I hopped on the red streetcar and took it to downtown Los Angeles and The Broadway department store.

Mom never knew. She just told me, "Be home by dinnertime."

See's candy store was usually my last stop of the day where I bought a few vanilla cream chocolates for the bus trip home. One time, I went to pay for the chocolates and didn't have my wallet. Frantic, I ran blocks back to the Sears and Roebuck store where I thought I had left it. Sure enough, it was buried in a bin underneath some bathing suits. Good thing, because I needed the ten cents in my wallet to get home.

The Christmas season was my favorite time of the year to go shopping. The store windows were beautifully decorated in winter scenes, Santa Clauses, elves, and snowmen. Red and green tinsel decorations dangled from wires stretched high above Brand Boulevard. In the gusty winds of December, the decorations flapped and twisted noisily, threatening to break free and fly away. The Salvation Army ladies, in their official uniforms and bonnets, stood at intervals along the sidewalk, ringing small handheld bells. Shoppers walking by dropped coins and dollar bills into their donation kettles and were rewarded with a sincere "God bless you."

While Christmas music played inside the stores, the rustle of the wind, whirling street decorations, and Salvation Army bells outdoors created a holiday symphony all its own. I thought it was a magical time of the year.

Pickwick Swim Park

Terry's backyard pool became less of an attraction as I got older. My friends and I started going to Pickwick Swim Park on Riverside Drive across from the Pickwick Stables. It was an easy walk from home and inexpensive.

The summer I was fourteen, I went shopping on Brand Boulevard for a new bathing suit to wear at the Pickwick pool. In a small store, I tried on several suits with the help of a nice saleslady. A salesman looking on gave his approval when I chose the one-piece Rose Marie Reid in a light-mocha color that complemented my dark suntan.

The next day the phone rang, and I heard Dad take the call. "How old do you think she is?" He chuckled. It was that good-looking salesman. He asked my father if he could take me on a date. My phone number was on the sales receipt. The salesman was surprised when he learned that I was fourteen, not eighteen as he thought. I was flattered and couldn't wait to tell my girlfriends, but I never went back in that store again.

Pickwick Swim Park was the most heavenly place on earth as far as I was concerned. The pool was enormous and perfectly round, and the low and high diving boards were in the exact middle of the pool. Park-like grounds covered in grass surrounded the pool with trees on the perimeter if we wanted shade. Sometimes I packed a lunch, but I usually bought a hamburger and a Coke at the snack stand. A covered dance area with a jukebox that played popular records was next to the snack stand. One of my favorite songs was "How High the Moon" by Les Paul and Mary Ford.

Chain link fencing cordoned off a sandlot adjacent to the pool. One time, circus apparatus appeared on the sand. I watched in awe as a troupe of acrobats and trapeze artists practiced their tricks. Mom brought Sally one afternoon, and my sister and I got the idea to try some of the tricks at home in our backyard. We mastered only one. I squatted while Sally stood on my thighs with her arms outstretched. She was small and skinny, so it didn't take any skill on my part to support her.

The kids today may have trendy water parks for thrilling rides down water shoots and hair-raising slides. Pickwick Swim Park had an unbeatable ambiance that you won't find around here anymore. We could hang out for the whole day, our towels spread out on the grass as we listened to the jukebox playing in the background. We swam, sunned, picnicked, danced, and relaxed in the tranquility of a slower time. Those were definitely happy days.

Glenna

Glenna lived up the street on Thompson Avenue across from Myrtle and Jimmy. She was a year older than me and the studious type with bright-red hair and freckles. The small, yellow stains on her teeth were permanent, according to her dentist. Glenna said they came from the drinking water in Lubbock, Texas, where she was born and lived before moving to Glendale. She often remarked cynically, "Lubbock is good place to be *from*."

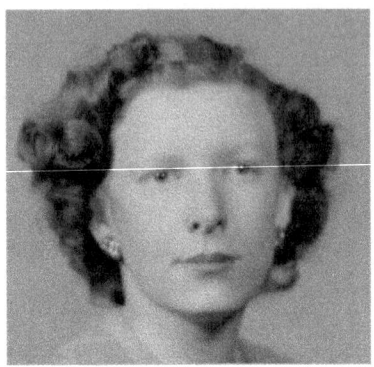

Glenna

Glenna had a slow Southern way about her. She wasn't interested in horseback riding or hanging out at Roger's corral. She was a homebody. Sometimes I stayed overnight at her house and shared her single bed. We stayed awake for hours talking. During one stay, I got up the nerve to say, "Glenna, I think you need to start wearing deodorant."

Glenna and I took tap dancing lessons together. I talked her into going with me after I saw a dance studio advertisement in downtown Glendale. Mom said she'd pay for lessons and tap shoes. Wearing the black patent leather tap shoes was the best part of dance lessons. I was still the girl who loved Mary Janes.

Mom had already taught me some basic dance steps. She was still a good dancer from her days as a showgirl at the Orpheum Theater. With some practice, I mastered step-ball-change and "Shuffle Off to Buffalo." Glenna and I learned more steps in class and prepared for a recital program. We practiced on my back porch and on Glenna's driveway. Glenna's mother made us matching dance outfits with bloomer pants. For whatever reason—maybe the cost—we stopped taking lessons, and that was the end of my dance career.

In the heat of summer, Glenna wasn't interested in outdoor activities. She preferred staying cool in front of the tabletop fan in her living room, devouring short stories in *The Saturday Evening Post* and the *Ladies' Home Journal*. She was an avid reader.

My passion for reading didn't catch hold right away. In school, I thought most of the required books were uninteresting. Going to the public library and doing research or trying to find a good book to read were chores made more tedious by having to look through the voluminous card catalogues. I wanted to be outside having real-life adventures.

Knowing that I wanted to write, Dad told me, "You can't be a writer, Susan, until you're a reader." That was discouraging, but he had a point. I thought laziness was my problem, but Mom wisely found the key that started me reading.

For several days, I was sick with a bad cold and had to stay home from school. I had nothing to do. Mom went to the library and checked out her favorite book from when she was a teenager, *The Good Earth* by Pearl S. Buck. I read it from cover to cover, savoring every page. This was my kind of book, and I thought Mom was a genius for knowing. We had a good discussion afterward about the Chinese culture and the woman's role in China.

The next book I read was *The Amboy Dukes*—at night, by flashlight, and under the covers because of its racy sexual content. That's exactly why it went underground, away from parents' eyes, and was passed from girlfriend to girlfriend until the pages were wrinkled and falling out. That was my kind of book too.

Glenna's mother was a wonderful cook. She brought her famous Southern fried chicken and potato salad to our picnics in the park. She made the best chicken ever.

Glenna often helped out with the cooking at home, and that resulted in a good story. When visiting from Texas, her grandmother was making dinner one night for the family. Glenna helped her by peeling the potatoes and putting them on the stove to boil. In a thick Southern drawl, her grandmother said, "Glenna Faye, don't forget to put a kiver on the pot."

"It's called a cover, Grandma," Glenna said.

Her grandmother shrugged and said, "Oh well, then just put a led on it."

Glenna's younger brother, Butch (real name Jesse), also had red hair and freckles. He was the opposite of a bookworm—fun loving, outgoing, and full of energy. Although Butch was younger than me, we got along great.

A new store selling refrigerators and stoves opened up on Victory Boulevard. The refrigerators came in tall boxes, and Butch and I knew exactly what to do with them. With our parents' approval, we planned a backyard sleepover at his house.

We dragged two of the refrigerator boxes down the street, placed them end to end on the grass in his backyard, and outfitted them with overnight supplies. That night, with flashlights in hand, we ran through the neighborhood until late before going to bed. We discovered that sleeping outside in boxes was uncomfortable. We heard strange noises, tossed and turned on the hard ground, shivered as the night air cooled, and stayed wound up from the candy we'd eaten. Still, we had fun talking. The next day, we took a long nap in our own comfortable beds.

Mrs. Kerr

Dad finally moved on from the Polish radio station and was hired by the Kerr Glass Manufacturing Company to write a promotional film. Ruth Kerr, widow of the founder Alexander H. Kerr, ran a successful home canning supply business. Alexander Kerr had invented a clever two-part lid to seal a mason jar that transformed home canning safety. The jars are still seen in stores today.

Dad had conversations at the dinner table about Ruth Kerr, saying he admired her Christian beliefs and ideals. They were incorporated into her company, and she was known for treating her employees well. "She's quite a businesswoman," I overheard him telling Mom.

Many of the employees were women who Mrs. Kerr promoted to management positions. I listened closely as my father spoke admirably of her. Being in an executive position was uncommon for women, and hearing about Mrs. Kerr's accomplishments made me feel that someday maybe I could be a successful woman.

In a write-up about her, Ruth Kerr was quoted as saying, "Anything I've done was accomplished because of what God has done."

I'm not sure if Mrs. Kerr had any influence on Dad's decision to convert to Christianity, but it's possible. Around this same time, Mom's cousin, Kermit Houck, moved west to take a ministerial position at a Christian community church in Burbank. He visited our home, and my father had discussions with him about religion. Dad asked Kermit to baptize him, which he did one Sunday morning as our family looked on.

Because of his Jewish heritage, Mom wondered about my father's sincerity. "I don't know if he's doing it for the right reason," she told me.

Somewhere along the way, Dad had come to this important decision, and I was proud of him.

After the Kerr Glass film, Dad wrote and directed a film for the City of Burbank entitled *Burbank, Story of a City*. After the script was finished and filming began, he invited some of the neighborhood kids to participate in a "playing in the park" scene. The filming took place in a Burbank park nearby, and we had fun that day being in the movie.

Butch was picked for the clean water scene, a segment touting Burbank's city-owned water company. That scene was filmed in our bathroom. Butch is seen scrubbing himself, standing in the large corner bathtub with the overhead shower running, for the shot. He was thrilled with his starring moment as "shower boy."

Lake Street Baptist Church

Lake Street Baptist Church played a big role in my life when we lived on Stanton Avenue. Barbara introduced me to the church when we were in the sixth grade. Dr. Minton was the Southern Baptist minister, and he attracted an active congregation that supported a wonderful youth program. Sally and I walked the few blocks to church for Sunday school every week and occasionally stayed for the church service. Our parents never went with us. Many kids living around Lake Street and in our immediate neighborhood attended Sunday school there, including Glenna and Butch, whose parents made sure they never missed Sunday school or church. Even Jerry, who was Jewish, went to Sunday school with us for a while because he didn't want to miss out on the fun activities.

Those activities included roller skating outings, vacation Bible school, ice cream socials, swimming trips, and summer camps in the San Bernardino Mountains. One time, we went to The Pike, an amusement pier at the ocean in Long Beach. A carnival booth featured flea races, and I could see the tiny fleas jumping, one after the other, as if racing. It was a strange sight.

Another time, we went to the Rose Bowl in Pasadena for a Billy Graham revival meeting. During the revival, a man sitting near us fell on the ground, shaking. We didn't know what was going on and stared as people tried to help him. Was he overcome by the Holy Spirit? "He's having an epileptic fit," one of the church leaders whispered. I'd never seen anything like that before, and I felt sorry for the man.

Barbara and I went to church camp together in the San Bernardino Mountains each summer after seventh, eighth, and ninth grade. Our first trip was to Forest Home. We then went to Thousand Pines and Tahquitz Pines, where I won first place in a swimming race. I met Bob at Thousand Pines, and we were an item that week. I loved going to camp. It gave me the chance to be away from home and on my own.

Forest Home and Mom's Drinking

At Forest Home, I came forward on the last night and accepted Jesus into my heart. Baptism was the next step. Dr. Minton did the honors during a church service a few weeks later. Wearing a heavy, white corduroy robe, I was baptized by full immersion in a baptismal font of water. I was given a Bible, which I still have. My parents were seated in the second-row pew as witnesses. They wore proud expressions and smiled, but I knew there was tension between them. It had been that way since my arrival home from camp.

The day I came back from Forest Home, I could hardly wait to share my camp experience. One step through the front door, however, and I knew something was wrong. My smile faded as Mom told me about the huge fight between her and my father while I was gone. She had fallen during the fight. "He pushed me," she said accusatorily.

A child never wants to know intimate details of fights between their parents, but Mom was never one to spare any details. It was one of her biggest faults. Thankfully, Sally had been present and saw what happened. "Mom started it," she told me later in private. "She was drunk, stumbled, and lost her balance. That's why she fell."

This incident played out again in a few years when my mother needed major surgery for a damaged kidney. The doctor said the injury might have come from a fall, and Mom was quick to blame my father, but Sally and I knew the real story.

The fact that Mom had a serious drinking problem became clearer to me and Sally at this point in our lives. While she surely had been drinking regularly in previous years, it escalated on Stanton Avenue. We were just kids, so we didn't know anything about alcoholism. We just knew that Mom liked to drink beer in those tall, green glasses. When she wasn't drinking, the clashes between her and my father were less frequent. After even one beer, however, her personality changed, and she could get real nasty. It seemed that she purposely egged my father on until he exploded. Since my parents made no attempt to hide their quarrelling, my sister and I were the unwitting audience to their drama. We heard personal things that children shouldn't hear. It affected us in many unseen ways far into our adult lives.

"I only drink beer," Mom said defensively when pressed about it. That was true for the time being, but I saw that even one glass of beer had an effect on her. With alcohol in her system, a deep-seated anger roared to life. At my young age, it was difficult to figure out why. I tried not to take sides, but sometimes it was easier to support Mom's point of view because she was a woman, and I could understand her better. Dad's quick temper and intense personality frightened me and made me nervous. I wanted his unconditional love and acceptance in the worst way, but he couldn't show it, and I couldn't tap into his softer side. Sally understood him better, so they were always closer.

As a kid, I was easily stressed and more emotional than Sally. Dad pinpointed my nature. "You're too sensitive," he said.

I didn't want to be, but I was. I wondered if I was adopted. One day, I caught Mom off guard with the important question on my mind. "Was I adopted?" If so, maybe that explained why I was so sensitive and didn't look like anyone in the family. I asked to see my birth certificate. "You're ours, Susan," Mom assured me.

There it was in black and white on my birth certificate. I was a Wise. Maybe there was something worthwhile in that. After all, the Wises did have those good writer genes.

While the storm clouds hovered over our home life, my outside world remained happy and carefree. Stanton Avenue was a safe harbor filled with friends and fun things to do. I loved school and my church. I talked about the problems at home only with Sally. We worried what the neighbors might think. Could they hear our parents quarrelling? Their fights were often long and loud.

More about Roger

Going to Roger's house continued to be a favorite pastime. We played hide-and-seek when there were lots of kids in the corral. Playing after dark was even more fun. One time, Roger and I stayed hidden in the hay loft for a long time, kissing.

Roger got a special drivers' license at fourteen. Sometimes, he drove an old black coupe around the neighborhood that belonged to his mother. It had a rumble seat and an ooga horn that made me grin. "Let's go for a ride," he said one day, and I jumped at the chance. We had fun driving up and down the streets, honking the ooga horn at everybody.

Another day, Roger and I went to a movie on Brand Boulevard and saw *The Fuller Brush Man* starring Red Skelton. I thought it was a real date until he treated me more like a pal than a girlfriend. His movie invitation came after he'd kissed me in the old Hudson, which was parked next to the corral, awaiting repairs. Roger was such a confusing boy. One minute he was affectionate, and the next, he treated me like a buddy.

As a teenager, I was blessed with clear skin. For my beauty regime, I used soap and water on my face and Noxzema cream. One Saturday morning, I decided to give myself an egg white facial like Mom did when she was a showgirl. As the egg white dried, it pulled my skin taut into a creepy-looking mask. When the doorbell rang, I had forgotten about the egg white on my face and opened the door. There stood Roger. He burst out laughing.

I was mortified and slammed the door in his face. "What are you doing here?" I asked stupidly through the closed door. I don't recall his answer.

I drove Mom crazy talking about Roger. It was Roger this and Roger that to the point that she pleaded, "Please, Susan, give it a rest. Let's see if you can go an hour without mentioning his name."

Those were the days when, after school, I wore boys' jeans with the legs rolled up to just below the knees and one of Dad's discarded white shirts with the sleeves rolled up and the tail hanging out. Joyce shoes were all the rage. They looked like nurse's shoes—white with a wedge sole. I couldn't afford the real thing and bought the cheaper knockoffs at Leeds Shoe Store.

The hairstyle I favored after school and on the weekends was faddish and ridiculous, never to return in popularity again, thank goodness. I made pin curls at each temple, held in place with bobby pins. I attached a silk scarf around my head, over the pin curls, with more bobby pins and tied it in back at my neck, letting the rest of the material hang loose. Only my curly bangs showed. I wore the scarves—mostly blue ones to match my jeans—day in and day out. Mom said I had beautiful hair that needed to breathe. "You're going to go bald," she said.

That never happened, but it did give me concern. I gave up the scarf wearing about the time I was ready for high school.

We didn't have good hair products in those days and no hair spray. Glenna's mother was nice enough to give me a home permanent, but the outcome was disappointing. My naturally wavy hair turned way too curly and looked like it did when I was a little girl. "I love it," Mom said. I had envisioned a more grown-up style.

One afternoon, Marlene and I got together at her house with a bottle of peroxide. We bleached a thick swatch of our dark-brown hair, hoping to achieve a nice blond streak. Instead, our bangs turned brassy gold. Mom was shocked when I walked through the front door. "What happened to you?"

"It'll grow out," I said, heading for my room.

The scarf wearing was an easy solution when I didn't know what to do with my hair. I also thought I looked older wearing the scarf, but I wondered what Roger thought.

One evening at dusk, I had a conversation with Roger's mother as we stood at the corral fence. Frustrated with his off-and-on attention, I confided in her about how much I liked him. I said, "He must be queer."

Shock and disapproval flashed across her face. "You shouldn't say something like that. Do you know what it means?"

I didn't know and felt ashamed. I thought it meant a boy who didn't like girls. That sure seemed the case when it came to Roger and me. I hoped that Daisy wouldn't tell him and was relieved when she moved away, taking my stupid remark with her.

At the end of October, Roger had a Halloween party in the corral. No costumes, just everyone wearing jeans. I was excited when he invited me and assumed I would be with him. I was in the ninth grade, and he was in tenth grade in high school. When I arrived at the party, he wasn't around. One of his friends said, "He went on an errand." When he returned, there was a girl with him: his date for the party.

Hurt and depressed, I left the party early and went home with tears in my eyes. The facts were plain. He didn't feel the same way about me that I felt about him.

Looking back, there's the slim possibility that Roger didn't know that I had a crush on him. He could have assumed that I was there for the horses more than for him. I wasn't confident enough to express my true feelings. As a young teenager, I wouldn't have said, "I like you." Sometimes I acted nonchalant with a hard-to-get attitude, because I thought that's the way girls were supposed to act around boys.

Dad told me that relationships were like mercury. "Hold the mercury gently in the palm of your hand, and it will stay there," he said. "Squeeze, and it will slip through your fingers."

In those days, Sally and I experienced holding mercury. Our parents, like others, didn't know mercury shouldn't come in contact with the skin.

I liked Mom's advice better. "If one boy doesn't like you, there's plenty more fish in the sea."

After that, I rarely went to Roger's house. It wasn't the same anymore.

Fun Things

Fortunately, there were other fun things to do. On Friday night, I went to the movies at the Cornell Theater in Burbank with Beverly and Patti. Saturday was a big night at the outdoor roller skating rink on San Fernando Road. It was packed with junior high boys and girls. The rink backed up to the railroad tracks with a sheet metal fence as the only barrier. When the freight trains roared by, the whole place shook, and we couldn't hear the music.

The next best thing to riding horseback in Griffith Park was riding there on my Hercules bicycle. I always rode with a group of friends for safety. Sometimes, we packed a lunch and stayed for the whole day. We rode on the merry-go-round and went to the zoo.

Occasionally, I rode my bike with friends to the Los Angeles River, which was shallow. We went wading for pollywogs, baby frogs, or whatever interesting things we could find. There were no fences, and the river's sandy bottom was fairly clean. It wasn't unusual to hear of young, inexperienced riders who rented horses and found themselves upside down in the river because their horse decided to go for a roll in the water.

Rapist in the Park

One afternoon, I got more adventure than I bargained for. About six of us girls headed to Griffith Park for a hike. We had just crossed the flat, grassy area that runs adjacent to the park road when we heard a girl screaming for help. I was first to see her on the hilltop. She was naked and struggling with a man.

"STOP," we shouted, shaking our fists. Another girl, fully clothed, was clinging to a bush on the side of the hill. Her feet were dangling and searching for a foothold. The man had apparently grabbed one girl and pushed her friend down the mountainside.

We ran back to the boulevard and tried to wave down a car. Two teenaged boys riding the trail on horseback saw our distress and stopped. Learning of the situation, they sped off on their horses to rescue the girls. A car pulled over on the shoulder with its engine on fire, and a police car showed up right away. Seizing the opportunity, we intercepted the policeman who radioed for patrol cars and the mounted police. The park was soon swarming with officers. The man scrambled away when he saw the boys on horseback, who were able to reach the girl in time. With their help, the naked girl retrieved her scattered clothing and got dressed. The boys made a human chain and rescued the girl hanging on the side of the hill. From below, we could see all of this going on as well as the park rangers who were methodically searching the hills on horseback.

We picked up some sticks and started walking through the park next to the roadway, thinking the man would flee in our direction. A lone car was parked on the road, and there was white underwear on the backseat. We figured it had to be his car and decided to stake it out, taking the smart approach by returning to the grassy area a safer distance away.

Before long, the man approached his car. He saw us and ran in the opposite direction on the grass, and we took off after him. We waved our sticks and yelled at him in what was later described in the *Glendale News-Press* as "A posse of young girls capture would-be rapist." Police officers who heard our shouts came quickly, apprehended the suspect, and placed his wrists in handcuffs.

After the arrest, several police officers gathered us girls together to take the report. The two of us who were first on the scene had to stay longer to provide more details. I was feeling shaky and tired by then from the adrenalin letdown, and I probably looked disheveled after running through the park. The sun was low on the horizon, and I knew Mom would be getting worried. "I'll be happy to drive the two of you home," one of the officers said, and we gratefully accepted.

Mom rushed outside with a serious look on her face when the police car pulled up. The story of our harrowing experience tumbled out of my mouth as her expression changed from worry to relief. "I told you Griffith Park could be dangerous," she said. "I'm glad you girls are okay."

My friend and I had to testify in a closed court session. Mom drove me to the superior court building in downtown Los Angeles. I met with the judge and a woman officer in private chambers, feeling uneasy and scared. As part of the procedure, I had to identify the suspect who was in court and shackled. He looked at me and snarled, "I'll get you for this," just like in a movie. Shivers ran down my spine. For years afterward, I was afraid he would get out of prison and find me.

Talk of the attempted rape quickly spread around school, and that's when I learned who the girls were. We were so upset and frantic that day that I never got a good look at their faces. To my surprise, both girls were ninth grade classmates of mine, and I knew them casually. I didn't say anything to either girl about being part of their rescue posse, as I thought it would be too uncomfortable for them. Nevertheless, I was proud of the job we did that day. We were called heroes, and I knew that was true.

Grandma Lovey Dies

It was a sad day when our family received word that Grandma Lovey had died in New York from cancer. Some of her things were sent to us in a large steamer trunk as keepsakes. The trunk might have been one that she used when she traveled by ocean liner from New York to Germany.

Sally and I were excited the day the trunk arrived and had fun going through everything. We found tablecloths and various linens. Some of the things were embossed with the letter "W." There were two velvet opera capes, one black and the other ruby red, that my sister and I later wore as costumes. We found three engraved silver serving spoons, miscellaneous items of clothing, and lace doilies. There were two silver jewelry boxes made in Germany that Sally and I kept for our own. Sally still has hers, but I foolishly sold mine at a garage sale. Some of the silver had rubbed off, and I didn't know it could be resilvered like new.

Fortunately, I saw Grandpa George one more time when we later visited New York, and before he passed away in 1959 at the age of eighty-eight. It was a peaceful death. On that day, he had lunch at his favorite delicatessen and enjoyed a pastrami sandwich and a glass of beer. Feeling some indigestion, he lay down for a nap and never woke up.

45 Records

In 1949, 45 rpm records were brand new in the stores. Sally and I shared a small, portable record player that played them. Collecting them was fun, and they were smaller and easier to store than 78s. I enjoyed playing my favorite songs over and over again instead of waiting for them to play on the radio. Some of the favorites in my collection were "How High the Moon" by Les Paul and Mary Ford, "The Tennessee Waltz" by Patti Page, "Cry" by Johnny Ray, and "Aba Daba Honeymoon" by Debbie Reynolds.

"A' You're Adorable" (The Alphabet Song) sung by Perry Como hit the top of the charts in 1949. This was special in our family because my uncle, Fred Wise, wrote the lyrics. His music career was going well. There were more number one hits in his future, including "Let Me Go Lover." He went on to write the lyrics for most of Elvis Presley's movie songs. He collaborated on many of his songs with other lyricists and the well-known pianist and composer, Ben Weisman.

Movie about Polio

Sally, about ten, was excited when Dad tapped her for a role in a movie he was making. The film was about the treatment for polio, the dreaded disease of our childhood. Sally was chosen because she was skinny enough to play the part of a recovering patient. She was in one scene, sitting in a therapy tank of warm water. This was a sponsored film.

New Bedroom

My parents ended up sleeping on the Murphy bed longer than expected. Almost two years passed before a contractor was hired to build a second bedroom. Square footage was added to the breakfast room at the front of the house, and that became the new bedroom for Sally and me. The dining table was relocated to the living room next to the rear windows where the Murphy bed was no longer needed. The downside to adding the bedroom was losing half of the front porch and with it the outdoor couch and chairs. Sally and I sure missed that porch when it was gone. It had been the perfect gathering spot for us and our neighborhood friends.

Enlarging the house was dependent on Dad getting more work. Gladding McBean & Company in Glendale hired him to write a promotional film, and that job funded the remodeling project. Gladding McBean produced beautiful ceramic tiles, pottery, and hand-painted Franciscan dinnerware. My cousin Beverly worked there for about a year as a pottery artist. While making the film, Dad got a good deal on two sets of dinnerware, a twelve-piece service for Mom and her sister. Mom chose the Apple pattern, and Aunt June took the Desert Rose pattern.

Cousin De Setta

Mom and De Setta were more like sisters than first cousins. They were street smart, independent, and pragmatic, while Aunt June was more emotional and a dreamer. She had an artist's temperament. Sometimes my aunt had an unrealistic approach to solving problems, which confounded and often irritated my mother. Aunt June believed in prayer and God's intervention, while my mother was inclined to believe that God helped those who helped themselves.

"I can't understand why my sister never learned to drive," Mom told me, thinking it made her too dependent on others, especially her husband. "De Setta and I see eye to eye."

De Setta visited us on Stanton Avenue with her first husband, Byron. Mom didn't particularly like him. "He's a con man," she said, talking about his shady real estate deals when he and De Setta were first married. Later, he owned a bookstore.

Byron could really turn on the charm, and he played the piano by ear like nobody's business. Sitting at our baby grand piano, he entertained us for hours, playing popular songs on request. Even my father had fun during our old-fashioned singalongs.

De Setta and Byron had two sons. Bob was the oldest. Don, the youngest, was eight years older than me and good looking. Sometimes he was at home when we visited De Setta in the Silverlake area, and he was always friendly. Don had a collection of handmade, balsa-wood model airplanes displayed in his bedroom. I thought they were special and wanted to learn how to make them. "I'll teach you," he said, but I thought he was just being nice.

The next time De Setta came to our house, Don came too. Sure enough, he brought some models, an X-Acto knife, and airplane glue. We put a few of the models together in our garage. It was easy with him working at my side but much harder on my own. I tried to finish the models but gave up, deciding that building model airplanes was a hobby best left to the boys.

After De Setta's divorce, Mark came into her life. Mom initially thought it was a terrible match. Her new husband was twenty years her junior, drove a Good Humor ice cream truck, drank heavily, had a jail record, and a temper that fueled hotter when he was drinking. He went by the nickname of Lucky. "I'm lucky at gambling," he told us, reminiscing about his many trips to Las Vegas. "That's how I got my name."

Despite his questionable past and shortcomings, Lucky was an outgoing guy with a big heart. He loved animals, especially dogs, and would give any friend the shirt off his back. De Setta might have been older than Lucky, but she looked girlish for her age with rosebud lips and bleached blond hair. She had a good head on her shoulders and worked hard as a practical nurse.

De Setta and Lucky were married at the Church of Religious Science in Studio City, and our family was there to celebrate the nuptials. For the wedding, she wore an ankle-length, lace-and-tulle formal in a lilac color. She looked lovely but a bit glitzy. Lucky spiked the fruit punch. Reception guests discovered that after noticing children going back for seconds and getting a little buzzed. When confronted, Lucky laughed his head off.

"It won't last," Mom said, but De Setta and Lucky stayed married for the rest of their lives. Over the years, I became close to De Setta and visited her often.

Uncle Arthur

My grandfather's younger brother and his wife relocated to Beverly Hills from Manhattan to be near their son, Nat, and grandson, Johnny. It was a big change for them in their later years.

We visited Uncle Arthur and Aunt Ruby several times at their Monterey-style apartment on Palm Drive. These are important memories now but were unappreciated back then. Uncle Arthur reminded me of my grandfather. There was a strong family resemblance, especially the prominent Wise nose. From my youthful perspective, he typified the affluent, sophisticated New Yorker. He dressed well in a tailored wool suit and impressed me as being intellectually sharp. You knew what was on his mind, and he told good stories like my father.

Aunt Ruby was soft spoken, cultured, and always wore a lovely dress or suit. Her passion was knitting. The rhythmic clicking sounds of her knitting needles drew our attention as we visited in their living room. Her fingers seemed to fly as she created knitted row after row of what ended up being a sweater, afghan, or pair of men's socks.

Uncle Arthur always slipped a crisp dollar bill into the palm of my hand. "How are you doing in school? Are you getting good grades?" he asked.

My grades were no match for his grandson's. Cousin Johnny was smart, the kind of kid who preferred chess over baseball and carried on intellectual conversations with grown-ups as if he were an adult himself. He graduated from Beverly Hills High School and later received a bachelor's degree from the California Institute of Technology in Pasadena.

No intellectual match for Johnny, I took solace in knowing that he came up athletically short. Unlike me, who'd been swimming since the age of five, Johnny was afraid of the water and didn't know how to swim. I teased him about that.

Unfortunately, I never gave any thought to Uncle Arthur and my grandfather growing up together in Manhattan. Uncle Arthur could have told me about the Wise family history and our German roots. Like most teenagers, I cared less and begrudgingly tolerated those obligatory visits. Inquiring about family history was the furthest thing from my mind. "Act polite," Dad said.

I answered Uncle Arthur's questions about school and tried to act mature. Though I felt awkward under the microscope, clearly Uncle Arthur and Aunt Ruby were glad to see us and interested in whatever I had to say. They were nice people, and I think my father cared for them deeply.

Richard

My friend Patti went steady for about a month with a boy named Richard. "He's the most popular boy in Burbank and knows everyone," she told me.

Richard sold newspapers on the weekend in front of the drugstore at the corner of San Fernando Road and Olive Avenue in downtown Burbank. The newspapers were bundled and stacked on the sidewalk. Richard sat on top of the pile and held court, so to speak, with the kids who came by to see him. The corner drugstore was a popular hangout for young teenagers, and he was a popular guy. Patti met him selling papers there.

After Patti broke up with Richard, she thought I should meet him. She made arrangements for us to meet one Friday night at the Cornell Theater. Richard was waiting in front of the theater when Mom drove Patti and me to the theater in the Nash Ambassador.

Patti introduced Richard to me, and I could tell right away why he was so popular. Pretty-boy handsome, he had jet-black hair and dark eyes that lit up when he smiled. He was polite, and my heart skipped a beat. We sat together during the movie and even held hands. Afterward, he asked for my telephone number.

The next day, Richard called, and we talked for over an hour. Talking to him was easy. I didn't have act phony or play hard to get. Before hanging up, he asked me to go to the movies with him the next Friday night. Of course, I said, "Yes."

Easter Sunday was the day after that first telephone call from Richard. I wore a new sleeveless dress for church that I'd recently bought in downtown Glendale. It was navy-blue cotton with a white sweetheart collar and white pearl buttons on the pleated bodice. My white ballerina flats went nicely with the dress, and I thought I looked pretty.

On that Easter morning, the sun shone brightly, and it was unusually warm for early April. I didn't need a sweater for the walk to the Lake Street Baptist Church. Along the way, I noticed the trees were leafing out, and some had pretty, pink blossoms. Birds in rare form skittered about, chirping loudly as they filled the landscape with their songs. Spring was in the air, and I was on cloud nine and over-the-moon happy, like only a girl can feel when she thinks she's met a special boy. My world seemed near perfect on that spring day when I was fourteen.

Patti was right. Richard was very popular. So was I just being with him, especially after he asked me to go steady. I liked being popular and the envy of the other girls. Richard was definitely a catch, and my confidence and self-esteem soared.

Richard had the indisputable reputation for being nice to everyone. That was why he had so many friends, including Ernie who was Mexican and wouldn't have been included in any other group of white kids. In those days, social segregation was the norm.

I met Ernie one day at Richard's newspaper stand. He called me a few times, and we had long talks. "I like you," he said one night during our conversation. "Richard's a lucky guy. I guess your parents wouldn't let you be with someone like me, a Mexican."

"Probably not," I told him. I was flattered but knew I would never cross the line. Besides, I was Richard's girl.

Richard had a twin brother named Rodney, and they looked nothing alike. Rodney was short with auburn hair and freckles, while Richard was taller with black hair. Sometimes Rodney acted tough, maybe to compensate for his short stature, but he was a nice guy. Richard possessed an unusual charm and ease with people for his young age. He probably got that talent and his good looks from his father. As a character actor in Hollywood, his father played dapper, continental villains, and noblemen with over four-hundred films to his credit, including many of Charlie Chaplin's comedies. He was in his sixties when he died about a year before I met Richard, which I didn't know at the time.

"What was the movie about?" Mom asked one Friday night after I'd been at the Cornell Theater with Richard.

"Oh, it was sort of a mystery," I told her, recalling the coming attraction. Richard and I had made out through the entire movie, and I had no idea what it was about.

The next Friday night, we were necking when I heard the distinctive smoker's cough belonging to my mother coming from the back of the theater. I sat up in my seat and looked around. "My mother's here," I whispered in Richard's ear. I was embarrassed that she'd been spying on us. Richard and I found seats as far away from her cough as we could get.

When Mom picked me up after the movie, she pretended she'd come straight from home.

"I know you were in the theater," I said, angrily.

She denied it.

"I heard you coughing, Mom."

"I just wanted to see what was going on with you guys," she said sheepishly.

Richard and I went steady for maybe two months. We talked on the telephone every night, went to the Friday night movies at the Cornell Theater, roller skated at the outdoor rink on San Fernando Road, swam at Pickwick Swim Park when the weather was warmer, and looked at the stars in Patti's backyard. During Burbank on Parade, we met up with Rodney at the Burbank Recreation Center and had a good time going on the carnival rides.

Then something happened. Richard broke up with me and asked my friend Marlene to go steady. Marlene? I hadn't seen that coming. Devastated, I spent one afternoon sobbing my eyes out.

Mom came into the bedroom and sat on the edge of my bed. "You'll meet another boy real soon," she said, trying to console me.

"What do you know about love?" I wailed through my tears. "You just met Daddy and got married."

She shrugged and said, "Oh, Susie dear" in that way of hers.

Richard went steady with Marlene for only a couple of weeks before he moved on to the next girl. About five years later, he curiously showed up in my life again when I was in college.

Susan, Richard, Marlene

Graduation

Graduation night was held in the Hoover High School auditorium across the street from Toll Junior High School. The girls were asked to wear party dresses. Dad took me shopping for my dress at Bullocks on Wilshire Boulevard, a ritzy department store perhaps like one on Park Avenue in New York. In the dress salon, we sat in overstuffed chairs while the saleslady brought out different dresses for me try on. One was a pink, organdy dress with a waffle pique bodice and a scoop neckline. The dress was sweet and flattering for a young girl like me who happened to be big busted. Dad preferred a white, sleeveless sundress that was low cut with ruffled shoulder straps. "The sundress looks beautiful on you," he said.

He wanted me to wear it for graduation, but I thought it was too casual and way too sexy. I chose the pink dress.

When I got home and opened up the box, both dresses were inside. "Surprise," Dad said, smiling broadly. "I couldn't resist the white one."

For graduation, I wore the pink dress with my first pair of high-heeled shoes. They were white platforms with about a three-inch heel. I'm sure I must have wobbled as I walked. The white dress was worn only a few times, drawing stares from boys and even grown men. I probably looked great in it with my buxom figure and dark tan. However, at fourteen, I didn't have the maturity or confidence to wear it without feeling self-conscious.

Sally's Birthday

Sally turned eleven that June, and Mom had a party for her in the backyard. We played 45 rpm records on our portable record player for dancing. Sally had a secret crush on Butch and looked forward to dancing with him. After he asked Myrtle to dance, Sally went into the house and cried.

"What's wrong?" Myrtle asked Sally when she found her alone in the bedroom.

"Butch asked you to dance. He likes you better than me," my sister said tearfully.

Myrtle shrugged and replied, "He asked everyone to dance."

Sally dried her eyes and returned to the party, but she was still unhappy. My little sister was growing up and close to that stage when it's all about the boys and trying to fit in.

Moving Away

By now, Dad had a good job as a writer for Cate and McGlone Productions in Hollywood. Ted Cate and Ed McGlone produced public relations films, industrial films, travelogues, and documentaries. The company had offices in the historic Crossroads of the World business center on Sunset Boulevard. With more money coming in, Dad got the bug to buy a bigger house. The summer before I entered tenth grade, we went house hunting again, this time farther west in the San Fernando Valley.

One Saturday, Dad and I were looking at houses together, just the two of us. We stopped for lunch at Kover's Bull Pen, a barbeque place on Ventura Boulevard in Sherman Oaks. Although it was blazing hot that day, the restaurant was deceivingly cool. I had a pork roast sandwich and chocolate pudding pie for dessert. That night I was deathly ill. By noon the following day, I hadn't improved, and Mom called the doctor, who made a house call.

"You've got ptomaine poisoning," the doctor said, and he gave me a shot to ease the pain and nausea.

That's the sickest I'd ever been.

Dad eventually found his perfect house in Studio City, and my parents bought it. We planned to move a week before school started and began packing with my grandmother's help. Nanny made one of her most endearing remarks while she was packing for the move. She had just finished filling a cardboard box with dishes that had been carefully wrapped in newspaper and said to my mother, "Mark the box fragilley." Of course, the word was *fragile*. Nanny's sixth grade education left her with gaps when it came to the English language. An avid reader, she pronounced the words as she saw them. We all laughed, and so did Nanny when we set her straight.

I thought the new house was beautiful. It was larger and grander than our little house on Stanton Avenue. Regrettably, it was far away from my friends and the neighborhood I loved.

"It's an opportunity to meet new friends," Dad said, hoping to convince me. In his opinion, my friends fell short of his standards. "I don't want you to turn cheap."

Some girls had their ears pierced, and that probably made them look cheap. Pierced ears weren't in vogue at the time. I wanted my ears pierced and asked a friend to do it. I wore dangly earrings for a couple of weeks before deciding I didn't want to look cheap after all and let the holes close up.

I defended my choice of friends, but Dad thought otherwise. He pointed out that many of the girls in my social group didn't seem ambitious beyond marriage and weren't headed for college like me. As it turned out, a few of them did marry early and had babies right away.

Sally and I faced the move to Studio City with lukewarm enthusiasm. The four years we lived on Stanton Avenue were the happiest and most carefree times of our youth. Sadly, there would be no going back.

CHAPTER 10

Bellaire Avenue

In August 1951, we moved to Studio City, and my life changed dramatically. Our new home on Bellaire Avenue was lovely and large, and I had my own bedroom for the first time, but that didn't make up for missing Stanton Avenue and my friends. Gone were the days of horseback riding and hanging out at Roger's corral, baseball games in the street, activities at Lake Street Baptist Church, swimming at the Pickwick Swim Park, going to the movies at the Cornell Theater, roller skating at the outdoor rink, and bike riding in Griffith Park. I was starting high school in a new town where I didn't know a soul. Mom kept on drinking.

The house was located north of Ventura Boulevard between Coldwater Canyon Avenue and Whitsett Avenue. Anything south of Ventura Boulevard was considered more prestigious, a reputation that endured throughout the years. Many celebrities still prefer the hillsides of Studio City with views of the San Fernando Valley. Our neighborhood wasn't in the hills, but its desirability endured because of the attractive, custom-built homes, shady, tree-lined streets, and proximity to many of the movie studios. Ours was the last house on Bellaire Avenue at the corner of Valleyheart

Drive, which runs parallel to the cemented Los Angeles River channel. The river was barely a trickle in the summer, but during winter storms, it could become a rushing torrent.

Across the street from our house, looking east, was a large undeveloped parcel of land with some tumbleweeds and a well-worn footpath leading to Ventura Boulevard. The lot eventually became the lush green links of the Studio City Golf Course. Unfortunately, the golf course wasn't built until years after we moved away. While we lived there, Sally, age eleven, and her friends enjoyed playing in the open field. After a winter rain, the soil burst forth with wild grass that was perfect for making hidden forts. With the field in front of our house and the river to the south, we were isolated from all but two neighbors. The seclusion might have been nice if I'd been an adult. However, as a girl in her teens, I felt isolated and lonely.

Living in this house was not about making good memories. It was simply the experience of residing in a beautiful home. The house had been designed and built by owners who had an eye for quality and had spared no expense. A shake-shingled roof and diamond-paned living room windows gave the home an English cottage appearance. In front, pink roses climbed against a tall, white picket fence, obscuring the side portion of the backyard where there was a paved badminton court. The brick entry path lined with flowers (daffodils in the spring) was at the corner of the property and sloped upward toward the front door. Visitors often remarked about the unique, heavy wooden door that was cut in half Dutch style and embellished with chunky iron hardware. Sometimes Mom left the top half of the door open to let in the breeze. We had no air conditioning.

My father could hardly tolerate summer in the San Fernando Valley when the heat was at its worst. One insufferably hot day, he came home from work and announced, "Get ready. We're going to the beach."

We hurriedly packed a few things and drove to Malibu where we had dinner and stayed overnight at a motel fronting the ocean. The waves crashing on the shore kept me awake, but it was sure cooler than at home.

A covered patio paved in flagstones was at the rear of the house. More flagstones were laid out on the ground, separated by dichondra grass. This created a place for additional seating, shaded in summer by a canopy of Chinese elms. A flagstone pathway led to the garage with its entrance on Valleyheart Drive. Another pathway led to the guesthouse, which had its own kitchen and bathroom. Mom fixed up the guesthouse and rented it to a young couple for a short time. Although the backyard was nicely landscaped, our family never entertained friends there or had a barbeque. Sally and I spent little time in the backyard and rarely played badminton on the paved court.

Our cocker spaniel, Taffy (Timmy was given away before we moved), gained the most benefit from the backyard. Living a comfortable dog's life, she ran around sniffing out smells, soaked up the sun on winter days, and dozed in the shade when the weather turned warm. Taffy was soon joined by a new pal when my parents acquired a German shepherd. Mom chose Lori as the puppy's name because she loved the song "Annie Lauri." Lori was sweet, gentle, and smart, wedging her way into our hearts right away. When Taffy died of old age, Lori became the number one dog in our family.

My mother was the main caretaker when it came to feeding, grooming, and clean-up for the dogs. Dad took charge of the obedience training. I could tell he loved dogs by the firm yet caring way he handled them. Lori was one of his favorites. Still, he could be tough and demanding. Our dogs had to be well-behaved in the house and weren't allowed to get up on the couch or sleep on the beds. They weren't supposed to beg at the table until my grandmother visited.

"Mama, why is Lori sitting alert at your chair? Are you feeding her again?" Dad always seemed to catch Nanny whenever she slipped food under the table. He then embarked on a lecture about how dogs are healthier and live longer when they don't eat table scraps.

"I won't do it again," my grandmother promised, but we all knew that she would.

Our living room was comfortable and decorated in an Early American style with a newly purchased sectional couch and, of course, Dad's favorite wingback chair. The room had a handsome stone fireplace, hardwood floors, wooden beams on the ceiling, a built-in bookshelf, and a perfect space for our baby grand piano by the diamond-paned front windows.

The dining room was separated from the living room by wooden posts. The French provincial table in the dining room was my father's place of choice for working on his scripts at night. His lined yellow legal pad and plethora of eraser-tipped pencils were the tools of his trade. He didn't know how to type and never owned a typewriter. Of course, there were no computers in those days. His movie scripts were handwritten and turned over to his secretary for typing. Martha Kitchen was the capable secretary he admired and relied on at Cate and McGlone.

There were many times when I said, "Goodnight, Dad," while he was writing at the table only to find him still there when I woke up in the morning. "I work better at night when the house is quiet," he always said.

Dad relied on black coffee and cigarettes—Camels or Chesterfields—to stay awake when he was working. Both of my parents were heavy smokers. In those days, the dangers of cancer and other lung diseases had not been documented as they are today. My mother instinctively knew that her nagging cough was from the cigarettes, and she beseeched Sally and me not to take up what she called "a dirty habit." Unfortunately, my parents' habits would one day catch up with them and cut their lives short.

In one of her argumentative moments, I overheard my mother admonish my father for using the amphetamine Dexedrine, and he didn't deny it. He said he used the stimulant only occasionally when a pressing deadline forced him to keep writing until his script was finished. Naturally, it made him more edgy than usual, but such was the life of a writer, I assumed.

My bedroom was at the front of the house next to the front door. It was a small room and originally intended as a den. My bed sat under the curved front windows, which were shaded outside by a green canvas awning. A built-in mirrored bar with glass shelving and indirect lighting was the perfect spot for displaying my perfume bottles and jewelry box. I had my own bathroom off the hallway that led to the kitchen.

Sally's bedroom was on the opposite side of the house. It was smaller than mine but big enough to hold her single bed, dresser, and the matching maple corner shelving unit that held her bronzed metal horse collection. An outside glass-paned door led to the covered patio.

The master bedroom was across the hall from Sally's room. My parents had a large, luxurious bedroom with its own fireplace and emerald-green carpeting. A separate dressing room led to the master bathroom that had a second door, giving Sally access from her bedroom.

Some of the rooms in the house were wallpapered in an Early American print, which was in style and went with our Early American furnishings. The expensive custom curtains we inherited from the former owners were an attractive feature. Most of the windows were covered in white, ruffled tiebacks of imported fine cotton, reminding me of fluffy, white clouds.

Here's another interesting thing about the house. In 1996, it was featured in several scenes from the movie *Two Days in the Valley*. When I saw the movie, I was surprised as heck to see our house on the big screen.

After we moved in, Mom was more noticeably under the influence of alcohol. When Sally and I came home from school, we could see that she had sleepy eyes and her speech was slurred. During dinner, after too many beers, she often started a fight with my father. Sally and I had to listen to our parents argue while we ate. Sometimes information that shouldn't have reached our ears was thoughtlessly tossed into the air. Worry over my mother's drinking and the nightly quarrels had a way of creeping into my thoughts, especially when I was sitting in a classroom trying to absorb a lesson. My confidence waned, and my studies suffered. Biting my nails was a habit that I couldn't break.

Taking geometry that first year in high school was the bane of my existence. I took geometry three times before finally getting a B grade in summer school. I put off taking the second semester of geometry until my senior year when dear Mrs. Rosen was my teacher. Knowing that I wanted to get into UCLA, she understood that I was mathematically challenged and took pity.

On the final day of class, I was the last student to leave the room and feared that I had flunked the course. Mrs. Rosen handed me the grade slip, rolled her eyes, and said, "Get out of here, and promise me you'll never take another math class." She gave me a C grade. I promised her with all my heart and grateful thanks. As promised, that was the last math class I ever took.

I didn't discuss the problems going on at home with anyone but Sally. I kept my worries to myself and hoped that my mother's drinking and the fights between my parents didn't reflect badly on me. I had little insight into psychological issues and internalized my feelings, believing I was different from my peers and somehow flawed. I thought everyone else's family was ideal, an erroneous conclusion for sure. More than ever, I missed my friends and the life I had left behind on Stanton Avenue.

I celebrated an unremarkable fifteenth birthday on Bellaire Avenue. Although I wasn't old enough to drive, I was already dreaming of having my own car. Out of the blue, Dad brought home an old Packard coupe with a cheap maroon paint job. It wasn't clear what he had in mind with the car, but he said to me, "It's yours to drive when you get your permit," and I was thrilled.

The car wasn't running right or the insurance cost too much, and to my disappointment, Dad got rid of the car.

For the next few years, I hoped and wished for a car as a Christmas gift. It turned into a game of sorts. On Christmas Eve, I'd start in on Dad. "I know you got me a car. I bet it's in the garage right now." After a few minutes of this, he'd stop me with an apologetic face and say, "I promise you, Susan, there's no car in the garage."

I had to look. After all, he was known for carrying out some great surprises, but, of course, there was no car. In all honesty, I knew he couldn't afford a car just for me. My parents were still sharing our family car and weren't able to buy a second car for Mom until I was nineteen.

Aunt June

Difficulties were emerging in the Clay family. Aunt June and Uncle Paul had moved from their rented farmhouse in Eagle Rock to La Canada where they purchased their first house.

Aunt June.

Growing Up Wise

Aunt June was thrilled to have her own home, though she had her hands full. Nanny was still living with them. My uncle's brother and elderly father had moved from Chicago and were now living in the guesthouse next to the garage. My cousin Gary was in junior high school, and my cousin Beverly was still living at home and working as a pottery artist at Gladding McBean. Aunt June kept more than busy cooking and cleaning for the whole bunch. During one of our visits, my aunt talked about the difficulty she had keeping food around and told us this story.

"They're eating me out of house and home. Pop's the worst. I hid a box of breakfast cereal in the washing machine, and he found it and ate the whole box. I decided to teach him a lesson. I emptied a can of Charlie's dog food into a nice dish, covered it with waxed paper, and put it in the refrigerator. Sure enough, Pop ate it." She laughed heartily and ended by saying, "He sure was surprised when I told him he'd eaten the dog's food."

Another one of Aunt June's stories described how she was nearly frightened to death one evening while washing the dinner dishes. It was dark outside, and she was staring mindlessly at the window over the kitchen sink. Suddenly the face of a monster popped up and looked her in the face. "I screamed bloody murder and thought I was going to faint."

It was Gary, her son, trying out his Halloween mask. Of course, we all burst out laughing. Aunt June had a way of telling stories that made them funny even if it wasn't her intention.

Things soon got more challenging for her. One day when I came home from school, Mom had something important to tell me. We went out on the patio to talk. "Beverly is pregnant," she said sadly.

Beverly wasn't married, and the father-to-be wasn't all that attentive. Upset, Mom figured this would diminish Beverly's chance of getting a good job and becoming something in life. She was a talented artist and had a bright future. "Let that be a lesson," Mom said. "Getting pregnant before you're married can sure put a damper on your life."

I took Mom's words to heart. I knew that having a baby out of wedlock could ruin a girl's reputation. I sure didn't want to be the bride in a shotgun wedding for the baby's sake, when the father agrees to marriage out of duty rather than love. I didn't want to drop out of school and go to a home for unwed mothers like some girls. This was enough to keep me and many young girls of my generation on the straight and narrow.

Aunt June soon had another person living in their already-cramped house when her grandson, Jeffrey, was born. Nevertheless, she embraced being a grandmother and adored her first grandchild, calling him "my little Jeffie." Jeff inherited significant artistic talent. As an adult, he worked for many years as a tattoo artist. Aunt June took care of Jeff temporarily. He lived with them in Hawaii when Uncle Paul was an executive in the purchasing department at Lockheed Aircraft on Oahu. Jeff was there when I visited in 1957.

Beverly married Jeff's father, but the marriage ended almost as soon as it began. She later married Bob Henry, and they had two daughters, Robin and Debby.

North Hollywood High School

My first day at North Hollywood High School turned out better than anticipated, thanks to meeting Marcia in the auditorium. We were both new to the area and initially hung out together during the lunch period. She was Jewish and, as nice as she was, continuing as her close friend wasn't an option. I couldn't risk someone finding out that I was half Jewish. I had never thought about it on Stanton Avenue, but high school was different. Getting in with the popular crowd was important to me, so I kept my Jewish heritage a secret. The humiliation inflicted by Sister Pascalita at the Catholic school was still fresh in my memory, and I hadn't forgotten Lynn's hateful bullying.

Hiding the fact that my father came from a Jewish background seems so silly to me now, but things were different then, and my perceptions were different. Prejudice against Jews was prevalent in the 1950s, and so was social segregation. California saw less prejudice than many other states, but there were still towns in California that had exclusionary covenants in place restricting the sale of homes to Jews and Negroes. College sororities were segregated both religiously and racially. I found that out later at UCLA when I was rushing a sorority.

Initially, I thought the older kids in the upper grades seemed pretty sophisticated. While I didn't feel out of place with the other tenth graders, my confidence wasn't what it had been on Stanton Avenue as if accidently left behind with the good memories. Soon I discovered there were clubs at school. Some were service oriented, and the rest were social clubs, somewhat like college sororities and fraternities before being outlawed in high schools. The social club members wore blazers to school each Wednesday, and the color of the jacket identified the particular club. I wanted to belong to a social club in the worst way, but I had no idea how to go about it.

One day, a girl sitting across the aisle from me in history class unexpectedly asked, "Would you be interested in coming to a Laudette rush party?" She was wearing a kelly-green jacket and belonged to one of the social clubs. I was thrilled and accepted her invitation.

Mom was my cheerleader and the person I went to for advice. When it came to the Laudette rush party, she gave me suggestions on what to wear and how to make a good impression. Despite her drinking problem, she was still there for me. Being younger than me, Sally didn't always get the help and support she needed growing up. She was shortchanged as the effects of Mom's drinking worsened year by year.

"You girls are the most important thing in my life," Mom always said, and we knew that was true. Unfortunately, it wasn't enough to keep her from drinking.

Dad gave me some good advice. One of his favorite sayings was "Better to remain silent and be thought a fool than to speak and remove all doubt." I took it to heart and made it my own.

Laudettes

Dad's advice and Mom's encouragement worked, because the Laudettes voted me into their club. I was ready and in my best pajamas when they came to get me early one Saturday morning. Off we went to Bob's Big Boy in Toluca Lake, stopping along the way to pick up more pledges. The new pledges, from every social club at our school, were at Bob's that morning, all of us wearing pajamas. Pledges had to do anything the actives requested such as take a big bite of the onion that they'd hung around our necks or do something silly and embarrassing in front of the boys. The traditional Hell Night took place a few weeks later, followed by the swearing-in ceremony.

I purchased my kelly-green jacket and started wearing it to school on Wednesday, paired with a pencil-slim, gray wool skirt. We wore matching green, sleeveless dresses with crinoline slips after the weather turned warm in the spring. The outfits were approved by the school and in line with its strict dress code. We were never allowed to wear long pants or capris, only skirts and dresses. The popular shoe styles were saddle shoes, penny loafers, and white buff oxfords. My favorite was the white buff oxford. Like the other girls, I carried a buff bag in my purse and applied white powder when the shoes got scuff marks.

Belonging to the Laudettes was the best thing about high school. I felt accepted and enjoyed having built-in friends. The club members were in all three grades—tenth, eleventh, and twelfth. As a tenth grader, I learned leadership skills from the older girls. This was a big advantage when I went to college. I was on my way to becoming a leader, but I didn't know it then. Sally joined the Laudettes four years later when she went to high school.

During lunch, the Laudettes sat together at a certain table in the quad area, and every club had its own table. The students who weren't in a club honored this unofficial assignment of tables to club members and found open seating elsewhere.

Wednesday night was meeting night for all the social clubs, including the Laudettes. We met alternatively at members' homes. The meetings were fun and a good excuse to get out of the house on a school night.

The best part of meeting night was afterward when we crammed into cars and headed for Bob's Big Boy. The drive-in was packed with high school kids coming from their various club meetings. The car hops were kept hopping with our orders of hamburgers, French fries, and cherry Cokes. Music blared loudly over the outside speakers with songs like "Unforgettable" and "Wheel of Fortune." Friends recognizing friends gathered in groups or crammed into cars. There was a lot of mingling and running around going on. If parking spots for the car service were scarce, we went inside the restaurant and squished six girls into a table for four. Sometimes we got a little rowdy and put sugar in the salt shaker and salt in the sugar container.

I put off having a Laudette meeting at my house for a while. Mom was more than agreeable, but I was worried that she'd embarrass me. By the end of the day and too many beers, there was no telling what might come out of her mouth. I could imagine her saying something like "I'm glad you accepted Susan into your club. She didn't have any friends."

When I finally did host a meeting, Mom was on her best behavior. I was on edge, as I always was when my friends were around my mother.

Sally and I often told Mom, "If you really loved us, you'd stop drinking." My greatest hope was that one day she'd find the courage to get sober and stay sober. I know now that she turned to alcohol as a refuge from an unhappy marriage and unresolved emotional problems stemming from her childhood. The mom that I had once admired for being fearless, capable, and strong was eroding away. Sometimes I'd get disgusted and curtly say to her, "I can see you're drunk again." I'd feel guilty, because I really did love her.

To her credit, Mom never neglected our home and the physical needs of our family. No matter how she felt, she got up on time in the morning, fixed breakfast, packed lunches, kept the house clean, did the laundry, and had a healthy dinner on the table every night. She was a fairly basic cook: meat and potatoes, because that's what Dad preferred. She made tasty roasts and steaks. Dad was primarily a beef eater and insisted on top-grade meat. Her Swiss steak with potatoes and carrots was a favorite meal.

Once, Mom tried to make matzo ball soup. The broth was fine, but the matzo balls came out heavy like golf balls. "There must be a trick to making them," she said sheepishly after noticing that Dad had taken only a few bites.

When Dad was away on business, Mom made a pot of chili beans, which she loved and he didn't. She'd serve them with a salad. Her salads were something else, and she had a way of announcing them like they were the most important part of the meal. "With dinner, we're having a nice green salad," she'd say proudly. The word *nice* had to be in there.

On top of her nice green salad would be leftover cooked vegetables—maybe peas, string beans, or carrots—and a dollop of cream cheese. When Sally and I grew up, we prided ourselves on learning how to make good salads sans leftovers and cheese balls, but in memory of Mom, we'd still laugh and say, "And with dinner, we're having a nice green salad."

If Mom had errands to run during the day, she finished them and was home by the time Sally and I arrived from school. Hers was a typical housewife's life for the era, made more mundane, I suspect, by the lack of outside intellectual pursuits or real social interaction with other women her age. Her friend Amelia Winters stayed in touch, but they didn't get together too often. Nanny continued to spend time at our house, although her visits seemed less frequent when we lived on Bellaire Avenue.

Mom enjoyed gardening, decorating the house, and refurbishing old furniture. While doing some gardening in the backyard, she happened to dig up a large, hand-carved wooden shoe that someone had buried there. It was quite a find. She cleaned and oiled the shoe, drilled a hole for wiring, bought a white linen shade, and turned it into a handsome lamp. "It's about as Early American as you can get," she said when she received compliments on the shoe lamp. Early American was the most popular decor of the day.

I always admired my mother's mechanical ability and her willingness to take on creative projects. She was the electrician, plumber, and handyman in the family. Being raised in a New York apartment, Dad was not good with his hands. However, he later developed an interest in gardening and created the most unique lawn when we moved to another house.

Our kitchen was large with Armstrong linoleum flooring in a red brick pattern. The window above the sink overlooked a sunny, south-facing rose garden. On the other side of the kitchen was an eat-in space next to a picture window that overlooked the covered porch and the yard. Mom found the perfect breakfast table and chairs at a secondhand store. She painted the set bumblebee yellow with an embellishment of red, blue, and green flowers. The table and chairs were cute but looked like a find from a Mexican store on Olvera Street. Bright!

Dad normally worked long hours, especially during the editing stage of a film. The filming phase often required trips out of town that could take him away from home for longer periods of time. Toward the end of our first year on Bellaire Avenue, Dad decided to take a well-paying temporary job with a company in San Francisco. He began commuting between there and home and was away a lot. Mom had her hobbies to keep her busy, but she was undoubtedly lonely. One evening she had a gentleman caller, the electrician who had done some work for us on Stanton Avenue. Their earlier phone conversations hadn't gone unnoticed, and I suspected something was up.

That night, Mom put on her lovely, crème-colored satin robe with the flowing sleeves and shrimp-colored lining that Dad had given her one Christmas. Putting two and two together, I went to bed but didn't go to sleep. In about an hour, I heard the front door open and a man's voice. Furious, I decided to intervene. Not wanting to come face to face with the man, I waited a few minutes and then called out loudly, "Who's there, Mom? Is someone there? Who are you talking to?" I threatened to get up and check. Minutes later, I heard whispering at the front door and hushed goodbyes as the electrician left.

I was angry and told Dad about it when he got back in town. The decision to tell was motivated more about wanting to gain his favor than a desire to protect him. Naturally, it created a huge blowup between my parents, and it sure didn't help me. In Dad's eyes, I was the bearer of bad news. I felt like an immature snitch and regretted my involvement. I vowed to stay out of their drama from then on. The emotional roller coaster of my life was careening downhill.

It was fortunate at this critical point in Sally's life that she met two wonderful friends in the sixth grade at Dixie Canyon Elementary School. Barbara and June were like Sally's soulmates. In one short year, they bonded and created some wonderful childhood memories. The three of them stayed in contact until after Sally married, but eventually they lost touch.

Eons later, Barbara and June miraculously came back into our lives after finding Sally on the internet. They have remained good friends of both of us for years now, and we've been able to see each other and stay connected through our daily email conversations. What a blessing!

Friends for the Weekend

My friends Marlene and Barbara from Glendale came for a visit one weekend. Sally had friends visiting as well. Dad was working out of town, and Sally and I took advantage of his absence to have our friends stay overnight, knowing things were more peaceful—no arguments—with him gone.

After dinner, we decided to play ring-the-doorbell-and-run-away for old time's sake. Off we went up the dark street, giggling and ready to have some fun. When it was Sally's turn to ring the doorbell, she entered the covered front porch of a tidy house and did the deed. The rest of us watched from our shadowy hiding places, ready to take off running. In her effort to make a swift retreat, Sally took a giant leap off the porch that was wet from just being washed off with the hose. Her foot slipped, and she went down on her stomach onto the edged corners of bricks that bordered the flower bed below the porch.

Sally said, "I lost my wind completely. As I staggered slowly forward, hunched over for lack of oxygen, the lady opened the door and asked, 'Are you okay?' I couldn't speak. I could only hobble away, grasping my stomach, as I tried to disappear into the evening twilight. I never turned around to say sorry but only wished to be invisible in this horrible episode of ding-dong-ditch gone terribly wrong."

The rest of us thought this was the funniest thing we'd ever seen. We laughed until our sides ached. Poor Sally was not a bit pleased that we were having so much fun at her expense.

Fun Things to Do

Ice-skating and shopping were still my favorite pastimes. Occasionally on a Saturday, I took the bus by myself to the Polar Palace in Hollywood for an afternoon of ice-skating. More often, I walked to the main part of Studio City and browsed through the shops along Ventura Boulevard.

During the summer, I made regular treks to the beach. I took the bus to Hollywood and then transferred to a streetcar headed for Santa Monica. My destination was Roadside Rest, a place on the sand named for the adjacent hamburger joint on Pacific Coast Highway. It was a quiet ocean road. In those days, anywhere along the coast was relatively crowd free and unspoiled. This particular stretch of white sand beach wasn't frequented by families with children, making it a favorite place on the shoreline for high school and college kids.

Beach volleyball was becoming popular, and I enjoyed watching the action on the sand courts at Roadside Rest. It was primarily a men-only sport, and the guys playing were usually the best looking and physically fit.

There were groups of kids who came to the beach regularly, and I made friends with them, including some of the boys who were there to bodysurf. None of them asked for my phone number, though secretly I had eyes for the lifeguards—gorgeous, bronzed hunks with sun-bleached hair, wearing dark sunglasses and their official red swimming trunks. They didn't give me a second glance.

Getting a dark tan was a priority. Using Coppertone suntan lotion or baby oil mixed with iodine, I slathered my body from head to toe and stretched out on my towel on the sand to let the sun do its work. The darker I got, the better. We didn't know anything about the dangers of skin cancer and the importance of wearing sunblock. It's a miracle that my skin survived that kind of abuse without any real damage showing up later in life.

When I wasn't suntanning, I went bodysurfing with the boys. I was usually the only girl in the water with them. It was exciting to wait for the perfect wave, ride its crest, and zoom to shore under the power of the foaming water. I stayed in the water for hours, not worrying about anyone taking my things on the sand: a beach towel, wooden canvas backrest, and small beach bag holding my brush, mirror, lipstick, coin purse, and suntan oil. I carried no watch because I could stay as long as I wanted.

I knew about the surfboard riders in Hawaii. My dream was to go there and learn how to surf on a long board. It wouldn't be until 1957, while visiting Aunt June and Uncle Paul in Oahu, that I had the chance. They lived in a house close to Waikiki Beach, and I took surfboard lessons from a Hawaiian beach boy.

Back in 1951, however, I didn't know that the sport of Hawaiian surfboarding had already reached Surfrider Beach in Malibu. A ragtag counterculture of surfers with handles like Lord Gallo, Thrifty Phil, Scooter Boy, Moondoggie, and Tubesteak were riding the waves on surfboards and developing a lingo all their own.

"Cowabunga!"

Bodysurfing called for strong arms and a good swimming ability, which I had. One afternoon, I hadn't paid attention to the growing size of the waves. Around four o'clock, the waves could go from regular to giant. I caught the crest of a wave and realized too late that I was on top of a mountain. Looking straight down, I could see the wet sand where the retreating water had been sucked into the wave. The wave let go, and I dropped hard to the ocean floor as the full force of the water fell on top of me. I rolled over and over and upside down, not knowing which way was up. The strap of my bathing suit snapped, and I ran out of breath as my body washed up onshore.

A strong hand grabbed mine and pulled me out of the water on my belly. One of the guys sitting on the sand had noticed my predicament and came to help. Coughing and snorting, my bathing suit curled up at my waist, exposing my breasts, I was embarrassed but glad to be alive. "Thank you," I said as I hiked up my bathing suit and staggered to dry ground.

From then on, I made sure that I was out of the water before those giant waves hit.

A Date with Joe

I went out with an older boy on a fix-up date that my friend Peggy put together. Dad met Peggy once and said she was cheap. He was right, as usual, but I thought she was fun, and that was all that mattered to me.

Joe was rough around the edges, and I knew he was a bad boy type. Still, I wanted to go on a date and accepted his offer for an afternoon drive. We ended up near Mulholland Drive in the Santa Monica Mountains where we parked to look at the view of the Hollywood Lake reservoir.

Joe kissed me and then got fresh. I put up a struggle and said, "Take me home, or I'm walking." I took a bobby pin out of my hair and held it in my fist as a weapon. It was a stupid thing to do, because he had muscles and strength. He laughed, made a few more moves, and finally took me home. He kept calling me for another date, but I wasn't about to make that mistake again.

First Job

The summer following tenth grade, I wanted a job and the chance to earn spending money for clothes. Not yet sixteen, I couldn't work in a dress shop or anything like that. I envied the boys who worked as box boys at the local grocery stores at fourteen. Girls were never hired for those jobs. We were stuck with babysitting mostly.

In the newspaper, I saw an advertisement for a summer part-time mother's helper. Mom drove me to the interview with Mrs. Gunter, and I got the job.

Mrs. Gunter was in her late twenties, married to a handsome man, and had two preschool children named Judy and Ricky. Her home was across the street from North Hollywood Junior High School where Sally would go in September. Mrs. Gunter was outgoing and fun. I worked four to five hours a day from Monday through Friday, helping her with the kids and household chores. Once we went to her sister's hillside home above the Sunset Strip for an afternoon of swimming. Mrs. Gunter was easy to be around. I felt safe opening up to her about some of the personal things going on in my life, and she was a good listener and empathetic. It was the perfect first job.

When the summer ended, I searched the newspaper ads for an after-school job and got one working for a married couple. Mr. and Mrs. Toplitt lived in a large, Spanish hacienda-style home not far from us. I took the bus there after school, and Mom picked me up after dinner. I had assigned housekeeping duties, which included washing the dishes after I ate dinner with the couple.

After such a positive experience with Mrs. Gunter, I didn't expect this job to turn out as badly as it did. My first challenge was learning how to wash the dishes in a kosher kitchen where certain foods and their serving dishes were kept separate. Mrs. Toplitt had recently lost a hundred pounds, and meals were healthy without starchy side dishes or desserts. She suggested that I needed to lose weight. At my sensitive age, I was taken aback but admittedly could have lost five pounds.

Conversations at the dinner table revolved around politics and current events. The couple involved me in their discussions and sought to explain the governmental process. I was more interested in talking about my school activities and friends. At fifteen, I cared little who was running for public office and dreaded having to sit through those heady conversations during dinner. Table talk in my house was never about politics.

Mrs. Toplitt was an odd duck. When I arrived at the house after school, the front door was unlocked so I could let myself in. She was normally sitting at a large weaving loom in the living room, the movements of her hands keeping rhythm to the strains of Wagner or Tchaikovsky playing loudly on the stereo. I nodded hello because I wasn't supposed to interrupt her.

Dusting the furniture and dry mopping the red tile floors were the daily chores. Mrs. Toplitt followed up by running her hand over certain places. I always seemed to leave a little dust behind on the floor, and her disapproval embarrassed me. Such fastidiousness made me appreciate Mom, who was more relaxed about her housekeeping.

One afternoon, I arrived to find a rack of freshly baked chocolate chip cookies cooling on a movable cart in the kitchen. Chocolate chip was my favorite cookie, and I couldn't resist. I took one and rearranged the rest.

Mrs. Toplitt came into the kitchen and said, "I made seventy-five cookies for my nephew in the army." She started counting. "One, two, three, four…"

"I ate one," I said, and she gave me a nasty look.

When I got home that night, I told Mom, "I never want to go back there again." The next day we drove over to the house, and Mom picked up my work clothes while I waited in the car. On the way home, I said I wanted to get a regular job. "Maybe I'll get lucky and find a job as a salesgirl in a dress shop."

Mom thought that was a good idea.

Dad's Work

One Saturday morning, Dad had a film shoot nearby, and I went along. He was the writer for an educational movie about safe driving. For about a block, Ventura Boulevard was closed off to traffic for a few hours. A skilled race car driver was directed to speed down the street, slam on the brakes, and spin the car in a circle. There were a couple of practice runs.

"How'd you like to be the passenger?" Dad asked.

"Sure,'" I said, jumping at the chance. It was a thrill to ride with the stunt driver, though my face wasn't visible in the finished film.

Dad's best friend for many years was Alan Stensvold. He was an accomplished cinematographer, TV camera operator, and founding member of the American Society of Cinematographers. Al was married to Vera, and they had two small sons, Mike and Larry. The family came to dinner at our house on several occasions. Al was down to earth and a genuinely nice man. Dad had great respect for Al and enjoyed working with him. They maintained a close personal friendship as well as a business relationship. They regularly talked on the telephone. I noticed that Dad's manner with Al was different than the way he spoke to his other friends, almost brotherly. "How ya doing, kid?" was the way my father usually started the conversation.

In 1958, Dad wrote the screenplay and Al Stensvold was the cinematographer for the movie *Thunder Road*. Robert Mitchum wrote the original story about bootlegging and produced and directed the film. The film has become somewhat of a cult favorite, especially in the South.

Dad's boss, Ed McGlone, and his wife were also dinner guests at our home. Ed had a son my age, and I looked forward to meeting him, but he was studious, quiet, and not my type.

I noticed a boy at school who I thought was cute. During lunch, he hung out with a group of kids who didn't belong to any of the clubs. I went out of my way to walk by him and tried to make flirty eye contact. I wised up after a friend said, "Forget it. He's Mormon, and they only date Mormon girls."

One evening, I had a blind date as part of a foursome. My girlfriend's date showed up with a newer convertible. The top was down, and it was one of those special nights in the San Fernando Valley—warm and balmy with a light wind blowing like the trade winds in Hawaii. We went miniature golfing and then to Bob's Big Boy for French fries and Cokes. Afterward, we drove the streets while talking, laughing, and singing as we enjoyed the starry night and the wind in our hair.

School Activities

I had adjusted to high school and was making friends. I declared English as a major and Spanish as a minor. I took Spanish for all three years of high school and another two years in college. The five years of study gave me a fluency in Spanish that I still enjoy. While geometry gave me the biggest headache, I found that I had a good ear for languages, and Spanish came easy if I did the homework.

I also took a typing class and was surprised when during roll call on the first day of class, the teacher called out a familiar name from my past. It was Judy from Bedford Drive whose mother served that wonderful potato soup. After class, we said hello and acknowledged the coincidence of winding up at the same high school after starting first grade together in Catholic school.

In those days, we only had four high schools in the San Fernando Valley: North Hollywood, San Fernando, Van Nuys, and Canoga Park. Rivalries were fierce, and I loved going to the football games and cheering for the North Hollywood Huskies. I had dreams of becoming a cheerleader or pom-pom girl. I tried out for the drill team with my best friend, Sheila. She made it, and I didn't. Later, she became a pom-pom girl. While she was dancing on the field, I sat in the bleachers with my other Laudette friends and enjoyed watching the games.

Looking back at my yearbook pictures, the first thing noticeable is the lack of black or brown people. The school was nearly 100 percent white. Today, it is probably only 5 percent white and 90 percent Hispanic with a representation of other nationalities including Asian, African American, and Armenian.

For one semester, a Negro girl went to our school. She was the only African American student to attend while I was there. Some Mexican students came from the Sun Valley area, all tough-looking with ominous reputations. They didn't mix with the white kids, but hung out on the football field, smoking cigarettes during the lunch period. The rest of us stayed in the quad area near the cafeteria. I had never heard of marijuana, but someone said they smoked it. The Mexican girls wore their hair teased and ratted high and were rumored to carry razor blades in the nests on top of their heads.

"They're Pachucas," my friend Sheila said. "Keep your distance."

One of the Pachucas named Rosie was in my Spanish class. Pachuca or not, Rosie was friendly and had a great sense of humor. I liked her a lot.

Being comfortable with Rosie paid off. One day, I walked into the gym bathroom and found myself alone with five Pachuca girls. They stared at me menacingly, their hairstyles bringing to mind images of razor blades. Several of them took an intimidating stance to block the mirror. Thinking of Rosie, I decided to say something. "Hola." I smiled. "Cómo está?"

They glared at me warily for a moment and then backed away from the mirror. It was a lesson in treating someone with respect and getting it back. From then on, I wasn't afraid of the Mexican girls.

We had a few fights on the school campus. One in particular was violent. Two muscled boys got into a fistfight like a couple of pit bulls. I found myself at the front of the onlookers' circle just in time to see a punch thrown and hear the sound of a nose breaking. Blood spurted everywhere. I gagged and almost threw up.

Sparring between some of the boys usually took on a more humorous aspect, ending with someone getting wedged into a trash can. Feet sticking up in the air, unable to move, the humiliated boy pleaded, "Help, someone get me out of here." The onlookers, of course, laughed their heads off, and finally someone helped the kid.

The annual theater productions at North Hollywood High School, as well as those at Van Nuys High School and Hollywood High School, took on a professionalism that often drew Hollywood talent scouts. Just regular students attending their neighborhood schools, some of the singers, actors, and actresses had exceptional talent and went on to have illustrious careers in the entertainment business.

As a tenth grader, I saw my first musical play, *Brigadoon*. Every year the school put on a wonderful musical production, and I developed an enduring passion for live musical theater. A North Hollywood student who became a top movie star was gymnast Russ Tamblyn, who starred in *West Side Story* and *Seven Brides for Seven Brothers*. Victor French, after graduation, costarred with Michael Landon in the television series *Little House on the Prairie* and *Stairway to Heaven*. Natalie Wood, Marilyn Monroe, and Jane Russell went to Van Nuys High School.

Dad had a contagious enthusiasm for live musical theater. He told captivating stories of living in Manhattan and seeing Broadway shows and going to the opera. He enjoyed the operettas of Gilbert and Sullivan and, as a writer, loved their clever, rhyming lyrics. When a production of *The Pirates of Penzance* came to Hollywood, he made arrangements for the family to go. A look of pure pleasure and excitement came over his face talking about it. "I want you and Sally to have exposure to great writing," he told me.

He had a love for words. I didn't fully appreciate the experience at the time, but that changed when I got older.

Earthquake

On July 21, 1952, we were sound asleep when the ground shook violently just before dawn. "Earthquake! Get under the doorjamb," Mom yelled.

I jumped out of bed and clung to the side of the doorway. Across the living room, on the opposite side of the house, I could see my parents and sister hanging onto the doorway. Our piano, which rested on small wheels, rolled back and forth across the hardwood floor like a child's toy. Bright flashes outside intermittently illuminated the room as electrical transformers went down. It was the scariest thing I had ever experienced. When the shaking stopped, we gathered together and turned on the television.

The epicenter of the earthquake was in Kern County at the southern end of the Sierra Nevada mountain range. The small town of Tehachapi had taken a big hit, experiencing heavy damage. Photos of its downed water tower became the symbol of destruction. Twelve people were killed, nine of them in Tehachapi. This was my first earthquake and a rude introduction to the hazards of living in California.

Moving North

By the beginning of the eleventh grade, the memories of Stanton Avenue were fading. I was enjoying the start of another high school year and my new friends. The Laudettes voted me sergeant at arms. I looked forward to replacing my after-school job with something better. An unexpected change came along, and my life zipped off in a different direction again.

During dinner one night, my parents announced that we were moving. Dad had grown tired of the San Francisco commute, and it looked like his temporary job was going to last longer than expected. "I've taken a larger furnished apartment in the building where I've been staying," he said, explaining it would accommodate our family.

The building was at the top of California Street on Nob Hill, a block from the famous Fairmont Hotel and Inter-Continental Mark Hopkins Hotel. The plan was to rent our house furnished and move to San Francisco.

"This will be an exciting adventure," Dad said. "You girls will get a chance to experience big city life, like in Manhattan where I grew up."

The house was rented quickly, and the day came for us to leave for San Francisco. With our clothes and personal belongings bundled, boxed, and stuffed into the trunk of the Nash Ambassador, we headed out before dawn on that memorable morning. Dad was at the wheel with Mom next to him. Our German shepherd, Lori, snuggled between Sally and me on the backseat. Reluctantly, Sally and I were about to become city girls. What would the future hold? We had no idea.

CHAPTER 11

San Francisco

The drive to Northern California was pleasant as I tried to imagine what my life would be like living in a city like San Francisco. Along the way, I enjoyed the scenery as it drifted by, lost in thought as early morning shadows gave way to sunshine. The rolling hillsides dotted with native oaks were beautiful. We passed agricultural hamlets and eventually a chain of small towns in what is now Silicon Valley. As we neared San Francisco, aged clapboard row houses appeared. Unlike the upscale Victorian houses found in affluent sections of San Francisco, these smaller, south-of-the-city, Victorian-style bungalows hugged hilly streets, looking faded and weathered in a place where fog brought its own dreariness. We were almost there.

California Street

At first sight, the city was breathtakingly beautiful: the notorious steep hills bustling with activity, views of the bay, two magnificent bridges, and the charming cable cars with their clanging bells. Our new home was not so appealing except for its spectacular location on California Street at the top of Nob Hill. The hill was often referred to as Snob

Hill because of its affluent apartment buildings, well-to-do people, classy hotels, and picturesque views.

Dad played up the advantages of living in an apartment hotel. "It has a front desk and weekly maid service. You girls won't have to do any housework." He failed to mention the age of the building.

"I'm worried about this place," Mom said as we toured our apartment. The building had been built before the 1906 earthquake with electrical wiring that was suspect.

Fortunately, there was a fire escape. Shortly after we moved in, Mom gave us instructions on how to get out of the apartment in case of a fire. We were on the second floor next to Jones Street, an uphill side street. The living room windows were only a half story above the sidewalk with a fire escape on the outside. Next to the living room was the bedroom that Sally and I shared. It had a window that also faced Jones Street and an eastern exposure that let in the early morning sun. If we stuck our heads out of the window, we could see the cable cars as they traveled up and down California Street.

Sally and I thought Mom was being overly cautious with her fire drills. However, about two years later, after we had moved away, our apartment was one of two seriously damaged by smoke in a fire. The building was eventually demolished and replaced by a tall, modern condominium.

Our apartment came furnished. It was clean but plain and cheerless. My parents shared a dark bedroom that had a curtained window overlooking the dead space between the buildings. There was a small, windowless bathroom and a dreary kitchen that had a window over the sink with the same ugly view of the dead space. The front door next to my parents' bedroom led to the second-floor hallway and the interior of the building. Unlike the modern apartments in Studio City with their outside entrances, picture windows, green landscaping, and swimming pools, this building had no redeeming features. It smelled musty and looked as old and tired as some of the residents. It was expensive to live there. In fact, anything in a decent area of San Francisco was extraordinarily expensive.

"This was a good find," Dad said with conviction, but I soon wondered how I'd ever adjust to living there.

Lowell High School

Through a friend, Dad secured my enrollment in Lowell High School. It was a prestigious public school and the only one of its kind in the city with an alumni roster of some of the most successful business leaders in the country. It offered only a college prep program, and entrance required a B average. Staying in the school meant maintaining that average. I started the eleventh grade at Lowell a few weeks after the fall semester had begun.

The high school was across town. To get there, I took the cable car, which stopped in front of our apartment on California Street, transferred to a southbound bus on Van Ness Avenue, and then took another bus the rest of the way. Unlike back home where the buses ran every thirty minutes, this was the city with convenient and rapid public transportation. Getting back and forth to school was not difficult.

Sally was in the seventh grade and in junior high school. She also rode the cable car and then transferred to a northbound bus on Van Ness Avenue. To show her the way, Mom accompanied Sally on her first day of school. The next day, Sally made the trip alone. She hadn't been gone long when she showed up back at our apartment. "I missed the bus," she tearfully told our mother. Mom replied, "Honey, the buses run every five minutes. If it happens again, just wait for the next one." Sally had no idea.

Interestingly, there was a girl from Sally's school whose father was a guard at Alcatraz Federal Penitentiary, the maximum-security facility on an island near the Golden Gate Bridge. Sally's friend came across the bay each school day on a ferry that brought people from the island to the mainland. The federal prison was home to such notable criminals as Al Capone, Mickey Cohen, Arthur R. "Doc" Barker, and Robert Franklin Stroud (the "Birdman of Alcatraz"). There was also housing for the Bureau of Prison staff and their families. The prison closed in 1963 and today is a popular destination for visitors on sightseeing tours.

Without friends to hang out with after school, Sally came home one afternoon and told Mom she was taking Lori for a nice walk. Everyone knew that walking in San Francisco could be challenging because of the steep hills, but Sally had to find it out the hard way.

She said, "I started walking down the hills toward Market Street, and after walking for about an hour, I realized that Market Street was way too far. By then I had entered a seedy part of town. Street people were checking me out, and one man asked what kind of dog I was walking. I was uncomfortable and glad to have a German shepherd at my side for protection. I turned around and headed for home only to find that it was way more difficult climbing those steep hills than going down them."

Two and a half hours later, Sally dragged herself into the apartment, exhausted.

"Where have you been all this time?" Mom asked in an angry tone.

She might have seemed upset, but Sally said, "I knew she was just worried. I told her what happened and vowed not to make that mistake again."

The Lowell High School curriculum was rigorous and required plenty of homework. I noticed that during the lunch period, students didn't waste time hanging out in the cafeteria or gathering in the walled-in recreational area that held a couple of basketball courts and benches. They studied alone in the library or huddled in study groups in the stairwells and along the hallways. No noontime socializing in this school like at North Hollywood High School. Tests were frequent, and the students were focused on getting into a good university like Stanford or the University of California, Berkeley. If I wanted to stay in the school, I had to buckle down and improve my study habits.

For Spanish, I had a Castilian teacher. He pronounced Spanish words with the distinct "th" sound that characterizes the dialect. I thought it was strange and missed my former teacher, Mr. Campos, who had a soft Mexican way of speaking Spanish.

My physiology teacher had students stand up when they answered a question. We were learning the bones and muscles in the body. The teacher pointed to something on the skeleton and asked, "What is this, Miss Wise?" You can bet that I came to class prepared. I didn't want to embarrass myself by not knowing the answer. I can still remember my efforts to learn the Latin term for the hip bone, *os coxae*.

Because of the colder weather, the girls' gym classes were usually held inside the gymnasium. Instead of shorts and white blouses like at North Hollywood High School, the girls wore old-fashioned blue bloomers with elastic around the legs, the kind Mom wore in her youth. Clean but previously used bloomers were available in a bin, and I picked one out for myself that fit. At first, I felt silly but soon discovered that bloomers were comfortable and didn't ride up like shorts. That was beneficial when I was playing a fast game of volleyball.

Winter brought with it my indoctrination to the San Francisco weather patterns. First, there was the fog. One school morning, I headed out without a scarf on my head, knowing that my naturally wavy hair became curlier and usually looked better on foggy days. The San Francisco fog was not like anything I had experienced before. They called it fog, but it could be so dense with moisture that it was almost like rain. By the time I got to school, my hair was dripping wet.

The rain was something else. The first rainfall of the season was light, but I noticed that many kids came to school wearing full-length yellow slickers and matching hats, the gear that fishermen wore. The next time it rained, I headed for school with my umbrella in hand, wearing a short coat as I did in Southern California. As I stood in front of our building waiting for the cable car, the wind blew fiercely up the hill and whipped my umbrella inside out. The rain was coming at me sideways. By the time I reached school, I was pretty wet.

Mom gave me the money to buy a yellow slicker, and I joined the fishermen. That's the way it was in San Francisco. The Northern California winter storms were mighty as they swept across the bay, bringing heavy winds that drove the rain into your body. Staying home from school when it rained was preferential, but I couldn't do that and risk falling behind in my studies.

Making friends at Lowell was a challenge. Students came from all over the city. The campus didn't have a close community feeling from my perspective as a new student. With lunchtime used for studying, it was hard to make friends, and in-class talking wasn't allowed. Lowell had a Big Sister Program to help the incoming new student adjust. My big sister was a senior and a popular school leader with plans to attend UC Berkeley. She was friendly, showed me around, and introduced me to a few of her friends.

I met a nice girl, also a junior, in the cafeteria. She had recently moved to San Francisco from Spokane, Washington. Her name was Elaine, and she became my new best friend and the only real friend I had at Lowell.

Elaine lived across town from me, near our school, in a tired-looking apartment building. Her parents were older than mine, and her siblings, including an older sister she talked about fondly, were all young adults. I visited her apartment once and decided that mine looked mighty good by comparison. Needing a friend mattered more to me than my fear of Mom being drunk, so I invited her over. Elaine sometimes visited me after school and stayed overnight a few times. Occasionally, we went shopping together on the weekend. Once we went on a double date to the amusement pier at the beach with soldiers who had been in the Korean War. One was a friend of hers; the other was a friend of his and my date. They were nice guys. My date had a wooden leg and had earned a Purple Heart.

I admired Elaine's good looks. She was pretty enough to be a movie star with large, dark eyes, flawless skin, a dimple in the middle of one cheek, and silky, shoulder-length, chestnut-brown hair. She had a gentle nature and pleasant sense of humor. During one sleepover at our apartment, she confided in me about her boyfriend in Spokane. They had been involved in a sexual relationship, and she missed him. I couldn't relate because I had barely dated.

A boy sitting in front of me in literature class was suave, smart, sophisticated, popular, and gorgeous. What I wouldn't give to go out with him, but Pete, like the lifeguards at Roadside Rest in Santa Monica, hardly knew I was alive. In my attempts to make clever conversation, I felt awkward and silly. He was a senior and way out of my league. No matter. I was head over heels for the guy.

As November neared, Mom asked me several times what I wanted for my birthday. "All I want is Pete," I'd tell her. That became my mantra. Mom teased me and referred to him as "Pete, Pete So Divine."

Getting to Know the City

Although I had school to keep me busy and Elaine and Sally for companionship, I was often lonely and depressed. The frequency of cloudy or foggy days was a downer. Sometimes the sound of the clanging bells from the cable cars, as they stopped and started along California Street, was the most cheerful thing about living on Snob Hill. Sadly, Sally didn't have even one friend outside of her school day. Dad kept busy with his work, but he didn't make any personal friends either. Uncharacteristically, he never spoke of his work the whole time we lived in San Francisco. I had no idea about the writing project he worked on beyond knowing that the job paid well.

Mom had no friends either, and no one to talk to other than a casual meet-up with a resident of the building or the proprietor of the small market where she shopped for groceries. The maid kept our apartment clean, and we ate many dinners out. Mom spent her days alone with little to keep her occupied. That kind of isolation and lack of purpose was the worst environment for anyone struggling with alcoholism. Her drinking substantially worsened. Instead of just beer, she turned to vodka and whiskey, starting out the morning with one or the other in her coffee.

Mom was rarely sober anymore, and her combativeness and anger toward my father escalated. Sally and I recognized the seriousness of her deteriorating condition, but we had no idea what to do. There was one horrible scene when Sally and I decided to pour all of Mom's liquor down the kitchen drain, as if this would solve the problem. We found bottles hidden everywhere—under the bed, in the cupboards, and even in the bathroom. Mom whined, pleaded, and threatened, but we kept going until the liquor bottles were empty. It was a sad day, but worse ones were yet to come.

As a family, we did have a few good times together in San Francisco. Dad did his best to expose us to the better things about city living. He loved good restaurants. We went to his favorite delicatessen one night for dinner, and he ordered each of us matzo ball soup with half of a cooked chicken resting in the bowl. It was delicious. "This is what I used to have as a boy in New York," he told us. "They have wonderful delicatessens there."

Another favorite place we frequented was in the classy Fairmont Hotel a block away from our apartment. We walked there for dinner in the Tonga Room where tropical rain showers intermittently fell from the ceiling into a catch pool. We also enjoyed strolling through Chinatown and having dinner at one of their many cafes. Dad made sure to take us to all the major sites and tourist attractions throughout the city. The Top of the Mark, a rooftop bar at the InterContinental Mark Hopkins Hotel with sweeping views of the city and bay, was a big tourist attraction. It was a short block away from our apartment, and occasionally my parents walked there for cocktails in the early evening.

Dad loved ships because they brought back good memories of his boyhood travels to Germany. On Sunday afternoons, we often went down to the piers along San Francisco Bay to look at the ships in dock. We'd find a nice seafood restaurant at Fisherman's Wharf and have dinner. Mom always ordered Lobster Newburg, which was her favorite dish.

The ships came to San Francisco from all over the world. Back then, visitors were allowed to go onboard, and Dad was able to get us tours on several ships. One was a Norwegian freighter that carried a small number of paying passengers. Dad said, "This is the most interesting way to travel." He preferred a working ship with a few passengers for traveling rather than an all-passenger liner.

Sally's friend Barbara, from Sherman Oaks, was visiting us for the weekend and came along the day we toured the Norwegian freighter. The captain in his spiffy uniform was charming and gracious as he took us on a tour. He ended the tour by giving us fresh-baked pastries from the galley. Dad was all smiles, enjoying the special treatment we were getting. Barbara remembers there was music, and some of the passengers were dancing. At one point, the captain said in his thick Norwegian accent, "Don't you think she is beautiful?"

I smiled shyly and replied, "Thank you."

Dad burst out laughing. "The ship, Susan, not you." I was so embarrassed.

One day, we took a ferry to the quaint seaside village of Sausalito. Another time, we drove north across the Golden Gate Bridge to see the sights and walk in the beautiful Muir Woods. Dad was a great tour guide, and I looked forward to our Sunday outings.

Left to my own devices, I often went shopping on Saturday. From the cable car on California Street, I transferred to the one on Powell Street and in no time was downtown where the major department stores were located. I learned quickly how to maneuver the sidewalks of San Francisco, which were far more dangerous than those in the sleepy San Fernando Valley. In San Francisco, like in other big cities, flat steel doors embedded in the sidewalks could suddenly pop open as smelly bags of trash rose to the surface from the bowels of a building. You had to pay attention or risk getting hit.

The sights, sounds, and smells of downtown San Francisco were unmistakable: cars honked, cable cars clanged, the wind howled, the fog horns wailed, and an eclectic mix of people scurried along the sidewalk. The odor of food cooking on grills in the many ethnic cafes wafted into the streets, converging with the salty air. The city was alive, and that's the way I felt when I went on my shopping excursions.

Every street seemed to have a hole-in-the-wall eatery selling sandwiches and salads. I usually got a sandwich for lunch and then stopped at a chocolate shop to buy a few pieces for the trip home. In those days, people dressed up to go downtown—men in suits and women in dresses or suits with hats and gloves. I enjoyed dressing up.

Flower stands selling fresh flowers were on some of the major corners, and I bought myself an armful one day. On the way home, the cable car driver noticed me holding the flowers and asked, "Are you a movie star?" I was flattered.

Chinatown was a favorite haunt of mine. I loved going there by myself, pretending I was actually walking the streets of China. I ate lunch at my favorite small café where I always ordered pork fried rice. One time, I went to pay for my lunch and recognized the girl standing at the check-out register. It was Carole, who had lived on Stanton Avenue for a short time. We had a nice chat and marveled at the coincidence of meeting up at some obscure hole-in-the-wall café in San Francisco's Chinatown.

Joe

Joe with the roving hands called me one night. He was now in the air force and stationed at Travis Air Force Base near Fairfield on the east side of the bay. My friend Peggy had given him my phone number. He sounded pretty nice on the phone and lonely. He wanted to take me to the movies, and, lonely myself, I foolishly agreed to go. He took me to a rundown establishment on Market Street where we sat in the middle of an almost-empty movie theater. He put his arm around me, and his hands started their wandering ways again.

What a big mistake I'd made. I remembered what Mom always told me. "If you're in trouble, grab a cab, and we'll pay for it when you get home." I told Joe I needed to use the restroom. Instead, I hurriedly left the theater and jumped into the cab that was sitting out front at the curb. I never heard from Joe again.

Turning Sixteen

The majestic Grace Cathedral and adjacent Huntington Park took up a whole block on California Street between our apartment building and the Fairmont Hotel. One drizzly evening, I headed to the church with my umbrella. Alone and depressed, I danced along the sidewalk, twirling my umbrella, singing the popular song "Singin' in the Rain" in an attempt to cheer myself up. I went inside the church and lit about a dozen candles, praying for a miracle and a speedy return to our home in the San Fernando Valley. I didn't know you were supposed to leave an offering for the candles. Maybe that's why our return home didn't come anytime soon.

What did come was my sixteenth birthday on November 21. "We're taking you to dinner at the Fairmont Hotel," Mom said cheerfully. "Here's some money for a new outfit. Find something nice and treat yourself."

At the Emporium on Market Street, I bought a tailored wool suit in a pinky-beige color that was on the sale rack. Right away I had second thoughts about the color and style, wishing I had chosen something more flattering. On the night of my birthday, having nothing better to wear, I reluctantly put on the suit and got ready to go out for dinner with the family.

As I waited in the living room, I noticed that my parents were dawdling. At the unexpected sound of the doorbell, Mom called out from her bedroom, "Susan, can you get the door?"

When I opened the door, there stood Pete with a corsage box in his hand. My Big Sister from Lowell and her boyfriend were standing next to him.

I was dumbfounded. My body began to quiver with an acute case of nerves. What on earth had my mother done? Devised a plan and tracked down my Big Sister for help with her crazy idea, that's what she'd done. Like the

Good Fairy, Mom found a way to make her daughter's wish come true. Pete, Pete So Divine was my surprise date and birthday present.

As we left the apartment for the Fairmont Hotel, my parents and sister were all smiles. "Have a good time," they called out as I struggled to hide my mortification.

The four of us walked the short block to the Fairmont Hotel with me on Pete's arm. We were seated right in front of the stage at a reserved table in the crowded main ballroom. I felt unprepared and tongue-tied as I tried to carry on a conversation. Thank goodness the three of them knew each other well and contributed more to the conversation than I could. Oh, how I wished I had bought a pretty dress instead of the plain, beige suit. We had dinner, I danced a little with Pete, and then the famous Will Mastin Trio, starring Sammy Davis, Jr., came on stage to entertain us. After a few songs, there was fanfare, and the spotlight moved to my surprised face as Sammy Davis, Jr. stepped off the stage to shake my hand. "Happy birthday, Susan," he said, and everyone in the ballroom clapped.

At this point, I was beyond embarrassed, but there was one more thing. From the entrance to the ballroom, I heard the distinct sound of my mother's smoker's cough. I turned in time to see her and Dad duck behind the curtains. They were spying on us.

The evening was surreal, and I had nervous jitters all night, but I did get to dance with my dreamboat. At school afterward, Pete was cordially distant, and I tried to pretend the whole fix-up had never happened. That was Mom for you. She meant well and only wanted me to be happy, but from then on, I was careful about what I asked for. Mom had proven that she could make the impossible happen. Once was enough for me.

After surviving my sixteenth birthday, I decided it was time to look for a job. It would keep me busy on the weekends and give me some spending money. I dressed in my new suit and went to some employment agencies. Without any experience and only rudimentary typing skills, I wasn't surprised that nothing came of it. I never got a call or had an interview.

My Friend the Tailor

There was a little European tailor shop a block down from our apartment. The store window featured a couple of slimline skirts that caught my eye, and I went in one day and talked to the tailor. "I have a narrow waist and wide hips," I said. "If the skirt fits me on the hips, the waist is too big." I mentioned my mistake in buying the beige suit.

"I would like to make you a skirt. No cost," he said, showing me some houndstooth fabrics. One piece went nicely with my light-blue sweater.

Mom went with me for the fitting. The skirt was a success and fit me perfectly with no gap at the waist. The tailor's kindness and friendship meant a lot to me.

Christmas

Christmas that year went down in history as the worst imaginable. On Christmas Eve, the presents sat wrapped under our small, decorated fir tree. Dad was in the living room reading while Sally and I were in our bedroom. All was quiet. Suddenly, my parents' voices erupted into a horrendous argument. Mom had been drinking heavily that day, and Sally and I rushed into the living room to see if we could calm things down.

At that moment, the lovely voices of Christmas carolers floated up from the street below. Mom threw open the window, leaned out, and bellowed, "Merry Christmas." Her words slurred, and she started yelling awful things about my father including how he ruined the spirit of Christmas.

I'm sure the carolers were appalled. Sally and I were beyond upset, and Dad was furious. He picked up the Christmas gifts he had wrapped for Mom and started throwing them out of the window. They hit the pavement, tissue paper flying as the contents spilled out. One was a beautiful, cream-colored knitted sweater that had batwing sleeves. It was an awful scene. The carolers swiftly moved on. Sally and I started crying. There was more quarrelling, and Mom decided to call the police. Several officers showed up at the door, and one of them noticed Sally and me standing in the background. He said, "Folks, it's Christmas Eve. Please think of your children."

We went to bed, and the next morning, life resumed to normal as it always did. Mom or Dad must have picked up the things on the sidewalk, because the sweater wasn't lost. Sally and I opened our presents as our parents maintained a stony silence.

Things got even worse. One Sunday afternoon shortly after Christmas, Sally and I were enjoying a movie at a theater nearby. Someone tapped me on the shoulder. It was Dad. "Come on girls," he whispered. "We have to go." As we walked through the lobby, he said, "Mom's gone. I found a note. She wants to kill herself." The urgency in his voice was alarming. Sally and I were upset and scared.

We drove the hilly streets, aimlessly looking for Mom, but it was futile. Not knowing what else to do, we went back to the apartment. There she was, curled up in a dark corner of the hallway near our front door. She was obviously very drunk. It was a huge relief to find her alive but devastating to realize that our mother had sunk to this lowest of low places in her life. She went to bed and slept it off, but Sally and I were left with a devastating memory.

New Apartment

Unexpectedly, Mom got a call from our neighbor on Bellaire Avenue saying that the renters had moved out of our house and might have stolen some of our possessions. Mom took an early flight home to take care of things, and Sally went with her. The sale of the house was a possibility. A decision was made to vacate our apartment and have Dad and I take a smaller apartment in the same building so I could continue high school at Lowell. With my parents living apart, I was happy knowing it would end the arguments and bring some peace into my life, at least for the time being. I looked forward to making dinner for my father and spending time with him.

After Mom and Sally left, Dad and I settled into our one-bedroom apartment. Before long, he started asking me about my friend, Elaine. "Why don't you ask her over? I'll take the two of you to dinner, and we can go shopping for sweaters."

Girls of my generation collected sweaters like girls today collect designer shoes. The more, the better. Cashmeres were the best kind.

"Maybe Elaine can spend the night," Dad added, his interest causing me to feel jealous and confused about his intentions.

At his urging, I arranged for Elaine to spend the night. We had dinner at a restaurant and relaxed afterward in our living room. I watched as the two of them talked, laughed, and carried on in a way that made me uneasy. Clearly, my father was flirting with her, and she was returning the attention. There was an obvious attraction between them despite their difference in age.

Feeling like an outsider, I decided to go to bed. "Goodnight," I said. There was no objection as I left the room.

I woke up the next morning feeling hurt and betrayed. Dad and Elaine said nothing about the night before, and I was left wondering what had happened after I went to bed. It seemed as if he had used me to spend time with her. It was clear to me that he had paid too much attention to Elaine and had been attracted to a woman my own age. I called my mother and asked to come home. Living alone with Dad was not working out. That afternoon, I was on a flight to Burbank Airport where Mom picked me up.

The incident with Elaine changed my relationship with my father from that day forward. Dad never apologized. He behaved as though nothing had happened and nothing was wrong. Elaine and I never discussed that evening.

I realized later in life that Dad was dealing with loneliness and a marriage gone bad. No matter. The episode left its mark on me.

Vallejo Street

My stay back home in Studio City was short lived. Within a week, Mom re-rented the house, and the family was back together in San Francisco. Dad found a furnished apartment on Vallejo Street, west of Van Ness Avenue, in upscale Pacific Heights. The apartment was on the seventh floor and had a spectacular view of the bay, Alcatraz, and the Golden Gate Bridge. Unfortunately, there was only one bedroom. A large, windowless, closet-like space next to the living room was just big enough to hold a bed and dresser for Sally. I slept on a convertible sofa bed in the living room.

During the time I spent in Southern California with Mom and Sally, Lori stayed behind with Dad in San Francisco. She went to work with him every day, and in the afternoon, he called a cab for her. Dad told the cab driver, "Take Lori to the grassy area in the marina area, and let her run around and do her business." For his trouble the cabbie received a generous tip with the fare.

"I had to smile when the cab left the curb," Dad told us. "There was this German shepherd sitting in the backseat staring at me with big, brown eyes."

The day we moved into our apartment on Vallejo Street, we went to great lengths to hide Lori. No dogs were allowed in the building. Dad had been desperate because he was unable find any other suitable or affordable place to live, and rentals were extremely scarce in San Francisco. "If we can't keep Lori here, I don't know what we're going to do," he said, preparing us for the worst.

After we settled in, Dad telephoned the building manager, Mrs. Monroe, and asked her to come meet the family. He mentioned offhandedly that we had a dog, hoping he had sufficiently charmed her—his forte—when he met her.

"What?" she said, annoyed. "How big is your dog?"

Dad replied, "Oh, just a medium size," which wasn't a total lie considering she was a medium-sized German shepherd.

We decided to stash Lori in the bathroom until we could bring her out quietly after Mrs. Monroe met the rest of the family.

The moment she entered the apartment, Mrs. Monroe demanded, "Where is the dog?"

"In the bathroom," Dad sheepishly said, pointing to the closed door.

Mrs. Monroe went straight to the bathroom and flung open the door. The next moment, she was on her knees, hugging and kissing Lori. "You poor thing, hiding here in the bathroom," she cooed as we looked on in disbelief.

It turned out that Mrs. Monroe loved dogs. She immediately fell in love with our gentle, sweet Lori. She said we could keep her but had to make sure that no one saw her coming and going. We promised. She had the building janitor clear the broken bottles, cans, and trash from the small vacant lot next door so Lori could safely relieve herself there.

Mrs. Monroe turned out to be a sweet lady. She brought doggie treats for Lori and homemade "people food" for us. For the time we lived there, we were the only tenant with a dog. If anyone mentioned to Mrs. Monroe that they had seen a dog in the building, she'd say, "Oh, that dog is just visiting."

Family life as we knew it continued uninterrupted despite the disturbing incidents preceding our move to Vallejo Street. Mom's drinking showed no sign of letting up. There were days when she drank less and appeared almost sober, and there were times when she smelled like beer and fell asleep on the couch right after dinner. Sally and I were kept busy with school, and Dad had his work. Mrs. Monroe was a welcome bright light, visiting our apartment almost every day to see Lori and otherwise being a friendly presence in the building as we came and went.

Chinatown

This leg of our stay in San Francisco was marked by several noteworthy experiences. The most unusual involved a night of mystery and intrigue.

One evening, Dad was working late, and Mom agreed to take Sally and me to Chinatown for dinner. While eating, we overheard a conversation between some Chinese men about communism or anti-communism. It wasn't clear. We glanced over in their direction.

As we finished our meal, one of the men came over to our table and asked, "Would you like to hear talks at 811 Clay Street?"

"No, thank you," Mom answered emphatically.

We left the café. As we were walking up the street, a car pulled up next to us and stopped. A man emerged from a doorway, crossed our path, and received a package from someone in the car in exchange for what appeared to be a wad of money. He disappeared back into the shadows, reminiscent of a Charlie Chan movie. "Maybe that was an opium deal going down," I said. Mom and Sally agreed.

On the drive back to the apartment, we talked about the strange events in Chinatown. Mom fell unusually silent and started driving faster than normal with determination. "There's a car following us," she said, fear in her voice.

Sally and I turned around and saw the trailing headlights. When we reached the front of the apartment building, Mom said, "Hurry upstairs, and lock the door. I have to pick up your dad. I'll be right back."

We hurried as fast as we could, trembling as the elevator rose to our floor. Once safely in the apartment, Sally and I were scared. Alone now, we wondered if we were being watched and stayed far away from the front window.

Mom headed back to the financial district near Chinatown where Dad was working. Here's where the story gets really strange. Mom said, "I parked the car and walked toward the building where Dad was. All of a sudden, two men stepped out from between two buildings and took my arms, one on each side. 'You come now to 811 Clay Street to hear talks,' one of them said. I managed to break free. My adrenalin was pumping as I ran around the corner and ducked into a small market. There was a clerk working behind the counter. 'A Chinaman is following me,' I told him, out of breath, but he just looked at me. He was Chinese, and I don't think he spoke English."

Mom said she fled the market with her heart pounding, all too aware that Dad was editing in a soundproof room. He probably wouldn't hear her if the door to the building was locked. She saw the figure of a tall man approaching. "Walter, is that you?" She gulped.

"Ethel? Yes, it's me," he said.

She ran to him. Mom made a call from Dad's office and told us they were on their way. After seeing no one on the street, they were able to make it to the car safely and head home. That ended a frightening, bizarre night. We never figured out what actually happened or, for that matter, confirmed that any Chinese men had actually followed us home, but to this day I remember the address 811 Clay Street.

The Pacific Heights neighborhood was more residential than California Street. Mom started taking Lori for long walks, and one day, she came home with this story.

"As I passed the little market on Van Ness Avenue, a cat leaped out of the doorway and landed on Lori's back. It was hissing and digging in with its claws. I screamed and hit the cat with my purse. I knocked it for a loop."

Hearing the commotion, the market owner rushed out. Mom learned that it was a mama cat protecting her kittens. They were sleeping in a box just inside the doorway. Poor Lori was traumatized. After that, she was noticeably wary when any of us took her for a walk.

Mom was the cause of one particularly terrifying experience. On a Saturday afternoon while Dad worked, she decided to take us on a nice drive, but the drive was anything but nice. We should have known better than to get in the car with her. She wasn't sober enough to drive. She decided to travel north across the Golden Gate Bridge, headed for Marin County. The bridge was confining with steady oncoming traffic and the treacherous water in the bay far below. Mom started weaving back and forth.

"Watch out," Sally and I hollered at once.

Just before exiting the bridge, the tires of the car hit the raised cement dividers and rode them going bump, bump, bump. "Get back in the lane," I yelled, frightened to death that we were going to wind up in the oncoming traffic. From my place in the front seat, I said, "Let me drive," reaching for the steering wheel.

Mom pushed my hands away and held the wheel more tightly. I didn't know how to drive, but anything seemed better than letting a drunk driver take us to our deaths.

Somehow we got home that day in one piece. It was a sad commentary on how alcoholism had changed our mother's judgment. In earlier times, our safety would have been her top priority.

Summer was long in coming, and when it finally arrived, so did the fog. Expecting warmer weather, I was disappointed that the summer months in San Francisco, except for a rare heat wave, could be cool and windy even when the sun was shining. Fog was synonymous with summer, and we had plenty of it. There were many days when I stood at the apartment window watching the ominous fogbank roll in from the ocean. The fog would quickly obscure the Golden Gate Bridge and then swallow up the city. The forlorn bleating of foghorns warning the ships trying to maneuver in the bay was a depressing sound.

All I wanted to do was go home. I felt trapped like the inmates serving time on "The Rock" at Alcatraz.

"I'm dying to see the sun again," I told Dad at dinner one night.

"I know just the place," he said. He was in a good mood. The following Sunday, Dad drove us to Walnut Creek on the east side of the bay, which was basking in bright sunshine. Sally and I stepped out of the car into what felt like ninety degrees and did a little happy dance. Before leaving, we had dinner at a restaurant known for its homemade walnut bread.

Having nothing better to do, I decided to attend summer school. It was held at Galileo High School, not far from our apartment on a hill above Fisherman's Wharf. I took the first semester of geometry for the third time, and my diligent studying paid off with a grade of B.

I also took a class in art appreciation, which was fun. For one take-home assignment, we had to create a still life using watercolors. I was surprised when the teacher held up my drawing for everyone to see. Instead of a compliment, he asked, "What is wrong with this picture?"

It looked fine to me, but some of the kids snickered. What I didn't see was that I had drawn the table legs suspended on the background. They didn't touch the floor. It's no wonder I had difficulty with geometry.

During the summer, Sally and I took advantage of any day that was sunny. Wearing our bathing suits, we rode the elevator to the roof of the apartment building and spread out our towels close to the edge of the roof. We hoped to block out the wind, doing our best to get a San Francisco suntan. We didn't stay on the roof for long, because all we seemed to get were goosebumps. One day, I was determined to get a suntan and shivered in the wind for too long. That was the day I got one of the worst sunburns ever.

One day, looking for a better place to sunbathe, I went by myself to the marina area next to Fisherman's Wharf. I spread out my towel on the hard, wet sand. It was a nice day, and I decided to dip my toes into the bay. It was freezing cold. Soon the wind came up, and I had to leave, missing the warmer, white sandy beach at Roadside Rest in Santa Monica.

Cousin Delphine

Sally and I were surprised when one day Dad announced, "We're going to dinner at my cousin's house."

I didn't know he had any cousins besides Nat Wise and Bennett Cerf. This new cousin lived in the Bay Area not far from us. Delphine Koshland was the only child of my grandfather's sister, Minnie (Wise) Rosenfeld. Another Delphine in the family!

We joined Delphine and her husband, Robert, for dinner at their lovely home in Hillsborough, south of San Francisco. The Koshlands were well off and had three grown children: Robert M., Susan (Sue), and Margaret (Peggy).

Delphine warmly welcomed our family as her long-lost relatives, and I thought it was wonderful to meet another member of the Wise family. It ended up being one of those stiff, formal gatherings where children are seen and not heard. The way wealthy people entertained, I rationalized in my unworldly way.

I thought it was brave of Dad to take Mom with us. Thankfully, she was on her best behavior. Sally, on the other hand, had an embarrassing moment. We had retired from the living room and were seated for dinner in the formal dining room. The table was elegantly set with white linen, bone china, crystal goblets, and sterling silverware. A large bowl in the center of the table held an arrangement of petit orange flowers. A maid working in the kitchen was about to bring out the first course, and Sally and I waited patiently while the adults talked.

All of a sudden, Sally burst into peals of laughter, causing the adult conversation to abruptly stop. "What's so funny?" Dad asked, smiling, as everyone turned to look at Sally.

"Nothing," Sally muttered through her giggles, her face turning red. It was an awkward moment, since Sally refused to say what was so funny. The adults resumed their conversation.

On the way home, Sally explained herself. She thought the orange flower resting in her finger bowl had escaped the arrangement and somehow flown into her bowl, but then she realized that everyone had an orange flower in their bowl. Her awkwardness around grown-ups was related to her young age (12 years old). "I made a fool of myself," she said.

That story reminds me of one of Dad's favorite jokes about the McCreary family.

They were expecting Uncle Joe for dinner. Since the kids had never met him, Mrs. McCreary made sure her children knew that Uncle Joe had a large, bulbous nose. "Don't make any comments about his nose," she said.

The dinner had gone well, and it was time to serve tea and coffee. Uncle Joe was sipping his tea when Mrs. McCreary passed the sugar. Without thinking, she asked, "Uncle Joe, would you like a little nose in your tea?"

Robert and Delphine Koshland were well known in the Bay Area, gaining prestige for long lives filled with significant business and philanthropic contributions. Oral histories and interviews posted on the internet are interesting and provide information about them that is worth sharing.

Delphine said that as a child, she made yearly train trips to New York with her mother to visit her grandfather, Nathan Wise. Her grandmother Delphine was no longer living, and her grandfather had remarried a woman named Bettie. When Delphine was fourteen, she and her mother stayed at the Cerf home when they visited Manhattan since Freda was Minnie's sister. Delphine said that on Saturdays, she and her cousin Bennett often bought tickets to nickel dances. There was a live orchestra for ballroom dancing. In those days, they were considered okay, because she and Bennett went in the daytime. They took the subway.

Dad was seven years younger than his cousin Delphine. They undoubtedly saw each other at family gatherings when his aunt Minnie and Delphine came to New York. The Wise family maintained close ties, something I didn't realize growing up on the West Coast. Dad sometimes flew to New York on business and used those opportunities to connect with his relatives. We didn't visit New York as a family until I was nineteen.

According to Delphine, her parents, Charles and Minnie (Wise) Rosenfeld, met and married in Manhattan before moving to Portland, Oregon, at the turn of the century. Delphine was born in Portland. Her father was employed in his Uncle Saul's cigar business, Rosenfeld-Smith Company. He and Minnie were members of Temple Beth Israel, although Delphine said they were not observant Jews or active temple members and didn't attend services. This continued a tradition where religion did not play a prominent role in their families, she said.

In her oral history, Delphine said she was brought up in a liberal household where social groups and friends were not limited to the Jewish community. She attended UC Berkeley from 1918 to 1920 and met her future husband, Robert Koshland, at a dinner party at his aunt's home in San Francisco.

Delphine volunteered at various institutions and hospitals. She lived a long life, passing away in 1995 three weeks before her ninety-fifth birthday. Her wishes were to be remembered as a good mother and grandmother.

Robert Koshland was a San Francisco native from a prominent family. He was a community leader and medical facilities planner for more than three decades, spearheading the building of the Peninsula Hospital in Burlingame when he was president of the Peninsula Hospital District. Before that, as a young married man, he and Delphine lived in Boston. He was a national buyer of raw wool, a business shared with his father and other family members. Robert and his father graduated from Lowell High School and UC Berkeley. His father served for many years as vice president and treasurer of Levi Strauss & Company. Robert passed away in 1989 at the age of ninety-six.

I have a good hunch that Robert Koshland was the person who secured my admission to Lowell High School.

Summer Ends

Summer was coming to a close, and I dreaded starting another year at Lowell High School. Sally and I had what seemed like futile talks with Dad. We wanted him to know how miserable we were in San Francisco. If only we could return home. We didn't care if he made less money. We were willing to make sacrifices.

One evening at dinner, he said, "I want you girls to be happy. I've decided to take a job back in Hollywood with Cate and McGlone Productions."

We were going home. Talk about happy! Sally and I were ecstatic.

Our stay in San Francisco left an indelible memory. For years afterward, I had a fear of moving. I used to think of San Francisco when faced with a life-changing event, especially a change of address. I had moved to San Francisco with an open mind, high hopes, and a positive attitude only to have things turn out so badly. My junior year of high school was a difficult one of isolation and an unhappy home life. On the positive side, I gained maturity, independence, and a greater ability to cope with adversity. I also learned something very important: bad times don't last forever.

CHAPTER 12

Magnolia Boulevard

Warm, sunny weather greeted us the day we returned to the San Fernando Valley. No fog! As soon as Dad stopped the car in front of our house on Bellaire Avenue, Sally and I jumped out, knelt down, and literally kissed the grass. It was wonderful to be home.

The fall semester of my senior year at North Hollywood High School was a week underway, but I fit in like I had never left. The late arrival, however, resulted in me being assigned teachers based on what classes still had room for students. That is how I got the crabbiest and hardest teacher for Spanish. I tried to transfer out of her class but with no luck. Fortunately, during the last semester of high school, I had Mr. Campos again, my favorite Spanish teacher.

My Laudette sisters welcomed me back, and I was soon voted vice president of the club. The good friends I made in the Laudettes and the club's various social activities were the highlights of my senior year. I was a better student, having learned some good study habits at Lowell High School. I also worked hard to bring up my grade point average so I could qualify for UCLA.

A few months after we returned from San Francisco, my parents decided to sell the Bellaire Avenue house, which meant selling Mom's treasured baby grand piano. Mom found an apartment to rent in a new building on Magnolia Boulevard in North Hollywood about half a block from North Hollywood High School. Though it was a convenient location for me, the apartment was another small living situation for our family with just two bedrooms and one bathroom. Sally and I had to share a bedroom again. With four people sharing the one bathroom, there were mornings when Dad got frustrated trying to get his bathroom time.

My mother made some friends in the apartment building, which was a welcome change from the isolation she experienced in San Francisco. She stopped drinking hard liquor in her coffee and went back to drinking beer. It was a busy time for her—moving, getting settled in the apartment, and looking for a house to buy. My perception was that she drank less while we lived in the apartment on Magnolia Boulevard, though she and my father continued to have loud arguments, which I worried were heard through the apartment's thin walls.

One day, I came home from school and was surprised to find Roger from Glendale sitting on the couch. I'm not sure how he knew where we lived, but there he was, talking to Mom and waiting for me. It was great to see him, but any romantic feelings I might have once had for my cowboy hero had long been outgrown. By then, he was just a good memory from the old Stanton Avenue neighborhood.

For my seventeenth birthday, I received driving lessons. I had a learner's permit before turning sixteen, but getting my license was delayed by the move to San Francisco. I was excited to have the instructor come to my door for an hour's lesson. I took the lesson in his car that had a stick shift, and that meant shifting smoothly and nailing the dreaded parallel parking exercise. I passed the test.

We still had one car in the family. Dad traded in the Nash Ambassador for a used Buick, which he drove to work and Mom used on the weekends. The Buick was older and different to drive than my instructor's car. It had an automatic rather than a stick shift, and turn signals had been added after it had been manufactured. The bar for the signals was on the right side of the steering column next to the automatic shift arm.

After some practice in the Buick, Dad let me drive the car to my lesson at Schramm's Ice-Skating School in North Hollywood. Sally went along with me for the company. On the way home, we approached a donut stand, and I said to Sally, "Want to get a donut?" She said no but then changed her mind.

I grabbed for the turn signal and instead yanked hard on the automatic shift arm, throwing the moving car into reverse. With a horrible screeching and grinding noise, the car came to a stop. Sally and I exchanged an "oh my God" look. I restarted the car and put it in gear. Miraculously, it moved forward and seemed to drive okay. "Don't say a word to Dad," I said. Sally promised she wouldn't.

About two weeks later, my father had this to say over dinner. "I had transmission problems and took the car to my mechanic. He said there was a hole in the transmission and asked if I'd put the car in reverse while it was moving. I told him hell no and then remembered that I let you use my car for the skating lesson."

I told him the truth, and remarkably, he was understanding and forgiving. The car repair bill had been a sizable one, but he paid it, and that was that. I never drove the Buick again. He didn't offer, and I didn't ask.

Over Christmas break, the Laudettes rented a cabin in Big Bear for a few days. There was a thin layer of snow on the ground, which wasn't good for sledding, but the lake was frozen. A couple of us brought our ice-skates, and we headed to the lake. There were lots of kids getting ready to skate, but I was the first one to step on the ice. I had moved only a few feet from shore when the ice gave way, and my right leg went down into the frigid water. I screamed for help, and one of the boys on shore somehow grabbed my hand and yanked me to safety. It wasn't too frightening because it happened so fast. I was in the freezing water, and then I was out.

After I went back to the cabin and changed my clothes, my friends and I walked around the main part of the mountain town and went shopping. I was in a store when I overheard someone say, "Did you hear about the girl who was ice-skating and fell in the lake and drowned?"

My friends and I looked at each in disbelief, knowing they must be talking about me. I'm glad the story going around town was inaccurate like a game of telephone. I was very much alive and a whole lot wiser about the dangers of skating on an ice-covered lake.

While in Big Bear, we met some college fraternity boys from Long Beach and attended a party one night in their large cabin. A nice-looking guy named Bill took a fancy to me, but I wasn't attracted to him. To avoid his repeated requests to dance, I hunkered down on the couch and accepted the free drinks that were being offered. It was my first experience drinking, and I chugged down two tall screwdrivers (vodka and orange juice), one after the other, like they were sodas. Next thing, I was dizzy and couldn't walk straight, and soon I felt miserably sick to my stomach with a pounding headache.

That's when the party ended for me and my Laudette sisters. Our chaperone, the mother of the club's president, thought it was time for us to leave. When we got back to our cabin, the girls gave me coffee to sober me up, and then I was just a wide-awake drunk. It made me wonder how my mother could drink and not feel as miserable as I did that night.

I didn't drink again until I was in college but experienced the same unpleasant dizziness and sick stomach after even one drink. I've often told people, "I don't drink because I have a hangover before the party's over." I didn't drink often during or after college, not knowing if it would make me feel relaxed and happy or nauseous with a headache. I subsequently learned that I have an intolerance to alcohol. From then on, I've had to be careful, and I rarely drink any alcoholic beverages except maybe a glass of wine on a special occasion.

One vice I did pick up in my senior year of high school was smoking. My best Laudette friend, Sheila, taught me how to smoke at Bob's Big Boy one night. We drove there in her new car, a Hudson that her father had given her. In those days, we didn't know how bad smoking was for our health. We thought it looked grown-up and sophisticated to have a cigarette dangling from our fingers. All of the advertisements of the day promoted that image. I ignored Mom's advice not to smoke and fell victim to peer pressure. I started smoking Marlboros regularly after that night and wasn't able to kick the habit until I was in my mid-thirties.

The last semester of high school, the seniors had to take a special class called Senior Problems. The teacher, Mrs. Evans, was well liked. The class dealt in issues we would encounter as an adult such as voting, building a resume, interviewing for a job, succeeding in college, and such. There was no homework, and it was an easy, fun class that we all looked forward to taking. What should have been taught were investment strategies, money management, and how to use a checkbook.

I was headed for college, but I had no idea what to choose as a major. I didn't know what I wanted to be in life except a wife and mother. Young girls commonly accepted the inevitability of limited career options and settled into standard jobs such as secretary, social worker, nurse, or schoolteacher. I wanted to be something, but what? Dad told me, "You're a good organizer," but as far as I knew, that skill didn't seem to translate into a job.

It was a common opinion among the girls that young men didn't want to marry girls who majored in the brainy subjects like science and mathematics. There was no chance I'd be left out of the marriage pool, since math and science were my poorest subjects. I did better in English, history, and Spanish. Thinking I must have hidden talents and strengths, I hoped to discover them. With that information, I could better choose a college major that would ultimately lead to a good job. Girls in my world didn't think in terms of careers—only a job until they got married and stayed home to raise a family. That all changed in the 1960s as women started entering the workforce in great numbers.

Mom learned of a company in downtown Los Angeles that conducted in-depth interviews and administered aptitude and scholastic testing designed to help college-bound students uncover their strengths. My parents paid for me to go through the intense, three-day program, and I could hardly wait to see what the tests revealed. I found out that my poorest skills were in math and science, and my strengths were writing, people skills, and organizational skills. Nothing new about that! According to the test results, the best choices for me were occupations as a teacher, social worker, or secretary. I was so disappointed that I had learned nothing new about myself.

"I guess I'll be a social worker," I told Mom, though I had no real interest in or passion for becoming a social worker. More to the point, I had no idea what the job entailed besides the notion that it involved helping people.

Over the Easter holiday season, I got a job at the May Company store in North Hollywood, working weekends as a salesgirl in the candy department. This was my first job outside of being a mother's helper. Working in chocolate heaven, however, was not the utopian job I thought it would be. I learned that the salesgirls were not allowed to eat any of the candy. A manager hovered nearby, watching our every move. People came to the counter and ordered small amounts of chocolate, as I often did at the See's Candy store. Measuring out candy on the scale in amounts less than a pound, I discovered, challenged my math skills. I worked there for two days and quit.

Still wanting a job and the extra spending money it would bring, I decided to look for work in a dress shop. I pounded the pavement along Lankershim Boulevard where all the shops were located. Without experience, no one would hire me. Exasperated after another day of job hunting with no luck, I said to a store manager, "How am I supposed to get experience if no one will hire me?" He was sympathetic and understood my dilemma, but he still didn't hire me.

I remembered there was a plaza with a few stores next to the May Company. I walked into Veeva Marie Sport Togs, and the owner surprised me with an offer to work part time on Saturdays. I was thrilled and enjoyed working there for a few months. The downside was that in its off-the-beaten-path location, the store drew few customers. Standing and waiting for customers was boring. I wanted more action.

With experience under my belt, I got a job at Remar's, a low-end dress store on Lankershim Boulevard that had a steady stream of customers. I enjoyed helping the customers, but working in high heels was challenging. During my break, I crossed the street and went into the Woolworth's five-and-dime store for a Coke. My feet hurt so bad that even while sitting on the stool at the counter, they were throbbing. I quit working at Remar's after a few months, deciding that I'd have to be content with the weekly allowance my parents gave me. There would be no more part-time jobs for a while.

My father still enjoyed going out to dinner, and we continued to do that often. One evening, we went to dinner at a Chinese restaurant in Toluca Lake. The waiter served our first course of soup in blue-and-white ceramic bowls. "I wonder if these bowls were made by Gladding McBean," Mom said, referring to the pottery company in Glendale that made her Franciscan Apple dishes.

Not thinking, Dad turned his bowl upside down to see what was written on the bottom. His soup dumped all over the table. The waiter rushed over to clean up the mess.

Laughing, my father tried to explain to the waiter why he did what he did. The waiter looked at him pokerfaced and continued cleaning. By then, we were all giggling. The waiter probably thought we were a weird family.

My parents started looking at houses to buy. Not far from the apartment in North Hollywood, they found a street where a young developer named Ray Watt was building about eight custom homes. They decided to have a home built and chose a lot. The construction of our new home started right away, and it would be ready shortly after I graduated from high school in June. This was an exciting venture for our family. We enjoyed driving by the property and watching the house go up during the construction phase.

As graduation neared, Sheila and I decided that we needed to do something mischievous to break a rule before the end of the year. We decided to ditch school. No sneaking off the grounds. After our homeroom period ended, we brazenly sauntered out of the main entrance and down the steps to freedom. No one even noticed.

Mom was surprised when we walked into the apartment to let her know we were going to the beach in Sheila's car. "Do you need a note from me to get back into school?" she said.

"Nope," I told her. "It wouldn't be ditching if we had permission from a parent."

When Sheila and I returned to school the next day, our homeroom teacher sent us to the vice principal's office, which was protocol for an unexcused absence. We were sitting smugly outside of her office when the vice principal walked in. "What are you girls doing here?" she asked. When we told her we ditched school, she said, "Oh for goodness sake. Have my clerk give you a note, and get out of here."

We were good students, and our attempt to break a rule didn't impress the vice principal one bit. She just laughed.

My father was working steadily for Cate and McGlone Productions during my last year of high school. It often took a year to finish a film project from the time the script was written to when filming ended and the editing process began. Dad always wanted me to join him in the editing room so I could learn the skill. "Editing is one of most important parts of good filmmaking," he said.

I didn't have the desire or interest to work that closely with him. He could be impatient and critical, and I wanted none of that.

Dad was often serious and preoccupied with his work. He endured the tension that came with pressing deadlines and delays perpetuated by writers' block. Film writing was not an easy profession. Dad was a freelance writer, meaning he was on his own and worked for various production companies. As one project ended, there may have been no other one in the pipeline. That was generally the way it worked out. It was difficult to pursue other opportunities while he was busy meeting the demands of a current film project. Being out of work between jobs for a spell was often a given, and unfortunately, those spells could last for months.

The challenge of staying employed and maintaining a steady income had to be extremely difficult and stressful. Though Dad was out of work between writing projects for relatively short periods, not knowing when the next project would come through caused my mother anxiety. I think those were the times that my parents quarreled the most.

Dad always found another writing job, and I have to hand it to him. He managed to keep working and writing motion pictures his whole working life. That says something about his skills as a writer and the ability to sell himself.

Graduation from high school, Class of 1954, was less exciting than I anticipated. It was held on the football field while parents and friends sat in the bleachers. I remember feeling sad, still unhappy that no one had asked me to the senior prom. In those days, you had to have a date or you couldn't go to the dance, which was held in the gymnasium

My parents and Sally had plans to take me to dinner after the graduation ceremony. We went to the Hilton Hotel in downtown Los Angeles. I had an unappreciative attitude that night. I wanted to be with my friends instead of my parents, and I acted sullen and didn't feel like talking.

Shortly after graduation, Dad's former boss, Shirley Burden, asked him to bring me by his office in Beverly Hills. I went and was intrigued by the photographs displayed on the wall of the lobby. Some had earned awards, and the one I liked best had been printed in *Life* magazine. Shirley was always kind and thoughtful. He gave me twenty-five dollars for graduation, which seemed like a thousand dollars at the time.

I was signed up to start summer school at UCLA one week after graduation. Going to a large university and making new friends was a scary thought. Little did I know my world was just beginning to open up.

CHAPTER 13

Rhodes Avenue

We moved into our new home on Rhodes Avenue in North Hollywood at the beginning of summer in 1954. It wasn't a large house, but it was well built and had the cozy, Early American charm that was so popular in the 1950s. It had three bedrooms, two bathrooms, and a small laundry room. My parents selected the inside finishes—maroon-and-pink tiles for the main bathroom, cocoa-brown tiles for the smaller bathroom that was mine, and Armstrong linoleum in a brick pattern for the kitchen and dining room.

The living room had beige carpeting and a brick fireplace. Placed against one wall was the delicate, French provincial desk with the tweaked leg, a favored and lasting piece of furniture from the early days of my parents' marriage. In the country-style dining room was a larger brick fireplace with a sitting ledge. The room had pine paneling and a vaulted, wood-paneled ceiling with exposed beams that was separated from the kitchen by a counter with barstools. Wallpaper in an Early American motif looked nice in the bedrooms.

Mom let me decorate my room and paid for the custom-quilted bedspread and matching cover for my cedar chest that was once hers. I had a maple bedroom set with a single bed, side table, and a student desk. The wallpaper I picked had petite, yellow flowers to compliment the decor. This was my first real decorating endeavor, and I thought it looked very nice.

Dad decided to do the landscaping himself. In the front yard, he went all out, and instead of regular grass, he planted Irish moss, a most unusual choice of ground cover that grows in clumps. He planted a variety of foundation bushes including three on the far side of the driveway that bloomed a bright yellow. In front of the house next to the narrow, one-lane road, he put up a low, spilt-rail fence and planted yellow climbing roses that eventually entwined the fencing. The front yard looked professionally landscaped when he finished. Mom expressed her surprise, since Dad had done practically no gardening in the past. He knew what he liked and created a lovely garden. People driving by the house and seeing Dad weeding his precious Irish moss stopped to inquire. He always received compliments.

House on Rhodes Avenue

Nanny visited us on Rhodes Avenue. One afternoon, she arrived with an older, sad-looking woman she'd met on the bus and had invited to dinner. Mom was not pleased and summoned Nanny into the dining room out of earshot and where I was doing my homework. Perturbed, Mom asked, "How is she supposed to get home?"

Nanny had a sheepish look on her face. "I didn't think you'd mind driving her, dear. She doesn't live far."

Mom rolled her eyes and finally agreed to let the woman stay—not that she had much choice, since the unwanted guest had made herself comfortable on our living room sofa. Making the point clear, Mom whispered, "Mama, don't ever do this to me again."

"Oh, I won't dear," Nanny said, giving me a wink.

It was a big deal when Mom got her own car, a 1953 four-door Ford in turquoise with whitewall tires. We were now a two-car family, and Mom had wheels. One weekend, she volunteered to take Sally and me with a few friends to Hansen Dam for a day of water skiing. Hansen Lake, in the north San Fernando Valley, was a small flood-control lake that offered swimming and boating. My friends and I had been there before and tried our best to entice some of the young boys with motorboats to give us a waterski ride, but no amount of flirting or looking sexy in our bathing suits worked. Mom, with her good ideas to make things happen, thought she could bring us better luck, and she was right. What was Mom's secret? Sandwiches and soda pop for the hungry boys. It worked every time.

While we lived on Rhodes Avenue, Dad worked on several movie scripts for Cate and McGlone Productions. One was a thirty-minute travelogue for United Airlines, *Holiday in Hawaii*. It highlighted travel in the Hawaiian Islands and is a fascinating look back in history, showing the lifestyle and clothing styles of the 1950s—a treasured tour of the islands before the late-twentieth-century expansion of condos, housing developments, and high-rise buildings, especially on the island of Oahu.

Another film, documenting the 1955 Mobil Gas Economy Run, was entitled *The Other Side of the Mountain*. He also wrote the script for *Christmas in the Holy Land*, documenting Art Linkletter and his family's tour of Israel. The film was a CBS Special shown on Linkletter's television show.

One of the most sensitive projects Dad worked on was about children with Down syndrome, who were referred to as "mongoloid children." He talked about meeting the children after visiting the institution where they lived. He said, "They were the sweetest and happiest kids. Nothing but smiles on their faces, just wanting to talk to me and be friendly."

He came away feeling deeply moved after the encounter with the children. The research was for a film commissioned by Roy Rogers whose daughter, Robin, was born with Down syndrome and lived only two years. I'm not sure if the film was completed, but Dad telling of his experience made a lasting impression on me. Today, because of the philanthropy work of Roy Rogers and Dale Evans, most children born with Down syndrome are raised at home instead of being institutionalized.

UCLA

Although I had a high-enough grade point average from high school, I wasn't accepted at UCLA. Instead, I was given the option of attending summer school in order to qualify.

I took English and music appreciation. Given the long bus ride to UCLA, and once again with poor study habits, I got a D in the music class, and that kept me out of the university.

When I met with the counselor, she said, "We made a mistake. You were actually accepted without needing to go to summer school."

In the fall of 1954, I was admitted as a regular student. I remember the feeling of exhilaration and happiness at the unexpected good news. Never mind that I was starting the university with a grade point deficit.

The cost per semester was twenty-four dollars. I listed sociology as a major, carrying through with my half-hearted decision to become a social worker. However, truth be told, I majored in parties and boys, hoping to get an "MRS degree." I still had no idea what I wanted to be in life except a wife and mother. However, I did want to join a sorority and went through rush. I met up with Carol Ann and Charmaine, friends from Catholic school, during the rush parties and was surprised and happy to see them again. I also learned that Lynn from La Grange Avenue was in one of the sororities, and that scared me to death.

The sororities were segregated, and Jewish girls, as well as girls of color, were not accepted into the regular Panhellenic sororities. I feared that Lynn would spread the word about me being half Jewish and I would be blackballed. Gratefully, that didn't happen, and I pledged Alpha Omicron Pi.

Being a sorority girl was fun. I made good friends among the large freshman pledge class, though I didn't feel close to some of the girls who were older with other interests. Looking back, I can see they were focused on their studies.

My parents couldn't afford for me to live in the sorority house, a beautiful, two-story mansion on Hilgard Avenue along sorority row, so I became a town girl. The girls who lived in the house had roommates and shared the many bedrooms. As a town girl, I stayed overnight on Monday night, which was our meeting night, and often on Saturday and Sunday nights as well. I slept in one of the bunk beds in a large room called the pledge porch. The other nights, I stayed at home and traveled to school with a friend who lived near me and had a car.

It was wonderful staying at the sorority house and getting away from the discord at home, even though the sorority had many more rules than my parents when it came to behavior and curfew times on school nights and weekend date nights. I learned quickly that I represented Alpha Omicron Pi, and my conduct was never to reflect badly on the sorority. My first semester, I was assigned volunteer hours at a center for patients who had rheumatoid arthritis. The second semester, I was a volunteer worker for a student body officer. The pledges from every sorority house were required to involve themselves in the community and on campus.

I enjoyed the process of rushing—meeting new girls and promoting my sorority—and became good at it. I was a human resources professional in the making, but I didn't know it then. Sororities added to their membership each semester, following explicit Panhellenic rules. Limits were set for the money a sorority was allowed to spend on rush parties. My sorority sisters came up with inexpensive and creative ways to make outstanding decorations for their themed parties, and I loved learning how to do that.

A flowchart, coordinated by the rush chairman working in a back room, enabled active members to meet as many rushees as possible. The actives were rotated through the seating areas where the rushees were located in the living room or card room. I mastered the system, and that would be useful in the future.

As a pledge, we had mandated duties in the sorority house. One assigned task was keeping the silver flatware and serving pieces polished, which meant giving up a Saturday afternoon to polish on occasion. On the Monday meeting nights, we had a formal dinner for members and alumnae guests. The pledges were in charge of setting the long tables covered in white tablecloths using the sorority's china dishes and silverware after learning the proper way to arrange a place setting—which knife, fork, and spoon went where.

Pledges took turns answering the house telephone, located in a phone booth downstairs, and taking messages for anyone not available. Pledges were not allowed to use the main staircase by the front door and, instead, used the back stairs.

Having a formal tea was a popular way of entertaining for rush parties and other occasions. One Saturday afternoon, Alpha Omicron Pi at the University of Southern California (USC) in downtown Los Angeles, our sister sorority, held an alumnae tea after remodeling the house. They asked for volunteers from the UCLA chapter to help with tours of the house, and I went with my friend, Dorothy. The house was packed with older women dressed to the nines, and I wore my favorite olive-green, circular-skirted wool dress with a bouffant crinoline slip underneath and high heels.

I took a group of women to the second floor for a tour and was coming down the wide staircase in full view of the ladies having tea in the living room when my heel caught on a step. It sent me tumbling and rolling into a heap at the bottom of the stairs in the foyer. All conversation stopped as someone helped me up. I attempted a hasty retreat but could only limp away, because the heel of my shoe had broken off. No one laughed, and I felt even more foolish as I giggled uncontrollably at the thought of how ridiculous I looked. So much for trying to act like a lady!

I liked the themed fraternity parties best. I missed a legendary one from the prior year when a fraternity sent an elephant down sorority row to pick up dates for a circus-themed party at the fraternity house. However, I attended many other outstanding fraternity parties including a spring dance at a country club in Palm Springs, all hotel and party expenses paid. My sorority held dances at country clubs as well. Every weekend I had a date, sometimes two, with boys I had crushes on, like Glenn and Jerry, or with boys who liked me better than I liked them, such as Ray, John, and other guys whose names I can't remember.

I went to every UCLA football game that year and took a train ride to a Stanford game with my pledge sisters Dorothy, Kitchy, and Joyce. We also took the train to San Francisco for the game at UC Berkeley. Joyce's parents picked us up at the train station in their Rolls-Royce. UCLA went to the Big Ten conference playoff in the Rose Bowl on January 1, 1955, and I was there. We were singing our victory song when, in the last two seconds of the game, Michigan State kicked a field goal, shocking the UCLA fans silent and winning the game.

The sororities and fraternities had Spring Sing every year, an acapella competition. One of my sorority sisters was a music major, and she trained the girls in our house and conducted the group on competition night. Everyone in the sorority had to participate. Some of the girls had good voices, and some were asked to mouth the music. I had a good soprano voice and was the lead in the soprano section. We sang a medley from Judy Garland's movie, *A Star Is Born*, that sounded terrific, but we didn't win that year.

I sat in the back of my large lecture classes such as psychology and anthropology, smoking a cigarette, which was allowed in the larger classrooms. I didn't keep up with the reading and crammed for exams at the last minute. I did better in the smaller classes like English and Spanish, where the professors knew me. After one year, I partied myself right out of college. The problem with flunking out, clearly due to terrible study habits, was the thought that I wasn't as smart as my peers. This erroneous conclusion left me feeling like a failure and didn't help my self-esteem. I wouldn't earn redemption for a few years. In the meantime, I decided to get a job.

New York

Before looking for work that summer of 1955, my dad took the family to Manhattan for the first time. It was an opportunity for my father to finally show off the city of his birth and boyhood, and, of course, we were going to visit the relatives at long last. What an exciting trip!

We flew out of Burbank Airport on a United Airlines four-propeller commercial airplane, and the flight took over seven hours.

Flight to New York

The constant, loud whine of the engines made my ears hurt. There was a comfortable lounge in the back of the airplane with about four tables and upholstered swivel chairs where we gathered and had refreshments, played cards, and stretched our legs.

We stayed at my cousin Susan's apartment in Manhattan while she and her young son vacationed on Fire Island. I had hoped to see her again and was disappointed that she wouldn't be in the city during our stay.

I hadn't seen my uncle or grandfather since I was six years old, and it was wonderful seeing them again. Uncle Fred was married to Elaine, and they had a daughter, my cousin Erica, who was four years old.

Elaine, Fred, Erica

Uncle Fred gave up his songwriting career to become a child psychologist. He found his work rewarding and discussed it with us. At the time, he was involved in an inkblot project and gave us all the tests. We looked at the inkblots and described what we saw from them. It was interactive and fun, and I enjoyed his intelligence and wit.

While in Manhattan, we alternated sightseeing excursions with Uncle Fred and Aunt Elaine (Erica came too) and my elderly grandfather George, who couldn't walk a long distance. For his advanced age, I thought Grandpa George was spry, and he was smiling the day he took us to his favorite delicatessen.

Susan, Grandpa George, Sally

It was exciting to visit my father's uncle Herbert. He lived on Riverside Drive in a penthouse with a great view of the Hudson River. Uncle Herbert was charming, and I was impressed by his swanky residence.

We were in Manhattan for a week. With my uncle and grandfather acting as tour guides, we saw many of the major sights including the Empire State Building, World Trade Center, Times Square, Waldorf Astoria New York, Greenwich Village, and Harlem. We bought slices of lemon meringue pie at the automat and took a short ride on the subway. The emphasis was on spending quality time with the family, and we did plenty of that.

One evening, my parents decided to have dinner for just the four of us, without the relatives. We went to a nightclub in Greenwich Village that had a live band and catered to bus tours. I wore an off-the-shoulder, black sheath dress that was flattering. I didn't see a handsome boy my age approach the table when he came over to ask my father if he could dance with me. We danced the whole evening. He was not only adorable and nice but a terrific dancer. It was a magical night. My dance partner was from Ohio, and we corresponded by letter a few times. I was disappointed when he stopped writing, though I did understand that living so far apart was geographically incompatible for dating.

Cousin Susan arranged for me to accompany an Ivy League college fellow to the tennis matches in Forest Hills, a double date on a cloudy afternoon with 99 percent humidity. Now I understood why Dad hated the summer heat when he was a boy in Manhattan. I felt like a real country bumpkin since I had never played tennis or been to a tennis match. I also had trouble making conversation with my three companions. Trying to impress, I told my date that I had gone to UCLA, and he said, "Where's that?"

"In Los Angeles," I said. "We were number one in football this year." I wondered if he was kidding, decided he wasn't, and wished I was somewhere else.

After watching him on *What's My Line*? I finally met Dad's cousin, Bennett Cerf. In the 1950s when television was still new, Bennett was a recognizable celebrity coming into our living room each week as one of the regulars on the quiz show. From New York, where the show was broadcast to the opposite coast in Los Angeles, his image was transported in real life as if by magic, giving me the opportunity to know him a bit even though the experience was one-dimensional.

We met Bennett in his publishing office at Random House, and I quickly noticed the life-size cardboard image of him standing next to his desk. A prop used for advertising, I figured. Bennett was warm and chatty just like on television, and his mannerisms were curiously similar to that of my father. I could see the Wise family resemblance, and I liked Bennett right away.

Before going to the theater to watch the filming of *What's My Line?* we stopped by Bennett's house to meet his wife, Phyllis. Bennett gave us a tour of his lovely townhouse on five floors with a brick patio sandwiched between two tall buildings. Once at the theater, I enjoyed watching the show in person and meeting the other celebrities: John Daly, Arlene Francis, and Dorothy Kilgallen.

After the show, we went to Sardi's for dinner. A man came over to our table to say hello. Though I had watched his television show every Tuesday night, I was surprised to learn afterward that it was the raucous comedian Milton Berle. He was so dignified and charming, dressed in a suit and tie, that I failed to recognize him.

We had hoped to see *My Fair Lady*, the hit show that was playing on Broadway, but not even Bennett, with his connections, could get us tickets for the sold-out show. Instead, we saw the musical *Fanny*, which was good, and we saw the dazzling performance of The Radio City Rockettes.

This wonderful trip—a first of its kind in my young life—was overshadowed by worry that my mother might drink too much, perhaps at dinner, and expose her worst side to our New York relatives. In my vulnerable adolescence, I was concerned that her behavior might reflect on how they thought of me. Above all, I hoped there would be no verbal confrontation with my father in front of everyone. Mom did have a drink or two with dinner, but she was careful and on her best behavior. As we headed home, I was relieved that there had been no unpleasantries during our stay in Manhattan.

I wouldn't visit Manhattan again for many years, and I wouldn't meet up with my cousins, Erica and Susan, for even more years until the internet made it possible.

Felix Chevrolet

When I returned from New York, I applied for an office position at Shammas Motors in Studio City, a used car lot. I was disappointed when another girl got the job, a bleached blonde who had gone to my high school and fit Dad's description of looking cheap. Fortunately, after a few weeks, she didn't work out. They called me, and I was hired.

A few months later, the owner, Nick Shammas, bought a large Chevrolet dealership with a full-service maintenance department, and I found myself working at Felix Chevrolet. The dealership was located at Twelfth Street and Grand Avenue in downtown Los Angeles and had a cartoon-based Felix the Cat sign grinning from the top of the building. I had my own desk in an alcove on the mezzanine as part of the finance department and reported to Mr. Shammas's brother-in-law. My job was to keep track of people making car payments. When someone fell behind in their payments, I got the go-ahead to call out the repo man to repossess the car. Such a feeling of power for a nineteen-year-old!

I loved working at Felix Chevrolet and took the bus there, which I caught a block from home. There were over a dozen car salesmen, and everyone was super nice, including the bosses and the mechanics in the service department. Being young, I attracted plenty of attention and often went to lunch with a group of salesmen. I had my eye on one good-looking salesman named Bob who was about twenty-eight and single. He flirted and even took me to lunch one day, but he likely decided I was too young for him, because the lunch was the only invitation.

I was fascinated by the large double switchboard run by a tough lady who learned her skills at the telephone company. She practically ran the place, fielding the incoming and outgoing calls and keeping track of everyone. I asked if I could learn the board, which included speaking over the intercom in a strong, singsong voice: "John Jones, you have a call waiting on line four. Line four, please, Mr. Jones."

She was willing to teach me during my lunch breaks, but she monitored me closely and wasn't thinking about turning the board over to me anytime soon. Another woman in the dealership was her regular backup. She got sick one day, and I was asked to take over for her. That was the day that Felix Chevrolet ran a radio advertisement. As soon as it aired, all twelve incoming lines lit up at once. I answered one after the other quickly. "Good morning, Felix Chevrolet. Please hold."

One by one, I transferred each call to a salesman waiting at a desk on the floor where the new Chevrolets were displayed. I did a great job that day, and from then on, I was the relief operator during coffee and lunch breaks. I loved working the switchboard and the adrenalin rush as the board got busy. All kinds of crazy things could happen—calls getting mixed up in a maze of crossed telephone cords—and it was fun keeping everything straight as my hands moved as fast as they could, reminding me of playing the piano.

One time, I got silly and answered an incoming call with a meow like a cat before saying the greeting. Thankfully, the caller didn't tell anyone. Another time, I paged the owner, Mr. Shammas, for an incoming call. His office was on the mezzanine. When the switchboard light came on from his office, I connected the call without first speaking to him.

Seconds later, a light came on from the service department, and when I said, "Yes?" the person on the line said, "This is Mr. Shammas. Do you have a call for me?"

Who had picked up the phone in his office? I listened in on the line and could hear the janitor, in his slow Southern drawl, saying, "I'll get the switchboard operator to connect you to Mr. Shammas right away."

Nick Shammas moved the dealership (along with the iconic Felix the Cat sign) to another downtown location a few years later. He went on to build an empire, including purchasing eight automobile dealerships and the landmark downtown Petroleum Building, which became headquarters of his Shammas Group.

After one year of working at Felix Chevrolet, and before it moved to its final location, I decided to go back to school. I enrolled at Valley Junior College, a community college offering a two-year undergraduate degree, which is now Los Angeles Valley College.

Valley Junior College

The morning I entered the campus, dressed in my shrimp-colored, pencil-slim skirt and cashmere sweater to match, I felt a heightened sense of confidence. I admit that I felt superior to the students attending there since I had gone to a university. The classes at Valley Junior College were held in temporary bungalows, and there was a regular gymnasium building. This was nothing like the handsome brick buildings and beautiful, sprawling hilltop campus of UCLA.

That first day, I met Barbara in the cafeteria. She was exceptionally nice, asked me to join her at the table for lunch, and welcomed me to the school. I discovered that she, like most of the other students, was on her way up in life and had elected to start with her undergraduate degree at a smaller college that was free. There was no charge at the time for Valley Junior College except for books.

Barbara invited me to rush a sorority and thought I'd be perfect for hers, Chi Theta. After my experience at UCLA, perhaps I should have resisted activities that interfered with my studies. I still liked the idea of belonging to a built-in sisterhood of friends, and my decision to join a sorority at Valley Junior College was a good one. It changed my life. I was accepted into the sorority and immediately made close friends.

The classes at Valley Junior College were small, and the professors were good ones and accessible. Along with the academic classes, I took shorthand and learned how to take dictation. I was already a good typist.

Mom said, "It's important to have skills to fall back on in case something happens later in life." She meant if my husband died or we got a divorce and I'd have go to work. It was good advice.

I had Mr. Puig for Spanish literature, my fifth year of Spanish, and was given the lead in a Spanish play. By then, I was close to being fluent in Spanish, which was a job advantage in later years. I was thriving in the small-school atmosphere and enjoying dates and fraternity parties while still keeping up my grades. I changed my major to business education, thinking I might like to be a teacher.

Phoebe, one of the girls in my sorority, was the commissioner of assemblies on the student council. She encouraged me to run for that position when her term ended. I ran my own campaign and won the election. I also was elected alternate cheerleader, getting to cheerlead at most of the football games with the three regular cheerleaders, all boys. That was the year I won the school's "Outstanding Woman of the Year" award and was one of three council members chosen to represent Valley Junior College in Sacramento at a conference of student council members.

I attended Valley Junior College for three semesters and, during that time, discovered my leadership talents. My Chi Theta sorority sisters, friends like Phoebe, encouraged me to become a leader and brought out the best in me. I was voted vice president of the sorority and served as rush chairman, introducing the rush rotation system I learned in my sorority at UCLA. The sorority was made of some of the best young women on campus, and Sally happily joined a few years later.

My close friend and sorority sister, Harlene, invited me to Yosemite for a camping trip with her family. It was my first trip there. She also invited me along on a vacation when her parents rented a mountain cabin in Lake Arrowhead. Waterskiing was offered at the lake, and I paid about twenty-five dollars for the chance to learn behind a classic Chris-Craft motorboat. Three falls or five minutes of skiing was the deal. I got up on the third try, and that was the beginning of my love for waterskiing.

I joined the Hollywood Presbyterian Church where Roy Rogers and Dale Evans attended. Hoping to join one of their two choirs under the direction of Charles Hurt, professor of music at USC, I asked our neighbor to help me prepare for the audition. Wally Popp was the musical coordinator for *The Danny Thomas Show* on television. With his guidance, I was accepted into the Chancel Choir and sang soprano with the choir for a few years.

Much later, as an adult, I auditioned for the Ventura Master Chorale and was accepted. I continued singing until a viral infection took away my ability to sing without my voice cracking. For a long time, I mourned the loss of my good singing voice and the enjoyment it brought me.

Pat was one of the cheerleaders at Valley Junior College, and he had a party at his house after a Saturday football game. I was his date, and we stayed after the party to clean up the house since his parents were out of town. He drove me home and said, "I hope you don't get in trouble for getting home so late."

It was about three in the morning by the time we pulled into my driveway. I told him it was okay, that my parents left it up to my good judgment, which was true. The front door flung open, and my father came rushing out of the house with a stern look on his face. Pat jumped out of his car and started babbling. "I'm sorry, Mr. Wise, but we had a party and…"

My father said, "Fine, fine. Please move your car. I'm late for my fishing date."

The next Monday at school, Pat told everyone the story, saying, "Thank goodness he wasn't going hunting."

As commissioner of assemblies, it was my job to bring talent on campus for entertainment. The famous singer and jazz trumpeter Louis Armstrong came the first semester I was on student council, an arrangement made a few years beforehand. Everyone thought I was responsible for bringing him on campus, and though unearned, I received the accolades. It was very special getting to meet Louis Armstrong before his performance.

The entertainer I brought to campus the next semester was the film and television star Spade Cooley and his Western band. It was an easy arrangement since his son went to the school. A few years later, Spade Cooley was arrested for beating his second wife to death and went to prison for the crime. Having known his son, it was a sad thing to read about.

I was walking out of campus one afternoon and was shocked to run into an old friend—Rodney, twin brother of Richard, my boyfriend from Burbank when I lived on Stanton Avenue. We talked, and he thought Richard would like to see me, so I gave him my phone number.

Richard called and invited me to go with him to the Burbank on Parade carnival, the same annual event we enjoyed when we were fourteen. He picked me up in his car, and it felt surreal being on a date with him. He looked about the same, still handsome and sweet, though by then we had both moved in different directions. I was a college girl, and he had experienced a failed young marriage and was working at Universal Studios.

We had a wonderful time that night and were on our way back to his car, walking in a dark parking lot, when he whispered, "Get ready to run. Some bad guys are following us."

I turned my head and out of the corner of my eye saw about four mean-looking Mexican guys carrying beer bottles a short distance behind us. One of them made a slurred comment, and I knew they were drunk.

Richard turned to face them and said, "Ernie, it's me, Richard. Remember me from school? This is Susan, remember her?"

Richard had recognized the voice of Ernie, the Mexican boy he befriended in junior high school and the boy who telephoned me, engaging in long conversations, when I lived on Stanton Avenue.

Ernie squinted and stared. "Who are you?" He then nodded as if he kind of remembered and said to the others, "Leave them alone. Let's go." They turned around and headed in the opposite direction.

Richard grabbed my hand, and we rushed to his car. We were stunned at what just happened, and I was so grateful that Richard's kindness to Ernie long ago paid off that night.

I never heard from Richard again, and at the time, it didn't matter. Over the years, however, I've thought of him and wished we could have stayed friends.

A good-looking boy named Jon was in Chi Theta's brother fraternity. He was two years younger than me, which made a difference to me at the time. Nevertheless, I dated him off and on because he was super nice and a terrific dancer. One time he was desperate to find a date for his fraternity party, and I jokingly suggested Sally, who was a senior at North Hollywood High School. He wanted to see her picture, and after I showed him the one in my wallet, he said, "Where have you been hiding her?"

Sally

Sally went out with Jon a few times and had a major crush on him. From then on, Sally and I were close, and the gap in our ages no longer made a difference. Sometimes we even shared friends and went out on double dates together.

I had an important date one night for a semi-formal dance and was concerned that my mother might say something embarrassing after she had a few glasses of beer. I could just imagine her saying, "Sue was hoping you'd ask her to the dance."

My sister still laughs at my attempt to control the situation. I assigned my parents and Sally their places to sit in the living room and cautioned them not to say anything more than hello and how are you. My date arrived, and I held my breath as the introductions went smoothly. Nanny came out from the kitchen. She grabbed both sides of her housedress, made a deep curtsy, and announced, "Hello, I'm the grandma." Everyone burst out laughing as my face turned red.

The next morning, my grandmother wanted to know all about the dance. "He was a nice-looking fellow," she said. "I hope I didn't act too giddy."

When I got home from a date, sometimes Mom was awake. She put on her robe and warmed up some Campbell's tomato soup, which she loved. We sat at the dining room table and shared the soup while I filled her in on my evening out. Those were sweet times.

I had an after-school, part-time job for a short while with Dr. Jackson Mayers, who was a sociology professor at Valley Junior College. He had an office in a musty attic room above the *Valley Times* newspaper publishing building in North Hollywood where he worked on his private research. To get to the room, I had to walk by the giant, spinning drums as they thundered noisily, churning out the pages of the newspaper.

Dr. Mayers was working on a research paper about future demographics in the San Fernando Valley and needed my typing skills. He had one of the first electric typewriters, which I hadn't used before. As I bent over the typewriter to erase a mistake, it started typing. In my naiveté, I explained what was happening and said to him, "I don't know why the typewriter does that. Does that happen to you?"

He cleared his throat and said, "No. I'm not built like you."

At the beginning of my third semester at Valley Junior College, I was elected student body secretary. I was thinking of applying to several universities to continue my education. The dean of students, who was the faculty advisor for the student council, encouraged me to apply for a leadership scholarship.

Things at home took a turn for the worse. My parents' arguments grew more frequent. Sensing that her marriage was ending, Mom faced the inevitable by drinking more. Dad arranged for her admittance to a treatment center, but after spending one night there, she decided she didn't need treatment and took a cab home. She surprised us during dinner as she unexpectedly walked in the front door. Concentrating in class and doing homework became more difficult. Familiar feelings of worry and uncertainty overtook my thoughts, and I dreaded going home after school. The emotional upheaval was too much, and I dropped out of Valley Junior College midsemester, saying goodbye to no one except the dean of students. Getting a job so I could move from home seemed best at the time.

I was almost twenty-one, and my experiences of "growing up Wise" were coming to an end. Soon I would make different kinds of memories and gain new wisdom as a wife and mother.

CHAPTER 14

Last Chapter of Our Family

The house on Rhodes Avenue was our last home together as a family. Sometimes, after a bad argument, my father left the house to cool off. After what became the final argument, my father left for good.

When Dad stopped by to retrieve some of his things, Mom made an attempt to win him back, saying, "Don't you know I love you?"

My father said, "Thank God you didn't hate me."

Dad rented a place of his own and quickly met his soon-to-be second wife, Dotty, who was working in a coffee shop that he frequented. She was a waitress, seventeen years his junior, and the mother of three young daughters. Dotty was artistic, a great Southern-style cook, and excelled in ceramics as a hobby. She had an edgy sense of humor and a hearty laugh that my father enjoyed. She liked to fish, and so did he. They enjoyed traveling and even went to Japan. Dad was happy in his new marriage, though I felt that Dotty could be disingenuous at times. That was unimportant, since neither she nor my father played a significant role in my life after they were married.

My father and Dotty lived in a newly built home in the San Fernando Valley. A few years later, after Dad inherited money from his Uncle Herbert, they bought a large, rambling ranch house with a swimming pool. Dad used some of the money to form a small independent film production company. During this time, he was writing classified films for the Pentagon.

Mom sold the house on Rhodes Avenue after the divorce and rented an apartment nearby, and her drinking continued. I lived with her for a short time before sharing an apartment with a friend. Sally stayed longer because she was younger. Our precious dog Lori was given away. Since Dad was gone, Mom began taking her anger out on me, which had never happened before. She left a note on the table one day for Sally to find, saying she had gone to the ocean and was going to jump off the pier, reminiscent of our troubling days in San Francisco.

After I left Valley Junior College, I went to work at Marquardt Aircraft Company as a secretary in the thermodynamics department and later was promoted to secretary in the advanced engines department. There were many young people working at Marquardt, including new engineers fresh out of college. We went in groups to the mountains for snow skiing and, in the summer, to lakes for water skiing. It was so much fun working at the company that I often said, "I ought to pay Marquardt for letting me work there."

I met my husband at Marquardt. He was a young aeronautical engineer, and we dated, broke up, got engaged, and married. A month prior to our wedding, we bought our first home on Wilbur Avenue in Reseda.

Sally followed in my footsteps to Valley Junior College and was there for one year. She joined the Chi Theta sorority and met her future husband at the college. She spent a year working as a secretary at Collins Radio in the engineering department before getting married.

After Sally and I both married and started our own families, we grew increasingly concerned about Mom's drinking. She continually talked ill of my father, miserable that he had found happiness and she had not. She took him to court for more alimony, which Sally and I strongly advised against. The action ended up in a reduction of her alimony instead of an increase, much to Mom's dismay. The discord in our family had broken Dad's spirit, and he made the mistake of asking Sally and me to take sides, which we couldn't. This led to an estrangement from him that lasted one year for Sally and six years for me.

It wasn't uncommon for Mom to drive under the influence of alcohol, thankfully not killing or injuring herself or anyone else. The lowest point came the day she showed up drunk at Sally's house, wanting to hold Sally's new baby. Sally and I had had enough. Together we made the toughest decision of our lives. We told Mom that unless she was sober, we no longer wanted to see her. We stuck to our resolve. If she killed herself, so be it.

That's what it took to motivate our mother to stop drinking. She went to her first Alcoholics Anonymous meeting and began the road to recovery. She never drank again, although she continued to smoke. Sally and I welcomed her back in our lives with open arms. Mom bought a little house next door to mine on Wilbur Avenue, which was wonderful. She got her real estate license, proud that she passed the test on the first try. Her sense of humor came back, and the talented and creative mother I remembered was slowly emerging. Unfortunately, her health was in jeopardy. The lack of good nutrition in favor of alcohol, coffee, and cigarettes had kept her at a low weight. When sober, her symptoms of emphysema became more apparent. In fact, by then, she was in the later stage of the illness. Though she tried to list and show houses, she had difficulty breathing and couldn't continue working in real estate. She was in and out of the hospital numerous times for breathing treatments. After the doctor's dire warning, she finally gave up smoking, but the damage had been done.

Mom passed away at sixty years of age after celebrating four years of sobriety. Alcoholism and heavy smoking had eroded her mental and physical health. They also stole her future and left an indelible mark on Sally and me. We loved our mother dearly and always missed what could have been.

Two years prior to my mother's death, Nanny peacefully passed away nine days short of her eighty-fourth birthday. De Setta, her niece and caretaker, said, "She was resting in a chair and lowered her head and closed her eyes as if falling asleep."

In the last years before Nanny's passing, she always had the same answer when I asked her how she was feeling. "I'm just fine, dear," she'd say, smiling. "I still have my good mind." Nanny left behind a legacy of love and treasured memories of the sweet and caring way she treated everyone.

I reconciled with my father after my mother died. We met for lunch at the Crossroads of the World where he used to work, and it was good to see him again. He was warm and affectionate and said, "I love you, Susan. You were my firstborn."

Dad retired from writing, and he and Dotty moved to a smaller home. While they were compatible, they did have disagreements. One time, Dad felt remorseful after an argument and went out to get ice cream for them. On the way home, a new tire on his car blew out on a freeway ramp, catapulting the car into the backyard of an adjacent home where it landed upside down. A woman living in the home found Dad awake, but he had a broken neck.

After a long hospital stay and many weeks recuperating at home, Dad recovered. However, he was diagnosed with lung cancer that had metastasized from the colon. He and Dotty moved to an apartment, and soon he was hospitalized again. Sally remembered fondly that he told her, "I have enough love to last me an eternity."

In his hospital bed, heavily medicated and barely able to hold a pen, Dad wrote a few last thoughts to me and my children. On lined paper, now yellowed with age, there is one line that reads, "There is a little river called the Wulda. You and your sister will have many hours…"

His pen stopped there. I always thought the note was a clue to the place where he had stayed in Germany as a boy, a faded memory of playing in a river long ago.

Dad passed away one month before his sixty-fifth birthday and several weeks before I married my second husband, whom he never met.

In the eulogy that Dad had written himself, he expressed his love for all of us and apologized for being too critical. I knew that he wanted Dotty to bring the family together, but that never happened. She moved to her mountain cabin in Wrightwood, bought years before from inheritance money. After that, Sally and I saw her only once.

Over the years, I had often thought about Dad's final words to me. Where was that river? When I finally decided to look for it, I learned there was no river in Germany named Wulda and was more puzzled than ever. The desire to solve the mystery prompted the beginning of my incredible journey of family research and discovery.

I found that little river for you, Daddy. It's called the Felda, and it's in Stadtlengsfeld.

AFTERWORD

My parents' lives were sadly cut far too short. They never saw their children become successful adults or experienced the joy of watching their five grandchildren grow up as they too became accomplished adults. Sally and her husband are still happily married and have two children and five grandchildren.

My first husband and I ended our marriage after eleven years. We have two daughters and a son, and are the proud grandparents of six grandchildren. My second marriage was also not forever, but we had many happy years together, enjoying family activities and vacations with our large blended family.

In my mid-twenties, I became a full member of my UCLA sorority post-collegiate. I was rush chairman for Alpha Omicron Pi when it established a new chapter at CSUN. During a discussion on whether or not to accept a girl who was half Jewish, I stood up and said, "I'm half Jewish, and I think I fit in just fine." It was a giant step for me. The girl was accepted into the sorority, and from then on, my days of secrecy were over. I have since embraced my Jewish heritage and am proud that I come from a long line of Jewish ancestors.

While working as a secretary at CSUN, I started taking classes and graduated with honors with a bachelor's degree in journalism. I became a corporate human resources manager, a career that brought me great satisfaction and suited my personality and talents. I taught human resources management at CSUN for four years in its Extended Learning Program. I am now retired and living in Camarillo, California.

Reflecting back on my life, I think I've lived up to the Wise name and have become wiser and stronger over the years through all that I've lived and experienced. I know that my parents loved my sister and me and did their best to give us a good life, no matter their problems or shortcomings. Growing up, I longed for parents who were happy together and had the perception that other families were perhaps happier and better than mine. Mom had a saying that she liked: "Every chimney smokes." I understand now that children play together in innocence without any knowledge of the problems that may exist in someone else's home. Discovering who my ancestors were, looking at my family's history, and rehashing some of the challenging times of my childhood has given me a better sense of who I am and why I am the way I am. Whether they rub you the wrong way or the right way, those experiences have the potential to polish your soul until it sparkles.

To those of you who read this story and are related to the Wise family and the Houck family, you may have noticed that your German ancestors came through tough times and perhaps were lacking in humor and lightheartedness. This may be true, but know that your ancestors were hard workers who had a dream and longed for a better life. They wanted more for their children, grandchildren, and generations of children they would never know. They did their best to be successful and create more opportunities for their family. Hopefully, through this story you have been able to know them in some meaningful ways and embrace a strong and proud heritage.

FILMOGRAPHY
Walter J. Wise

1936 *How to Train a Dog* (writer-short)
1936 *Sinner Take All* (writer-screenplay)
1937 *Bad Guy* (contributor to treatment-uncredited)
1938 *Arsène Lupin Returns* (cowriter)
1940 *Look to Lockheed for Leadership* (writer)
1943 *P-38 Flight Characteristics* (writer)
1946 *The Runaround* (writer-story)
1952 *Great Discovery* (writer-screenplay)
1958 *Thunder Road* (writer-screenplay)

Sponsored Films and Documentaries

1949 Gladding McBean & Company (writer)
1950 Kerr Glass Manufacturing Company (writer)
1950 *Infantile Paralysis* (writer-untitled film)
1950 *Burbank: Story of a City* (writer and director)
1951 *Driving Safety* (writer-untitled film)
1954 *Holiday in Hawaii* (writer-United Airlines Travelogue)
1955 *The Other Side of the Mountain* (writer-Mobil Gas Economy Run)
1958 *Christmas in the Holy Land* (writer for Art Linkletter-aired on TV special in 1959)
1960 Classified films for the Department of Defense

Note: Dates of films may differ from actual release dates.

www.ingramcontent.com/pod-product-compliance
Lightning Source LLC
LaVergne TN
LVHW011756060526
838200LV00053B/3612